Modern Language Testing

SECOND EDITION

Modern Language Testing

SECOND EDITION

REBECCA M. VALETTE

Boston College

HARCOURT BRACE JOVANOVICH, INC.

New York   San Diego   Chicago   San Francisco   Atlanta

ISBN: 0-15-561926-8

Library of Congress Catalog Card Number: 76-49392
Printed in the United States of America

Preface to the Second Edition

When *Modern Language Testing* appeared ten years ago, its aim was to introduce teachers to a diversity of testing techniques based on the teaching and testing theories and practices of the mid-1960s. This revised and expanded edition represents a natural extension of that basic objective. It is a handbook for classroom teachers of both modern foreign languages and English as a second language. It should help them understand the terminology used in reports of ongoing testing research and, more importantly, should suggest ways for improving and broadening their own classroom tests.

Several changes characterize the new edition of the handbook. First, it reflects contemporary concerns in measurement and evaluation. Part One introduces the classroom teacher to some of the terminology in current testing theory and practice, while Part Three presents recent trends in this field. Second, the handbook reflects contemporary changes in teaching aims. The growing interest in language as a means of interpersonal communication has led to the development of a variety of tests of communicative competence. Chapters Five through Eight of Part Two all end with sections devoted to the evaluation of listening, speaking, reading, and writing as communication skills. Chapter Nine describes a broad range of techniques for measuring student progress in the area of culture. The testing of literature is the topic of a new Chapter Ten. Finally, Chapters Eleven and Twelve touch lightly on new developments in testing and the role of evaluation in bilingual programs. The Bibliography and Appendix have, of course, been expanded and brought up to date.

Modern Language Testing in its revised form represents the distillation of years of reading, of teaching, and of testing. This new handbook is the by-product of hundreds of conversations, conferences, workshops, and classes. Often it has been impossible for me to assign credit for specific item types, for with various modifications they are being used in many parts of the country. Therefore, let me acknowledge my indebtedness and gratitude to all

v

those teachers and students with whom I have worked over the past decade: this book is dedicated to each of you.

I would like to offer my special thanks to Professor Randall Jones of Cornell University for his critical review of the entire manuscript, and to Professor Howard Lee Nostrand of the University of Washington for his suggestions on the culture chapter. I would also like to acknowledge Renate Schulz and Walter Bartz, who have kindly let me reproduce their rating scales for speaking tests. Finally, let me express my appreciation to Albert I. Richards of Harcourt Brace Jovanovich for his fine editing and helpful guidance through the publishing process.

REBECCA M. VALETTE

Preface to the First Edition

In the past twenty years a number of new methods of teaching language have appeared. These methods have been based largely on the results of research in learning theory and linguistics; their acceptance has been helped by an increased use of electronic equipment and by the financial and intellectual backing of the federal government, the Modern Language Association, and farsighted members of the profession. The foreign-language teacher now has available to him an abundance of texts and other instructional materials that suggest the sequential development of the four fundamental skills of listening, speaking, reading, and writing.

It is clear that these new methods of teaching require new methods of evaluation. This handbook introduces the teacher to a diversity of testing techniques based on modern measurement theory; the book's emphasis, however, is on the classroom situation, theory being introduced only when it has a direct application for the teacher. Many examples have been given to help the teacher prepare tests that will effectively evaluate proficiency in the four fundamental skills. A special section also discusses literature tests.

The terminology of traditional grammar has been used in most instances instead of the more precise vocabulary of the linguists so that even teachers without formal training in modern linguistics will find the handbook convenient and useful. With a better understanding of measurement through the development and interpretation of the types of objective classroom tests suggested, the teacher should also be better able to evaluate commercial tests in relation to the goals he has set for his class.

REBECCA M. VALETTE

Contents

introduction
How to Use This Handbook

To obtain maximum assistance from a handbook, the user must be familiar with its organization. Since this book is not intended to be used with one particular course of study or for one particular level of instruction, we have adopted the following format:

Part One presents the principles upon which tests should be constructed, a description of procedures, and an explanation of the terms that will be used in the remainder of the book. The last chapter in this section treats the topic of test analysis. It may be that readers will want to skip this chapter until they have prepared and administered tests and are ready to study the results.

Part Two contains practical suggestions for the construction of classroom tests. We realize that all textbooks or courses introduce vocabulary and the elements of grammar in slightly different sequences; the sounds of the new language are presented in various ways; and in going beyond the elements of language, each program also treats the communication skills somewhat differently. Certain teachers stress communication with beginning students, whereas others emphasize communication more heavily in the intermediate and advanced levels. Rather than adopt the order of presentation of any single textbook or course, we have classified the types of tests and sample items according to the four language areas: listening, speaking, reading, and writing. Although these skills are obviously intermingled in the second language, and subsequently in its instruction, it seems most logical to treat these areas separately.

Learning a language necessitates the acquisition of language elements (sounds, words, structures) on the one hand, and communication skills (listening, speaking, reading, writing) on the other. In each of the skills chapters, the first sections suggest ways of testing the elements of the language, while the latter sections focus on communication. The language skills chapters are followed by chapters on testing culture and literature.

The types of items shown offer a generous sampling of the various methods at the teacher's disposal for assessing the progress of the students, but these suggestions are by no means exhaustive. The purpose of this book is to introduce the teacher to the wide possibilities of testing. Not only should the variety of tests help teachers to construct more precise examinations, but it should enable them to offer their students livelier and more challenging tests. This handbook is intended for language teachers at all levels— elementary, secondary, and college. Some of the items are not suitable at all levels, but the teacher will be able to select those which are appropriate for a given class.

Part Three introduces the interested reader to some of the current developments in the area of language testing. The topics include aptitude testing, affective goals, and bilingual testing.

The appendix gives an annotated list of currently available commercial language tests. The bibliography suggests selected books that focus on language testing. Finally, a comprehensive index at the end of the book will allow the teacher to find easily the appropriate items to test the material being studied in a given course unit. Boldface page numbers indicate pages on which terms are defined.

part one
Principles and Procedures

outline

1.1 THE ROLE OF TESTING IN THE CLASSROOM

    1.1.1 Defining course objectives
    1.1.2 Stimulating student progress
    1.1.3 Evaluating class achievement

1.2 TYPES OF TESTS

    1.2.1 The aptitude test
    1.2.2 The progress test
    1.2.3 The achievement test
    1.2.4 The proficiency test

1.3 TYPES OF TEST ITEMS

    1.3.1 Multiple-choice items
        1.3.1a The item
        1.3.1b Passage items
        1.3.1c Discrete items
    1.3.2 Short-answer objective items
    1.3.3 Communication items

1.4 GENERAL TESTING TERMINOLOGY

    1.4.1 Test and quiz
    1.4.2 Objective and subjective test items
    1.4.3 Speed and power tests
    1.4.4 Formative and summative evaluation
    1.4.5 Norm-referenced and criterion-referenced tests
    1.4.6 Grading and evaluation
    1.4.7 Discrete point and global testing
    1.4.8 Testing linguistic competence and communicative competence
    1.4.9 Abstract vs. situational context
    1.4.10 Pure vs. hybrid test items
    1.4.11 Pretesting and posttesting

one

Modern Language Testing

Testing is a topic of concern to language teachers, both those in the classroom and those engaged in administration or research. While classroom teachers usually have no intention of becoming measurement experts, they realize that tests can improve their teaching and stimulate student learning. Furthermore, in a traditional school environment, teachers must periodically evaluate student performance and prepare reports on student progress.

The first half of the chapter introduces the reader to basic testing concepts. What is the role of testing in the classroom? What are the common types of language tests? The second half of the chapter defines testing terminology and explains item types.

1.1 THE ROLE OF TESTING IN THE CLASSROOM

Classroom testing is the topic of this handbook. Although the teacher is primarily concerned with teaching rather than testing, classroom tests play three important roles in the second-language program: they define course objectives, they stimulate student progress, and they evaluate class achievement.

1.1.1 Defining course objectives

Students, particularly older ones, are quick to observe the types of tests given and to study accordingly. Thus, much as the teacher may emphasize oral fluency in the classroom, if all the tests are written tests the students will soon concentrate on perfecting the skills of reading and writing. If the teacher explains to the students that the course is intended to teach them how to manipulate the language with near-native fluency and then persists in giving tests composed of translations and declension tables, the students will continually refer to traditional grammatical terms and English equivalents.

Therefore, in a very real way the classroom tests define the short-range course objectives of the teacher. If beginning students are expected to develop primarily the skills of listening and speaking, then listening and speaking tests must be given in proportion to the relative importance of that objective. (For a further discussion of objectives, see Section 2.1.)

1.1.2 Stimulating student progress

As much as possible, the time given over to classroom testing should provide a rewarding experience. The test should furnish an opportunity for the students to show how well they can handle specific elements of the target language; gone are the days when the teacher designed a test to point up the students' ignorance or lack of application.

Tests should be distinctly announced in advance to permit the students to prepare adequately.

If the students themselves are expected to demonstrate their abilities, it is only proper that they should learn as soon as possible after the test how well they did. The test best fulfills its function as a part of the learning process if correct performance is immediately confirmed and errors are pointed out.

The aim of the language course is the development of communication skills. Communication is a meaningful activity, and the test items should, as much as possible, be presented in a meaningful situational context. Sentences that switch from one language to another in mid-stream and groups of items in which the topic changes from sentence to sentence are to be avoided. The language test is difficult enough without placing additional comprehension obstacles in the students' path.

1.1.3 Evaluating class achievement

Through frequent testing, the teacher can determine which aspects of the program are presenting difficulties for individual students and for the class as a whole. By analyzing the mistakes made on a given test, or more precisely on given items of that test, the teacher can determine where to concentrate extra class drill and how best to assist each student.

At the same time, testing enables the teacher to discover whether the class objectives are being met. Through tests the teacher can evaluate the effectiveness of a new teaching method, of a different approach to a difficult pattern, or of new materials.

The most familiar role of the classroom test is to furnish an objective evaluation of each student's progress: his or her attainment of course objectives and his or her performance in relation to that of the rest of the class.

1.2   TYPES OF TESTS

There are four basic types of language tests: aptitude tests, progress tests, achievement tests, and proficiency tests.

1.2.1   The aptitude test

The *aptitude test* is conceived as a prognostic measure that indicates whether a student is likely to learn a second language readily. It is generally given before the student begins language study, and may be used to select students for a language course or to place students in sections appropriate to their ability. (See Section 11.1 for a detailed discussion of the development and use of aptitude tests.)

1.2.2   The progress test

The *progress test* measures how much the student has learned in a specific course of instruction. The tests that the classroom teacher prepares for administration at the end of a unit or end of a semester are progress tests. Their format reflects the various components of the curriculum. This handbook is written specifically to help teachers improve their progress tests and evaluate those which commercial publishers distribute to accompany their materials.

1.2.3   The achievement test

The *achievement test* is similar to the progress test in that it measures how much the student has learned in the course of second-language instruction. However, achievement tests are usually not built around one set of teaching materials but are designed for use with students from a variety of different schools and programs. For example, the afternoon tests of the College Board battery are achievement tests. Dictations given over unfamiliar material may also be considered achievement tests when they are used to compare students across different programs.

1.2.4 The proficiency test

The *proficiency test* also measures what students have learned, but the aim of the proficiency test is to determine whether this language ability corresponds to specific language requirements. For example, placement tests are proficiency tests: is the student proficient enough to enter Course 301, or would it be better to place him or her in Course 251? The reading-knowledge tests for doctoral candidates are also proficiency tests: is the student able to read professional literature in another language with a specific level (such as 90 percent) of accuracy? The Foreign Service Institute has developed a set of proficiency tests that indicate to what degree a candidate can function in the foreign language: can the candidate only carry out polite exchanges in the language, or can he or she handle technical discussions? The proficiency tests, in fact, usually report student language ability on a continuum that reflects a predetermined set of categories.

1.3 TYPES OF TEST ITEMS

The questions on a test are called *items*. The word *item* is preferred because it does not imply the interrogative form. The most common types of items used in language classes are multiple-choice items, short answer items, and communication items.

1.3.1 Multiple-choice items

Multiple-choice test items are designed to elicit specific responses from the students. Since there is only one right answer (or in some rare cases more than one, or even none), the scorer can very rapidly mark an item as correct or incorrect. More important, when a group of scorers is reading the same test paper, each of them arrives at the same score. (This agreement is called *scorer reliability*; see Section 4.2.2.)

The reliability of multiple-choice items and the increased use of electronic computers have led to widespread acceptance of the machine-scored answer sheet. Such multiple-choice tests have proliferated throughout the United States and have been applied to a broad range of subject matter. The items present the students with four or five options from which they must select the correct answer. Although the scorer reliability of these machine-scored multiple-choice tests is almost perfect (allowance being made for occasional mechanical failure), the validity of each test or each section of the test must be determined separately. Just because a test is "objective," it is not automatically a "good" test. Before using any standardized objective test, the teacher should carefully go over the specifications to determine whether they correspond to his or her own reasons for giving the test.

1.3.1a THE ITEM

In a multiple-choice item, the *stem* is the initial part: either a partial sentence to be completed, a question, or several statements leading to a question or incomplete phrase. The choices from which students must select their answers are known as *options, responses,* or *alternatives.* One response, the *key,* is distinctly correct or more suitable than the others. Incorrect responses are called *distractors* and should be so worded that they seem attractive to the uninformed or poorly informed student. If a distractor is so obviously wrong that it is never selected, it plays no useful role in the item and should be eliminated or replaced by a new alternative.

1.3.1b PASSAGE ITEMS

Passage items, as the name suggests, are two or more items that refer to a single "passage": a paragraph, a poem, a conversation, or a visual. The passage may be printed in the test booklet, recorded and played over a phonograph or tape recorder, or projected on a screen. The items that accompany a linguistic passage evaluate how well the students understand what they have just read or heard. Effective passage items should be so constructed that an intelligent native speaker could not arrive at the correct answer without having read or heard the passage. In other words, students should not be able to answer passage items merely with common sense and a knowledge of the target language.

Visual passage items consist of a group of items referring to a single picture, slide, or film. The meaning of the visual should be clear to the students, while the linguistic problems to be tested are found in the responses.

1.3.1c DISCRETE ITEMS

Discrete items stand alone. The most common discrete items are utterly independent of each other, and their order on a given test could be transposed without changing their effectiveness. To obtain greater economy in test administration, a series of discrete items employing identical options could be presented as a group.

Here is an example in English, where the stem is understood.

> Indicate whether the following statements refer to past events or to present events. Mark your answer sheet as follows: A = past, B = present.
>
> 1. They sing beautifully.
> 2. We came together.
> 3. You went with my car.

Correct responses: B, A, A

Discrete language items may also be developed around visual stimuli: drawings, a sequence of clock faces, overhead transparencies, flash cards, etc.

1.3.2 Short-answer objective items

An *objective test item* is any item for which there is a single predictable correct answer. Whereas the multiple-choice item format is most often selected for standardized tests, the classroom teacher typically makes heavy use of short-answer items. These items may require one-word answers, such as brief responses to questions (oral or written), or the filling in of missing elements. At other times, several words or full sentences may be required.

Like the multiple-choice items, the short-answer items may be classified as passage items (for example, questions on a reading) or discrete items. The stimulus may be printed, spoken, visual, or a combination of these presentations.

In order to assure the objective nature of short-answer items, the teacher must prepare a scoring system in advance. In a spoken vocabulary test, is credit given for a properly identified expression poorly pronounced? Or is the student also scored on pronunciation? In a written test of verb usage, is credit given for a verb in the appropriate tense even if there is a minor misspelling? Is credit given for the sentence if a nonessential element of the sentence is misspelled? Where possible, the students should be told exactly how their performance is to be evaluated.

1.3.3 Communication items

In tests of communicative competence, it is usually impossible to predict precisely how students will respond, for communication allows and indeed encourages creativity on the part of the students. Although one can develop objective items to evaluate listening and reading comprehension, tests of oral and written self-expression elicit free responses that must be scored subjectively.

Communication items are not, therefore, as objective as multiple-choice or short-answer items. However, through the development of an appropriate scoring procedure, it is possible to evaluate student performance with a good degree of objectivity. If communication is one of the major goals of the foreign language course, teachers must give the students the opportunity to demonstrate their ability to communicate, even if such tests are not totally objective.

1.4 GENERAL TESTING TERMINOLOGY

The literature on language testing contains terms often unfamiliar to the classroom teacher. The most important of these terms, frequently used in contrasting pairs, will be defined and discussed in this section.

1.4.1 Test and quiz

Both tests and quizzes play a role in the language classroom. The distinction between test and quiz is one of dimension and purpose rather than of item content.

The test is announced in advance and covers a specific unit of instruction, be it part of a lesson or several lessons. In reviewing for a test, students pull together the work of several class periods. Classroom tests may be given every two or three weeks—in some cases, every week. Such tests may be constructed to last the entire class period; in this case, optimum learning efficiency requires the teacher to return and discuss the corrected test as soon as the class meets again. Some teachers prefer preparing a shorter test so that items may be reviewed rapidly at the end of the same class period.

The essence of the quiz is brevity. In contrast to the test, it may be unannounced. Frequent quizzes encourage students to devote time regularly to their language study. Moreover, the quiz enables the teacher to acquaint students with types of items that will subsequently be used in tests. Students may be told to expect a quiz every period, although on some days the quiz might be omitted. A written or oral quiz may be given at the end of the period (to highlight work done in class). A regular brief laboratory quiz at the end of the laboratory session can be effective in maintaining student attention during the period.

Individual grades on daily quizzes are not of primary importance. The value of the quiz lies in its positive effect on student learning and the practice it affords in the art of test taking; such practice helps reduce the negative element of nervousness often affecting performance on longer tests.

The value of the test, on the other hand, lies in the completeness with which it examines the material under study. The relative weight given certain elements or skills should therefore accurately reflect the class objectives.

1.4.2 Objective and subjective test items

The terms *objective* and *subjective* when applied to test items refer to the manner in which the item is graded. An *objective item* is one for which there is a specific correct response; therefore, whether the item is scored by one teacher or another, whether it is scored today or last week, it is always scored the same way. Multiple-choice items are objective items. Fill-in-the-blank and short-answer questions are also objective items.

A *subjective item* is one that does not have a single right answer. A short composition or an impromptu interview may be scored in different ways by different teachers, and even by the same teacher scoring the answer twice under different circumstances. Test questions where students may give a variety of responses, each somewhat different from the other, are called subjective items.

1.4.3 Speed and power tests

On a *speed test*, the student works against time. A typical speed test is the typing test in which the student tries to improve his or her rate of words per minute. A language test that is so long the students are unable to finish within the time allotted and that contains items of more or less equal difficulty throughout the test would be considered a speed test. For instance, the reading and translation test given for doctoral candidates is frequently a speed test: the candidates must finish the translation within a specific time limit.

On a *power test*, the student is given sufficient time to finish the test. Some students may not answer all the questions, but this is because they are unable to do so, not because they were rushed. Most classroom tests are power tests: the length has been set to permit all students to complete the test.

1.4.4 Formative and summative evaluation

Benjamin Bloom has developed the concept of formative and summative evaluation.[1] The *formative test* is given during the course of instruction; its purpose is to show which aspects of the chapter the student has mastered and where remedial work is necessary. The formative test is usually graded

[1] See Benjamin S. Bloom, J. Thomas Hastings, and George F. Madaus, eds., *Handbook on Formative and Summative Evaluation of Student Learning* (New York: McGraw-Hill, 1971). Of specific interest to language teachers is Chapter 22 by Rebecca M. Valette, "Evaluation of Learning in a Second Language," pp. 815–53.

on a pass-fail basis, and students who fail are given the opportunity to study and then take the test again.

The *summative test*, on the other hand, is usually given at the end of a marking period and measures the "sum" total of the material covered. On this type of a test, students are usually ranked and graded.

1.4.5 Norm-referenced and criterion-referenced tests [2]

The *norm-referenced test* compares a student's performance against the performance of other students. On the classroom test, the student's performance is often graded on the curve. On a standardized test, the student's performance is compared to that of other students who have completed a similar language course, and the results are expressed in terms of percentile rankings (see Section 4.2.3). (The summative test is a type of norm-referenced test.)

The *criterion-referenced test* indicates whether the student has met predetermined objectives or criteria. Has the student mastered the rhythm and accent of the target language? Can the student rewrite a paragraph from the present tense into the past tense? The student's performance is typically graded on a pass-fail basis and the opportunity for retesting is provided. (The formative test is a type of criterion-referenced test.)

The test given at the end of a unit is a criterion-referenced test based on specific material. In broader terms, the criterion-referenced test may be conceived as a placement or proficiency test. According to the student's scores on the test, he or she is placed on a specific course or given a rating that indicates, for example, his or her speaking ability. (The College Board examinations are norm-referenced tests, while the Foreign Service Institute tests are criterion-referenced tests.)

1.4.6 Grading and evaluation

In the traditional school system, students are "graded." This concern for grades and ranks parallels the use of norm-referenced tests. The current trend in some schools is to replace grading with "evaluation": the student is told what he or she has learned with reference to the subject matter rather than in comparison with others in the class. Criterion-referenced tests are usually used in the evaluation of student progress.

It is obvious, however, that the scores on criterion-referenced measures may also be interpreted in such a way as to rank students. Although the

[2] For further reading, see Norman E. Gronlund, *Preparing Criterion-Referenced Tests for Classroom Instruction* (New York: Macmillan, 1973).

teacher focuses on evaluation procedures, the students themselves may translate relative progress into grades. In an individualized program where students may progress at their own rate, both Susie and Mary may be doing B-level work, but if Susie has completed seven chapters and Mary has completed only four, Susie's performance for the year will be superior to Mary's.

1.4.7   Discrete-point and global testing

Discrete-point tests measure whether or not the student has mastered specific elements of the second language. Items that test the control of phonemes, intonation patterns, vocabulary items, structural patterns, and the like are discrete-point tests. Most multiple-choice items are discrete-point items. (However, multiple-choice interpretation questions based on a longer listening or reading selection can focus on global aspects of the language. Longer speech and writing samples, in themselves global measures, can be scored on the basis of specific elements in a manner that parallels discrete-point items.)

Global language tests measure the student's ability to understand and use language in context. The dictation test based on unfamiliar material is a global language test. So is the reading test in which random words have been omitted (the cloze test[3]). Tests in which students are presented with a situation and must express themselves, and in which their performance is evaluated in terms of their communication effectiveness, are also termed global tests.

1.4.8   Testing linguistic competence and communicative competence

The *test of linguistic competence* determines the breadth and accuracy of the student's command of linguistic elements: pronunciation, vocabulary, and structures. Tests of linguistic competence are equated with discrete-point tests, in that the student is evaluated on specific aspects of the second language.

The *test of communicative competence* focuses on the student's ability to communicate in specific situations. The student is scored, not on linguistic accuracy, but on his or her ability to produce or comprehend a message. In this context, linguistic errors are counted only if they interfere with communication. Tests of communicative competence may be considered global language tests, even though the latter category also includes indirect measures of language proficiency, such as dictations.

[3] For a description of the cloze test, see Section 7.8.4.

1.4.9   Abstract vs. situational context

Most standardized and commercial classroom tests present items in an *abstract context*: the students are instructed, for instance, to select or provide the appropriate forms of suggested adjectives. Although full sentences are often used, these sentences when read in sequence have little relationship to each other. Students can perform well on such tests without understanding the meaning of the individual sentences.

With the growing emphasis on the importance of meaning in foreign language acquisition, teachers are beginning to realize the necessity of placing test items into a *situational context*. Although the situational test may include the same elements as the abstract test, the former is more effective as a learning tool. Here is an example:

Abstract context: Complete the sentences with the past tense form of the verb in parentheses.
1. I _____ (buy) a record yesterday.
2. John's parents _____ (write) him a postcard from New York.
3. We _____ (pay) the paperboy two dollars.

Correct responses: bought, wrote, paid

Situational context: Richard is out of luck! Whenever he asks his friends to do something, he finds out that they have already done so. Complete the answers with the past tense form of the underlined verb.
1. Richard: Do you want to go to the movies?
   Sally: Sorry, I _____ to the movies last night.
2. Richard: Do you want to see "Jaws" with me?
   Paul: I _____ "Jaws" last week.
3. Richard: Do you want to do your math homework at my house?
   Mary: I _____ my math this morning.

Correct responses: went, saw, did

1.4.10   Pure vs. hybrid test items

On a *pure test item*, the student uses only one skill. In a *hybrid test item*, two or more skills are used. For example, in a listening comprehension test, students might be asked to listen to a short conversation. If they then hear a series of true-false questions about the conversation and mark "true" or "false" on an answer sheet, this test would be considered a pure test. However, if they hear questions about the conversation and select the appropriate answer from among three printed options, this test would be a hybrid test, for it involves both the skill of listening and the skill of reading.

In the 1960s language test writers tried to produce pure tests as far as possible. Dictations, for example, were often discarded because they were hybrid forms, mixing listening and writing. With the present interest in communication and global testing, there is a return to certain hybrid test forms. It is now felt that since speakers of the second language naturally tend to use their language across two or more skills, hybrid test items are consequently valid measures of the students' mastery of that second language.

The hybrid test may introduce the problem of double jeopardy. For instance, the student may be able to read a passage with understanding but may receive a low grade on the test because of errors made in writing out answers to comprehension questions. In this example, the poor command of writing has jeopardized what would have been a strong reading grade.

1.4.11 Pretesting and posttesting

The *pretest* is given prior to teaching a course or a unit of instruction. It is similar in form and content to the *posttest* that is given at the end of the course or the unit. The scores on the pretest form a baseline against which one can measure the progress that students have made during the course.

The pretest is usually not given in beginning courses, unless there are some students who have had prior language experience (language spoken at home, travel or residence abroad, etc.). In intermediate or advanced courses, however, the pretest helps the teacher ascertain the students' level at the beginning of the course. It may be that certain students are so qualified that they may waive the course entirely or proceed to a higher course in the sequence. In research projects, a comparison of pretest and posttest scores enables the teacher to determine how much the students have learned in one class as opposed to another.

outline

two

Preparing The Classroom Test

All too often tests (and, even more frequently, quizzes) are put together haphazardly shortly before they are to be administered because the teacher is overworked and unable to devote much time or thought to their preparation. In addition, once the tests have been graded they are likely to be forgotten or discarded by the students, for the busy teacher finds even less time to discuss the questions and results with them systematically. Such situations are unfortunate, to say the least.

This chapter will provide suggestions for the establishment of an efficient testing program. Since most school systems change textbooks infrequently, the additional work required during the first year will permit a substantial saving of time in subsequent years. Even if different books are introduced later, many of the items, with minor revisions, can be used with the new texts.

2.1 COURSE OBJECTIVES

Before determining a testing program for a specific course—indeed, before setting out to teach a course—the teacher should clearly envision the course objectives. By so doing he or she will be sure that the teaching will be rationally oriented and that the tests will indicate how close each student has come to attaining the objectives.

2.1.1 Long-range goals

Long-range goals help define the nature of the second-language program. A major goal of most language programs is to enable the students to use the new language for communication: students should acquire the ability to engage in face-to-face conversation or to enjoy movies in the second language; they should learn to appreciate the literature written in the second language or to read specialized articles in the field of their choice. Some programs stress the goal of cross-cultural understanding and an intensified awareness of the broad linguistic and cultural heritage of the United States. It is also hoped that students, in gaining a certain proficiency in another language, will learn to appreciate more deeply the vital role of language in all human activity.

2.1.2   Short-range performance objectives

Performance objectives are precise descriptions of what students should be able to do as the result of a particular sequence of instruction.[1] There are two types of performance objectives: formal objectives and open-ended or expressive objectives.

2.1.2a   FORMAL PERFORMANCE OBJECTIVES

Formal performance objectives are stated in four parts: purpose, student behavior, conditions, and criterion. They describe student output in terms of predictable and observable student performance. Here is a sample:

> To demonstrate the ability to understand prices in spoken French, the student will write down the prices mentioned in fifteen separate statements. Each statement will be read aloud only once. To pass, at least twelve of the prices must be written correctly.

> Cette jupe coûte cent quatre-vingt-quinze francs.   *This skirt costs 195 francs.*

> Response: 195 Fr.

Formal performance objectives are brief descriptions of language tests. They can be equated with discrete-point tests and measures of linguistic competence. They frequently use multiple-choice or short-answer items.

2.1.2b   OPEN-ENDED OR EXPRESSIVE PERFORMANCE OBJECTIVES

Open-ended or *expressive performance objectives* describe the nature of the student performance without describing the precise form the output will assume. Open-ended objectives are usually stated in three parts: purpose,

---

[1] For a detailed presentation of performance objectives in second-language learning, see Rebecca M. Valette and Renée S. Disick, *Modern Language Performance Objectives and Individualization: A Handbook* (New York: Harcourt Brace Jovanovich, 1972). Hereafter this book is cited as *Mod. Lang. Perf. Objs.*

student behavior, and conditions. The criterion is often somewhat subjective. For example:

> To demonstrate the ability to relay telephone messages, the student will hear a recording of a French woman leaving instructions for her neighbor. The student will note the important elements of the message and then relay the gist of it orally to the evaluator. Student performance will be scored on the amount of information accurately transmitted.

In this case, the teacher cannot predict which lexical items and which structures the student may use in responding. The important factor is the relaying of accurate information.

Open-ended performance objectives can be equated with measures of communicative competence and frequently involve global measures of language acquisition.

2.1.3 Classification of language goals and objectives

Not all language goals are of equal complexity and importance. A classification system allows the teacher to visualize the relative roles of the various objectives being considered.

2.1.3a THE VALETTE-DISICK TAXONOMY[2]

The *Valette-Disick subject-matter taxonomy* organizes objectives from the simplest behaviors (Stage 1) to the most complex (Stage 5). Moreover, a distinction is made between internal behavior (primarily the receiving of messages—listening and reading) and external behavior (primarily the sending of messages—speaking and writing). The taxonomy is summarized in Figure 1.

2.1.3b THE RIVERS MODEL[3]

Wilga Rivers has developed a model of the processes involved in learning to communicate (see Figure 2). *Skill-getting* requires the acquisition of knowledge and intensive practice. *Skill-using* occurs as the result of purposeful conversation exchange. Like Valette and Disick, Rivers insists that language acquisition is not a sequential process in which students slowly move up the ladder toward communication; rather there is constant interplay from the outset between skill-getting and skill-using activities.

---

[2] For a complete discussion of the taxonomy, see Valette and Disick, *Mod. Lang. Perf. Objs.*, Chapter Two. The figure is taken from page 41.

[3] See Wilga Rivers, *A Practical Guide to the Teaching of French* (New York: Oxford University Press, 1975), pp. 3–5.

Figure 1

SUMMARY OF THE SUBJECT-MATTER TAXONOMY

Stage	Internal Behavior	External Behavior
1. **Mechanical Skills:** The student performs via rote memory, rather than by understanding.	*Perception:* The student perceives differences between two or more sounds or letters or gestures and makes distinctions between them.	*Reproduction:* The student imitates foreign-language speech, writing, gestures, songs, and proverbs.
2. **Knowledge:** The student demonstrates knowledge of facts, rules, and data related to foreign-language learning.	*Recognition:* The student shows he recognizes facts he has learned by answering true-false and multiple-choice questions.	*Recall:* The student demonstrates he remembers the information taught by answering fill-in or short-answer questions.
3. **Transfer:** The student uses his knowledge in new situations.	*Reception:* The student understands recombined oral or written passages or quotations not encountered previously.	*Application:* The student speaks or writes in a guided drill situation or participates in cultural simulations.
4. **Communication:** The student uses the foreign language and culture as natural vehicles for communication.	*Comprehension:* The student understands a foreign-language message or a cultural signal containing unfamiliar material in an unfamiliar situation.	*Self-Expression:* The student uses the foreign language to express his personal thoughts orally or in writing. He uses gestures as part of his expression.
5. **Criticism:** The student analyzes or evaluates the foreign language or carries out original research.	*Analysis:* The student breaks down language or a literary passage to its essential elements of style, tone, theme, and so forth. *Evaluation:* The student evaluates and judges the appropriateness and effectiveness of a language sample or literary passage.	*Synthesis:* The student carries out original research or individual study or creates a plan for such a project.

Figure 2

PROCESSES INVOLVED IN LEARNING TO COMMUNICATE

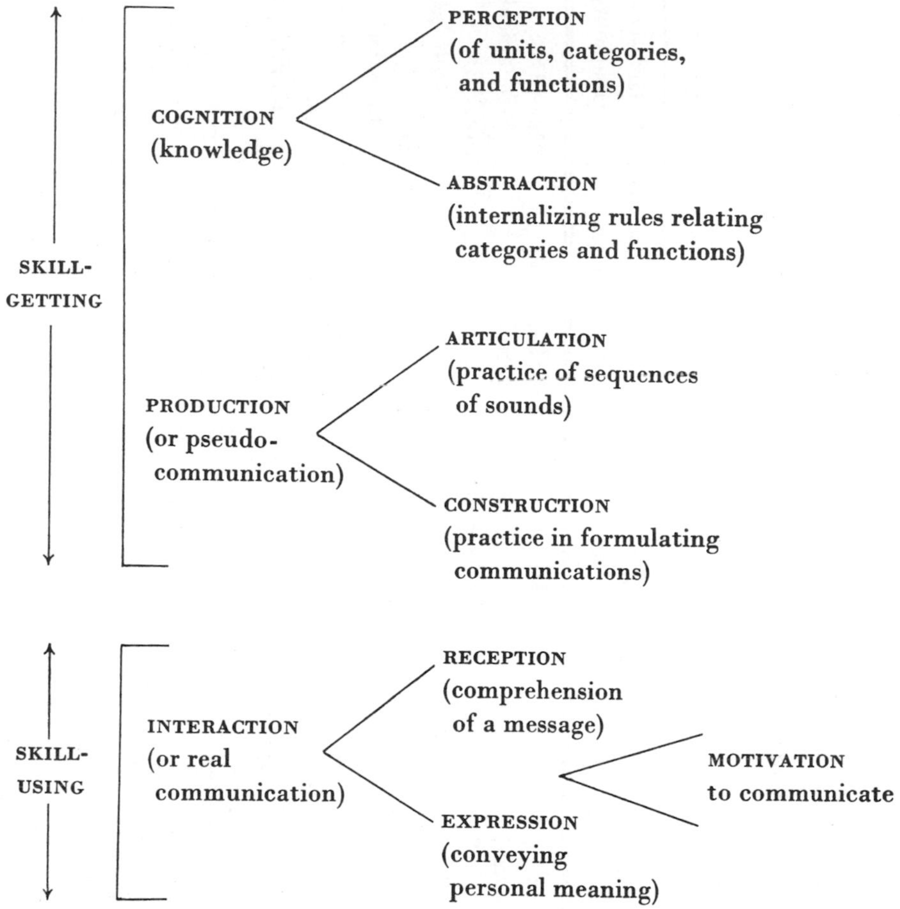

SKILL-
GETTING

COGNITION
(knowledge)

PERCEPTION
(of units, categories,
and functions)

ABSTRACTION
(internalizing rules relating
categories and functions)

PRODUCTION
(or pseudo-
communication)

ARTICULATION
(practice of sequences
of sounds)

CONSTRUCTION
(practice in formulating
communications)

SKILL-
USING

INTERACTION
(or real
communication)

RECEPTION
(comprehension
of a message)

EXPRESSION
(conveying
personal meaning)

MOTIVATION
to communicate

2.1.4 Matching goals and item types

Although language testing experts use a broad range of terminology, the general parameters of the topic can be reduced to a single chart. Figure 3 shows the relationship between item types and classification systems.

2.1.5 Selecting unit objectives

In selecting unit objectives in preparation for test construction, the teacher must consider the needs of the students and the general goals of the course. Most second-language courses at the beginning and intermediate levels are

Figure 3

Test type	Item type	Competence	Performance objectives	Rivers model	Valette-Disick taxonomy
discrete-point tests	multiple-choice and short-answer items	linguistic competence	formal performance objectives	skill-getting activities	Stage 1: Mechanical Skills Stage 2: Knowledge Stage 3: Transfer
global tests	communication items	communicative competence	open-ended performance objectives	skill-using activities	Stage 4: Communication

designed so that students master certain new structures and lexical items while developing their ability to communicate. The determination of unit objectives can be considered an operation in four steps.

2.1.5a STEP ONE: DETERMINING THE LINGUISTIC CONTENT OF THE UNIT

The teacher studies the unit and picks out the new structures and the new vocabulary items that the students are to master. This information may be tabulated on a sheet of paper. For instance, vocabulary items may be grouped by parts of speech; nouns could be subgrouped by gender and verbs by conjugation.

2.1.5b STEP TWO: DETERMINING HOW THE STUDENTS ARE TO DEMONSTRATE MASTERY OF THE LINGUISTIC CONTENT

The teacher plans how the students are to handle the new vocabulary and structures. Should the student be able to identify the new tense, for instance, when hearing it used in a series of sentences? Should the student be able to conjugate verbs in the new tense? Should the student be able to manipulate the new tense in speaking exercises or utilize the tense in rewriting a paragraph? Each type of activity selected might be accompanied with a sample test item.

2.1.5c STEP THREE: SETTING COMMUNICATION GOALS

The teacher uses the context of the unit as the point of departure for creating communication situations. In what way can the students use the material in the lesson for free expression?

2.1.5d STEP FOUR: MATCHING THE SAMPLE TEST ITEMS AGAINST THE TAXONOMY

The teacher classifies the sample items according to the Valette-Disick taxonomy or other classification system. Is there a good balance between language usage items and communication items? If the course emphasizes all four skills, are these skills represented in the test in proper proportion? If weaknesses appear, they should be rectified before the entire test is put together.

2.2 CONSTRUCTING THE TEST

Once the objectives of the course have been determined, the general parameters of the testing program become evident. Test construction consists of translating these general statements into specific tests and quizzes.

2.2.1   Setting the test sequence

Most teachers work with a specific syllabus that shows at which rate the course will progress through the term. (In some individualized courses, this rate of progress may be variable.) The school calendar typically gives the dates for major exams, or at least indicates dates on which grades must be submitted.

In setting the test sequence, the teacher will first indicate the dates for the term and midterm tests, with an approximate indication of the number of units or chapters to be covered. Then the dates for the unit tests are determined, and perhaps even dates for shorter quizzes.

2.2.2   Outlining the course content

In a basic language course, much of the course content is defined in terms of vocabulary items and grammatical structures. It is an excellent idea to prepare a notebook that corresponds to each basic text. This notebook would be divided into chapters and would contain the vocabulary and grammatical points covered in the course.

The vocabulary listing would be divided according to parts of speech: nouns (subdivided by gender, if appropriate), verbs (by conjugation), adjectives (regular and irregular), prepositions (and the case they govern), adverbs, conjunctions (and the verb forms they require), etc. The grammatical headings might also be divided into noun phrases, pronouns, verb tenses, etc.

These listings are very convenient when writing quizzes and tests. First of all, they let the teacher see at a glance whether certain expressions or structures have already been introduced. Secondly, they provide a checklist that lets the teacher see if certain words and structures are being overused, while others are being left out. Language learning is a cyclical and cumulative process; the classroom test can help reinforce prior learnings if the test items consciously reenter previously presented material.

2.2.3   Writing the items

Ideally, the classroom test should be written a few days before it is to be administered. This allows the teacher to read the test over with a fresh eye before preparing the stencil (and tape, if appropriate). On a second reading, one often notices ambiguities and errors that slipped by unnoticed when the test was first written. If possible, a colleague should read the test critically and a native speaker should be invited to check for correctness of language.

If alternative forms of the test are needed, for instance as a makeup test or second test, it is advisable to prepare these related tests at the same time. In this way, the teacher can be sure that all forms are of equal difficulty and equal length. Moreover, it is much faster to prepare several equivalent tests at the same time than to prepare each test separately.

2.2.4   Planning the scoring system

Once the entire test has been drafted, the scoring system should be determined. For multiple-choice tests, the teacher should fill out an answer key in advance so that any unbalanced distribution of correct responses can be remedied by shuffling the distractors.

For writing tests, scoring tables should be planned. Anticipated responses to essay test items should be listed, together with the appropriate number of points to be given for each part of a directed item or aspect of an essay subject.

For a speaking test, a different kind of scoring sheet is needed. If several questions are to be asked of each student and if different aspects of each response are to be judged, then it is often best to prepare individual scoring sheets. In an informal classroom test, when relatively few questions are to be asked, a single scoring sheet may contain the names of all students, perhaps in random order so that they cannot anticipate their turns.

The following guidelines will help the teacher check over a midterm or final exam prior to typing the final stencil:

1. Add up the number of points on the test. How many points (what percent) test grammar? How many test vocabulary? How many test communication? etc. The balance of the test items in the exam should reflect the proportions assigned to the various course objectives.
2. Check the content of the test items against the outline of material covered in class. Does the test cover all the essential points? Are the basic patterns given much more importance than the exceptions?
3. Take the test yourself, writing out all the responses. This should take you no more than half the time allotted for the actual test administration. Shorten the test if needed.
4. As you write the answers, check to see that the correct responses have not been accidentally used in another part of the test. For instance, if the students must write out the past tense form *he came*, you should make sure that the form *came* does not occur in another item.
5. As you take the test, try to determine whether an item might have more than one correct answer. Rework any ambiguous items that you uncover.

2.2.5   Test construction in multisection courses

Making comprehensive classroom tests is a highly technical task, demanding both concentration and time. In a department offering several sections of a given course, a common test program may be initiated. The construction of tests can be coordinated in the following way:

2.2.5a   ROTATION OF RESPONSIBILITY

Each teacher assumes responsibility for a specific examination during the year. He or she plans a tentative outline and asks the other instructors to contribute a specific number of items to each section. He or she also has charge of editing the script, cutting the stencil, and recording the tape.

2.2.5b   SMALL COMMITTEE

A small committee with a rotating membership prepares the common examinations. Each member either constructs certain portions of the test or contributes items to each portion. The committee also handles the mechanics of test preparation.

2.2.5c   ONE EXAMINER WITH RELEASED TIME

In a college department, one professor may be given a lighter teaching load in order to construct semester, and perhaps midterm, examinations. This system is especially effective for unifying the objectives and methods of instruction in first- and second-year language courses.

2.3   THE MULTIPLE-CHOICE ANSWER SHEET

Although the prepared answer sheet necessitates a slight investment in paper and the use of a duplicating machine, it more than pays for itself in terms of hours saved. Four copies of Figure 4 can be typed on a single stencil; then the printed tests can be cut lengthwise into columns with a paper cutter. When taking the test, the students indicate their choice of answers by completely blackening the corresponding letter with a soft pencil. If a student changes a response, the first mark must be completely erased. If two black marks appear for the same question, that question is counted wrong.

  The box at the top of each column allows the students to make a note of

Figure 4

Name					
Class					
Test number					

	☐	☐	☐	☐	☐
1.	A	B	C	D	E
2.	A	B	C	D	E
3.	A	B	C	D	E
4.	A	B	C	D	E
5.	A	B	C	D	E
6.	A	B	C	D	E
7.	A	B	C	D	E
8.	A	B	C	D	E
9.	A	B	C	D	E
10.	A	B	C	D	E
11.	A	B	C	D	E
12.	A	B	C	D	E
13.	A	B	C	D	E
14.	A	B	C	D	E
15.	A	B	C	D	E
16.	A	B	C	D	E
17.	A	B	C	D	E
18.	A	B	C	D	E
19.	A	B	C	D	E
20.	A	B	C	D	E

	(2)	(3)	(4)	(5)
A___	19-20,	19-20,	18-20,	18-20
B___	17-18,	16-18,	15-17,	15-17
C___	15-16,	13-15,	12-14,	11-14
D___	13-14,	11-12,	9-11,	8-10
F___	0-12,	0-10,	0-8,	0-7

additional instructions. If A = true and B = false, for example, the students are first told to enter a T in the box above column A and an F in the box above column B. Similarly, if A = past time, B = present time, and C = future time, the students will make the appropriate annotations in columns A, B, and C before taking the test.

In preparing to score the test, the teacher makes a scoring grid by marking the correct answers on a copy of the answer sheet. The blackened letters are punched out with a paper punch. To facilitate placing the grid accurately on each student's answer sheet, the numbers 1 and 20 are also punched out. The bottom part of the grid is cut off. To correct a test, the teacher places the grid over the student answer sheet, counts the number of visible black marks, and enters a check next to the appropriate grade at the bottom of the sheet. The grade is dependent on the number of possible responses. Thus, the only steps required for grading each test are aligning the grid, totaling the visible black marks, and drawing a checkmark (see Figure 5). Grades may then be entered directly in the record book.

The suggested grades for the numerical scores take into account only the "guess" factor for a 20-item test. A person with no language training will be able to guess an average of 10 correct responses out of 20 when only two choices are allowed. He would average a score of 6 or 7 out of 20 when given three choices, and 5 out of 20 when presented with four choices. To cancel this element of chance, the score for a passing grade must be at least three points above the average score obtained through pure guessing. Column 2 on the answer sheet gives the grades for tests with two choices, column 3 is to be used with three choices, and so on.

Some words of caution should be introduced at this point. First, there is nothing sacred about a 20-point quiz; on some days the teacher may wish to include only 15 items, or perhaps only 7 or 8. The same answer sheet would still be used, but the teacher would write the number of correct responses at the bottom of each student quiz. Second, the suggested grade–score correspondences at the bottom of the answer sheet are valid only for quizzes of moderate difficulty. On quizzes that are quite easy, the teacher might prefer to establish a cut-off point, such as 18 on a 20-item quiz, and merely mark the papers as "passing" or "failing." On very difficult quizzes, the teacher would write the number of correct responses at the bottom of the answer sheet and determine an appropriate grade–score scale.

Some teachers are concerned with the possibility of cheating. When the answer sheets are used with classroom listening tests, students can sense the movement of pencils. Thus, if the correct response on a four-choice item is B, many students will be marking their sheet while the teacher is reading C and D. The poor student would tend to mark B also, getting that item right for the wrong reasons. This problem can be minimized by asking students not to mark their papers until all options have been read. In the language

Figure 5

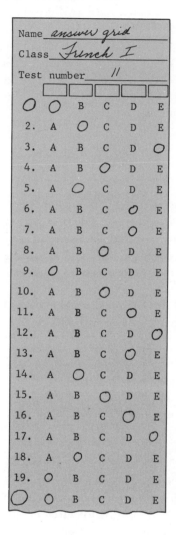

		(2)	(3)	(4)	(5)
A	____	19-20,	19-20,	18,20,	18-20
B	____	17-18,	16-18,	15-17,	15-17
C	✓	15-16,	13-15,	12-14,	11-14
D	____	13-14,	11-12,	9-11,	8-10
F	____	0-12,	0-10,	0-8,	0-7

laboratory, the dividers between booths greatly reduce visual communication between students.

Although it is possible that on a single test a poor student may make enough good guesses to receive a high mark (which in that case would be an unreliable estimation of his or her ability), the general pattern of daily grades over a period of time can present quite a reliable record of that student's achievement. The validity of this evaluation, however, is *always* dependent on the specific content of the quizzes themselves.

2.4　THE ITEM FILE

The purpose of a *test-item file* is to enable the teacher to keep items for easy reference and to allow quicker and more efficient test construction. Although many teachers simply file old exams by date of administration, it is more convenient to keep a second file in which items are grouped according to content and type, for example, vocabulary questions based on Chapter 3 of *A-LM French*, Second Edition.

The choice of format for the item file will depend on the teacher's preferences. The main considerations are easy accessibility and quick retrieval.

2.4.1　Card format

Each question or item is typed on a file card or piece of paper. The advantage of paper is that it occupies less space, but cards are sturdier and are easier to handle and file.

The file cards may be 3×5, 4×6, or 5×8. For long multiple-choice items, the largest card is the most convenient. Plain paper is available in pads of many different sizes, but the 5×8 (or $5\frac{1}{2} \times 8\frac{1}{2}$) is again the most convenient. (Typing paper can be cut in half if desired.) It is often helpful to get cards or paper of different colors to facilitate classification.

If each card contains only one item or set of items, the teacher may record the results of the item analysis on the back of the card. If the item is used more than once, additional results may also be entered on the card. As the new test is being put together, the cards may be shuffled, thus varying the order of the questions from previous tests (see Figures 6 and 7).

Each card is classified according to type of test, textbook and chapter, type of item, and item content. The cards are then filed in such a way that they may be easily retrieved. Probably the teacher would group items from a given text and chapter together, and then subgroup them according to test type.

Figure 6

French: Written Grammar

Valette FFM:2[4]

Chapter 5

taxonomy: Stage 3 = Transfer
type: Transformation
content: reflexive verbs, passé composé—
emphasis on agreement of past participle

Anne et Pierre s'aiment.
Dites qu'ils ont fait toutes les
choses suivantes hier. Mettez
les phrases au passé composé.

1. Ils se téléphonent.
2. Ils se parlent.
3. Ils se disputent.
4. Ils se donnent rendez-vous.
5. Ils se préparent.
6. Ils s'embrassent.

Anne and Pierre are in love.
Say that they did all the
following things yesterday.
Use the passé composé.

1. *They telephone each other.*
2. *They talk to each other.*
3. *They argue.*
4. *They arrange to meet.*
5. *They get ready.*
6. *They kiss.*

Figure 7

Correct answers:

1. Ils se sont téléphoné.
2. Ils se sont parlé.
3. Ils se sont disputés.
4. Ils se sont donné rendez-vous.
5. Ils se sont préparés.
6. Ils se sont embrassés.

Number of errors/number of papers:

Date		Date	
1.		4.	
2.		5.	
3.		6.	

---

[4] Adapted from Jean-Paul Valette and Rebecca M. Valette, *French for Mastery: Book Two* (Lexington, Mass.: D. C. Heath, 1975), p. 219.

2.4.2 Typing-paper format

In the typing-paper format, each item or set of items is entered on a separate sheet of paper. The easiest way to prepare such a file is to cut apart extra examination papers. The classification is typed at the top of the sheet of paper, and then the appropriate test section is glued in place. For writing tests, the correct answers can be entered in ink of a different color, and the item analysis can be written in the margins.

For listening tests, two sheets of paper would be used. One sheet would contain the tape script, while the second would contain the student answer sheet corresponding to that part of the test. For convenience, the two sheets would be stapled together.

The items would be sorted by textbook and chapter, and then grouped in folders according to item type.[5] In a foreign language department, all instructors could take the responsibility for cutting apart their tests and filing the various sections appropriately: vocabulary via listening; oral communication; written grammar; etc. These files would be accessible to any teacher making up a new exam.

[5] If desired, the chapter divisions and subheadings of Part Two of this handbook could serve as the framework for a classification system.

outline

3.1 TESTS IN A TRADITIONAL PROGRAM

    3.1.1 Timing
        3.1.1a Elementary schools
        3.1.1b Secondary schools and colleges
    3.1.2 Reinforcing correct responses
        3.1.2a Reinforcement on quizzes
        3.1.2b Reinforcement on tests

3.2 TESTS IN AN INDIVIDUALIZED OR COMPETENCY-BASED PROGRAM

    3.2.1 Flexibility in scheduling
    3.2.2 Rapidity of scoring

3.3 TESTING IN THE LANGUAGE LABORATORY

    3.3.1 Advantages of language-laboratory tests
    3.3.2 Disadvantages of language-laboratory tests
    3.3.3 Planning the language-laboratory test
    3.3.4 Types of language-laboratory tests
        3.3.4a Listening
        3.3.4b Speaking
        3.3.4c Reading
        3.3.4d Writing

three

Giving The Classroom Test

The classroom test should contribute to the learning process by enabling the students to demonstrate their acquisition of skill rather than impede it either by frightening them or by presenting them with test items that do not accurately reflect the course objectives. Undoubtedly, the content of a test is most important, but the effective administration of a test is a definite factor in its success.

3.1 TESTS IN A TRADITIONAL PROGRAM

In a traditional program, all students in a class take the tests at the same time and receive grades that reflect their progress relative to the other students in the course.

3.1.1 Timing

The big tests, midterms and finals, are usually scheduled by the administration and pinpointed on the school calendar. The teacher enjoys a certain amount of leeway, however, in planning classroom tests—short quizzes and unit tests.

3.1.1a ELEMENTARY SCHOOLS

In elementary schools few quizzes and tests are given. Class time is spent almost exclusively developing the listening and speaking skills: songs, short poems, dialogs, oral questions and answers all form an integral part of the instruction. The main contribution of Foreign Languages in the Elementary Schools (FLES) is the development of proper speech habits (pronunciation, intonation, and stress patterns) and of a positive attitude toward language learning. During the first years, testing is of interest primarily to the teacher, helping him or her to evaluate the effectiveness of certain methods and procedures. When the FLES program has been initiated on a trial basis, the administrators will also be interested in observing student progress in order to assess the effectiveness of the program and its role in the educational process.

Informal testing occurs whenever the teacher requests an individual response from a pupil. Short quizzes teach the pupil what procedures and types of questions will make up the more formal tests. The quizzes can be introduced as games or as opportunities to show off how much has been learned; they should be easy enough so that most pupils perform very well.

The few formal tests of the year should be announced well in advance, and their exact scope should be specified. Only those aspects of the language that have been thoroughly practiced in class should be incorporated into the test. A variety of stimuli such as oral cues, pictures, or situation dialogs may be used. Sufficient examples should be given so that all students are at ease before the test begins. The easiest questions should be given first to allow all students to build up confidence before attacking more difficult items.

3.1.1b   SECONDARY SCHOOLS AND COLLEGES

In secondary schools, and even more in colleges, outside work is required. With a variety of academic subjects and extracurricular activities vying for the student's time, the discipline of daily quizzes often proves effective. Some teachers find that an occasional surprise quiz maintains student alertness.

Unit tests should be given distinct advance notice, and the material to be covered should be clearly defined. The test that is given should correspond to its announced description, for students receive satisfaction from having prepared certain material carefully and then having the opportunity to show how well they have learned it. If new material is included in the test, or if sections of the announced material are omitted, the students may become discouraged.

3.1.2   Reinforcing correct responses

The testing program can become a particularly effective component of the teaching program if the students receive positive reinforcement for their correct responses and good performance. They should also be able to go over a test and profit from their mistakes.

3.1.2a REINFORCEMENT ON QUIZZES

Short quizzes lend themselves very well to immediate reinforcement. Whether the quiz is given at the beginning or end of the hour, the teacher should allot a few minutes for a rapid review of the items. On occasion the students may exchange their papers and correct the quizzes themselves, but often this procedure is overly time-consuming. Moreover, the students, even the more conscientious ones, often make errors in grading, and in any case the teacher must go over the papers too. Generally it is more efficient for the teacher to collect the papers and to review the test orally. On spoken tests those students who have performed poorly may be corrected individually or in a small group after the period; the entire class should not sit idly while one student is being corrected, nor should that student be subjected to the possible humiliation of being corrected at length on his or her test performance in front of the whole class.

3.1.2b REINFORCEMENT ON TESTS

With tests immediate reinforcement becomes more difficult. It is possible to allow ten minutes at the end of the period to go over sections of the test—a practice particularly effective for listening-comprehension tests or for written tests with oral cues. If the test involves primarily the skills of reading and writing, then the students usually profit most from review if they can see their corrected papers. The teacher should therefore make every effort to correct such tests within a day or two and, when the papers have been handed back to the students, to go over the questions that posed particular difficulty. Some teachers have the students rewrite in their entirety the items in which they made errors. If the students are quite sure of the correct responses, such a practice provides desirable reinforcement. However, if the poor students do not understand where and why they made mistakes, they gain nothing from spending additional time on wrong forms; these students would profit more from concentrated drill or homework in the areas in which they are weak.

With motivated students, the teacher can provide immediate reinforcement of a written examination by giving each student two copies of the test paper.[1] The students complete one test for the teacher and also enter their answers on the second copy. When they leave the class, they can discuss the test among themselves and look up questions they are uncertain about. Even if the teacher is not able to correct the tests for the next class period, the second copy can serve as a basis for a quick class review of difficult sections.

[1] Suggestion of Professor William J. Nolan, Western Kentucky University, Bowling Green, Kentucky.

3.2   TESTS IN AN INDIVIDUALIZED OR COMPETENCY-BASED PROGRAM

In an individualized or competency-based program, tests are used to ascertain whether or not the student has attained specific objectives. Students receive credit according to the progress they have made and the amount of material they have mastered, rather than according to their standing or rank within a class.[2]

3.2.1   Flexibility in scheduling

If students are permitted to take tests when they feel ready to do so, the teacher must establish a flexible system for administering tests. If the teacher always meets his or her classes in the same classroom, it is usually possible to set up a "testing corner" where students may take tests when ready. In a semi-individualized program, certain days and times may be set aside for testing, and the students would be expected to work within this prearranged schedule.

If aspects of the mastery-learning strategy are applied to classes, in a traditional program the teacher will want to schedule all tests and final examinations somewhat earlier than the prescribed dates. In this way the teacher will be able to correct the examinations and return the results to the students *before* the official dates. Students who are dissatisfied with their grades may take a second examination (retest) at the regular examination times. Those who scored well on the first test have more time to devote to tests in other subjects during examination week.

3.2.2   Rapidity of scoring

If students are allowed to take a test over as often as necessary for them to demonstrate that they have mastered the material being tested, it is essential that they be informed of their test results as quickly as possible. Therefore, the scoring of such tests should be carried out with a minimum time lag. It is usually advisable to give a series of short tests rather than one long test: in this way the student who experiences difficulties will retake only that short test or those specific tests that caused the problems. The teacher is also saved the time involved in rescoring a long test several times.

[2] For a more detailed description of test administration in an individualized classroom, see Renée S. Disick, Chapter 13: "Testing, Grading and Record Keeping" in her book, *Individualizing Language Instruction: Strategies and Methods* (New York: Harcourt Brace Jovanovich, 1972).

3.3   TESTING IN THE LANGUAGE LABORATORY

Many schools have language laboratories that can be used for administering tests. Many of the following remarks refer to tests in which the cue is recorded in advance and where the students respond by reading, writing or marking an answer sheet. (Such tests can also be administered in a traditional classroom with a tape recorder or cassette player.)

3.3.1   Advantages of language-laboratory tests

Language-laboratory tests possess a high degree of objectivity. All students get the same questions, asked the same way and at the same speed. For the teacher there is the added convenience that all students progress together and finish at the same time. At the college level, make-up tests can be self-administered. The test itself, if given at the end of the laboratory period, can be an incentive to the students to apply themselves more seriously to learning the lesson material.

3.3.2   Disadvantages of language-laboratory tests

The language laboratory does not present the student with a "real-life" situation. Indeed, the artificiality of the classroom becomes even more marked in the laboratory, for the classroom at least has the advantage of offering the oral give-and-take of conversation, and the student's comprehension is helped by gestures and facial expressions.

Language-laboratory tests have the additional disadvantage that it is technically difficult to immediately confirm correct answers for multisection classes once the test questions have been administered and the students have recorded their answers. As a solution, the proctor or teacher could post the correct answers for multiple-choice or written tests on a bulletin board close to the exit door. If the test is administered only once, answer sheets could be distributed as soon as the test papers have been collected.

3.3.3   Planning the language-laboratory test

Since students cannot ask questions or show by a quizzical look that they have not understood, the directions for the language-laboratory test must be extremely clear. It is advisable to read the directions twice. The directions should be in the native language until the teacher is convinced that even the slowest student will understand instructions in the target language.

The laboratory test is prepared as carefully as other language tests. Once the items have been written, the script is typed in page form and the recording made, preferably by native speakers.

Before giving a major test, the teacher should check the equipment carefully to insure that all students hear the oral cues properly. If a spoken portion of the test is to be recorded by the students, the equipment for this should also be checked.

3.3.4 Types of language-laboratory tests

3.3.4a LISTENING

Listening-comprehension and sound-discrimination tests can be administered very effectively in the language laboratory. If desired, a slide projector, opaque projector, or wall chart can furnish additional visual cues. The students indicate their answers to oral multiple-choice questions on an answer sheet. It is also possible to prepare printed answer booklets in which the students respond either to printed multiple-choice questions and answers or to oral questions and printed responses.

3.3.4b SPEAKING

The speaking test in which students record their responses should be administered only in a laboratory with high-fidelity equipment. Both students and teachers become discouraged when they discover that some machines have not been working properly or that responses were occasionally inaudible.

Cues for the speaking test can be oral, written, or visual. More advanced students may also demonstrate their proficiency by reading aloud; the text is distributed, and the students are given several minutes to prepare the reading before recording it.

Informal speaking tests may be given frequently in the laboratory if the teacher regularly monitors the class (as is usually the case in junior high and secondary schools). The following effective method has been suggested. The first or second time a lesson tape is used, the students hear and repeat the confirmations of the drills. A second two-phase tape, the same as the first but minus the confirmations, is prepared. This latter tape is used on the last day of the lesson. The teacher tunes in to the various student positions at random and grades student production. Such an informal testing system greatly stimulates better performance in the laboratory.[3]

[3] Virginia Cables, "The Language Laboratory, Boon or Bane?" *French Review* 39 (February 1966), pp. 618–22.

3.3.4c READING

It is possible to have all students work through a reading test at the same speed by using the laboratory. Each student is given a passage to read silently; after a signal the student is presented with a series of related oral questions on tape to determine how well he or she understood the text.

3.3.4d WRITING

The laboratory can be used to administer writing tests based on oral material. Dictation, pattern drills requiring written response, and directed paragraphs are all variations that can be adapted for use in the language laboratory. More advanced students can be graded on their ability to take notes on a recorded lecture.

outline

four

Evaluating Classroom Test Results

O nce the teacher has given a classroom test, he or she will want to evaluate the results. The manner in which results are interpreted depends on the type of test selected.

The *norm-referenced test* is used to rank students and to assign grades. Traditional measurement and evaluation techniques help the teacher improve classroom tests of this type. All measurement includes units and standards. To say that a book is worth 100 means nothing until the unit or standard of measure is defined (dollars? cents? francs? pesos?). Similarly, to say that a student scored 30 is of no significance until we know the length of the test (30 items or 150 items), how difficult the test was (is 30 a low score or a high one?), and what material the test covered.

The classroom teacher should be familiar with some very rudimentary concepts of measurement as they are applied to foreign languages. The first three sections of this chapter will define basic terms that are of use in discussing classroom tests and will suggest methods for making a simple analysis of both student scores and tests themselves.

The *criterion-referenced test* measures students' performance against a preestablished criterion or set of objectives. Such tests provide results that let the students know where they stand and where their weaknesses are. The evaluation of results on criterion-referenced tests stresses the diagnostic function: the student must be made aware of his or her level of achievement and must be told how to strengthen the weak areas.

Communication tests are *global language tests* rather than *discrete-point tests*. Although such tests may be used to rank students, they do not permit the same type of interpretation or item analysis as the objective *norm-referenced tests*. Frequently the teacher will want to adapt error analysis techniques (discussed in Section 4.5) to discover where student weaknesses lie.

4.1 BASIC CONCEPTS

Some tests are poor under any circumstances. But the results of even a good test are meaningful only if properly interpreted. The two essential characteristics of a good test are:

1. *reliability* (It must yield a dependable score.)
2. *validity* (It must measure what it is supposed to measure.)[1]

A third concept that plays a role in test score interpretation is *correlation*.

4.1.1 Reliability

Test *reliability*, expressed by test publishers in statistical terms, refers to the consistency of the examination scores. Presumably, if the same test were given twice to the same group of students, the performances of each student would show little variation. The requisites of a dependable test are the following:

1. multiple samples
2. standard tasks
3. standard conditions
4. standard scoring

4.1.1a MULTIPLE SAMPLES

For students' mastery of a complex body of knowledge to be reliably evaluated, they must be asked many questions. They must be given enough opportunities to demonstrate their familiarity with the various aspects of the subject. Learning a foreign language entails not only the acquisition of vocabulary and manipulation of a new grammatical system, but also the mastery of the skills of listening, speaking, reading, and writing. Consequently, a language test, in order to yield a reliable score, must be long enough to provide a generous sampling of the area or areas tested. While the scores on one short quiz cannot be expected to furnish a reliable appraisal of a student's achievement, the average score of a series of quizzes becomes more and more dependable as the number of quizzes increases.

It is also important that there be a wide spread in the level of difficulty of the items. A 75-item test containing items of similar difficulty will be a considerably less sensitive instrument of evaluation than a test of equal length

[1] For a more detailed presentation, see Henry Chauncey and John E. Dobbin, *Testing, Its Place in Education Today* (New York: Harper & Row, 1963), Chapter 4.

that contains a wide variety of levels of difficulty. The following example will clarify this essential concept:

Figure 8

Student	Test A (100 items)	Test B (20 items)	Test C (100 items)
1	97	20	85
2	92	20	86
3	80	20	85
4	73	19	84
5	66	20	85
6	60	19	83
7	52	17	82
8	43	18	82

The results of Test A are much more reliable because there is a much greater range in the scores than in Tests B and C.

4.1.1b STANDARD TASKS

If the test scores are to provide a dependable means of comparing student performances, then all students must be given the same items or items of equal difficulty. A brief oral test in which each student is asked a different question will yield a reliable score only if each response is scored according to a system that functions independently of the specific content of the items. The concept of standard tasks furnishes the basis for standardized tests: not only are the questions identical (or equivalent), but the format, too, is the same.

4.1.1c STANDARD CONDITIONS

The reliability of the test score can be assured only if all the students take the examination under identical conditions. In a listening test, for example, all students must be able to hear the items distinctly. On the individual level, the score of a student who was exhausted or ill at the time of the test will be an unreliable indication of his or her overall ability.

Occasionally a student is so nervous at the prospect of a test that he or she consistently performs significantly less well than his or her classroom participation would predict. A student under this kind of psychological stress is unable to take a formal test under the same conditions as the others in the class, and therefore that student's test results are unreliable indicators of his or her ability. The simplest solution in such rare cases is to excuse the student from taking tests and to find other means of evaluating his or her performance.

4.1.1d STANDARD SCORING

All tests must be scored in an identical manner. The advantage of multiple-choice tests rests on the fact that a mechanical error is the only element that can lower the dependability of the scoring. The least reliable test scores tend to be those given essay questions. Not only will different teachers disagree about the classification of a group of papers, but an individual teacher, reading the same papers on two different days, may assign different grades to the same essay. Speaking tests also present similar scoring problems. Methods of improving scorer reliability are described in Part Two of this handbook.

4.1.2 Validity

Test *validity*, that is, the relevance of the examination, is the area on which many of the testing controversies have centered: objective tests are criticized for their failure to measure this or that aspect of a subject. The publishers of commercial tests are often at fault for having omitted a detailed description of precisely what the tests presume to evaluate. For example, three different tests may be designated as "first-year Spanish tests," and yet all three may be entirely different: one might be appropriate for use in junior high school, another in senior high school, and a third in college. One might be a listening test with written alternatives for the student to choose from; one might be a reading test with questions in English about Spanish vocabulary and grammar; another might be a written test entirely in Spanish with emphasis on questions of reading interpretation and general cultural knowledge. Thus, the teacher must assess the content validity of a test before administering it. In constructing their own tests, too, teachers must evaluate the validity of the various items in relation to their course objectives. If the teacher wants his or her college class in elementary German to attain equal proficiency in the four language skills, and if the tests are all written ones, then the test scores will not be *valid* evaluations of the professed objectives.

For the language teacher, the degree of test validity is not derived from a statistical analysis of test performance, but from a meticulous analysis of the content of each item and of the test as a whole.

4.1.3   Correlation

In testing, the correlation coefficient describes the relationship between two series of scores. For example, a *high* correlation exists between two tests if the students scoring high on one generally score high on the other, and if those scoring low on one also generally score low on the other; .89 is a high positive correlation. The correlation is said to be *perfect* if the changes in one score always correspond exactly to a predictable change in the other score; ± 1.00 is a perfect correlation. When the scores on one test correspond in no predictable way to variations of scores on another test, then the correlation is defined as zero. Low correlations range from $\pm .01$ to .30.

The concept of correlation can help the language teacher in two specific areas: determining the relationship between the various language skills and determining the reliability of a specific examination.

Correlation may be represented graphically on a scatter diagram; the pattern of the marks gives the teacher a general idea of the degree of correlation between two variables. Here are some small scatter diagrams: A perfect correlation is a straight line, whereas zero correlation shows no trace of a grouping of points.

Figure 9

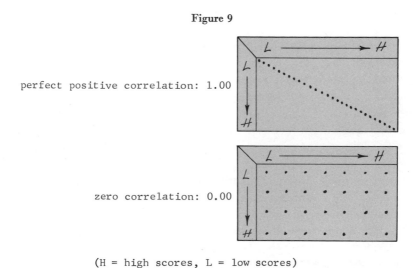

perfect positive correlation: 1.00

zero correlation: 0.00

(H = high scores, L = low scores)

The following chart shows a good positive correlation between the performance on the dictation part of a German examination and the score on the remainder of the examination (listening, reading, and writing). Statistically the correlation coefficient of the scatter plot has been evaluated at .90, an extremely high correlation.

Figure 10

Dictation score	Examination score									
	40 -49	50 -59	60 -69	70 -79	80 -89	90 -99	100 -109	110 -119	120 -129	130 -139
11				/						
12		/	/	/	/					
13			/	//	//					
14			////	＃ /						
15	/	/		//	//	/	/			
16			/	＃	/	///	/			
17				////	///	＃				
18				/	/	/	////	///	/	/
19						///	////	＃ //	＃	//
20									////	/

Although a good correlation cannot be taken as proof of a causal relationship between two variables, the teacher in the above case could arrive at the following conclusions: Given the conditions under which the class had been taught, the materials used, and the skills emphasized, the dictation grade furnishes a reliable evaluation of the student's proficiency in the other skills. On the other hand, the dictation could be suppressed because it changes very little the student's total score on the examination. In arriving at these conclusions, however, the teacher must be cautious not to go beyond the specific limitation of the case under study. It cannot be concluded from the above information that dictation could serve as a complete final examination in any German class. Perhaps the correlation between dictation and overall performance was high because the students were sure they were being graded on a comprehensive two-hour examination; had these students thought that their entire grade would depend on the dictation, they probably would have spent time practicing dictations. Perhaps their score would not have correlated so highly with overall language proficiency under different conditions.

4.2 ANALYZING THE SCORES: THE NORM-REFERENCED TEST

The raw scores on a norm-referenced test are usually calculated in numerical terms. Before converting the scores into grades, the teacher must first organize this collection of numbers into a manageable form.

4.2.1 Adjustment for guessing

On a multiple-choice test, the teacher may wish to adjust the raw scores to correct for guessing. This is particularly true in speed tests.

4.2.1a SPEED TESTS

On a *speed test* even the better students know that they will probably not be able to finish. Their score will depend not only on knowledge and comprehension but also on the speed at which they progress. In order to discourage indiscriminate guessing on a speed test, the numerical scores are often modified:

two options (for example: true-false)
    adjusted score = number right − number wrong
three options
    adjusted score = number right − $\frac{1}{2}$ number wrong
four options
    adjusted score = number right − $\frac{1}{3}$ number wrong
five options
    adjusted score = number right − $\frac{1}{4}$ number wrong

The rationale of this adjustment is the following. Let us assume that out of 100 items with four options, Steven had finished 60 items when he realized that only thirty seconds remained. He quickly marked Response A for Items 61 through 100 on his answer sheet; he hoped to get about one out of four correct and thus raise his score by 10 points. If we assume that Steven actually did make 10 correct guesses and 30 wrong ones, then his adjusted score on Items 61 to 100 would be

$$10 \text{ right} - \tfrac{1}{3} (30 \text{ wrong}) = 0$$

Thus, Steven gained nothing through his wild guessing.

4.2.1b POWER TESTS

On a *power test*, sufficient time is allowed for even the slowest student to finish, even though he may not actually do so because of the difficulty of the items. In grading a power test (and most classroom tests are power tests), the teacher is interested in seeing how well each student has done, what his or her total score is, and what grade best describes his or her performance. If the items are arranged in order of increasing difficulty, then it is not necessary that all students finish; a student's own stopping or slowdown point may be taken as an indication of his or her proficiency. Even with additional time the student would probably not have improved his or her performance significantly.

On the power test, therefore, an adjustment for guessing is not necessary. No student would have to answer a long series of items by blind guessing in order to finish the test before the time limit.

4.2.2 Describing the scores

Let us look at the various ways of handling the scores of a hypothetical 90-item test administered to 51 students.

4.2.2a RANGE

By finding the highest and lowest scores the teacher can determine the test range. At the same time, the teacher notes the maximum possible score. Thus, if the highest score on our hypothetical test is 86 and the lowest 53, the range is from 86 to 53 (or 34) and the maximum possible score is 90.

4.2.2b DISTRIBUTION

The distribution of scores can best be visualized by listing all possible scores within the range of the highest and lowest scores achieved and then recording after each score the number of students who achieved it. The score distribution of our hypothetical test looks like this:

Figure 11

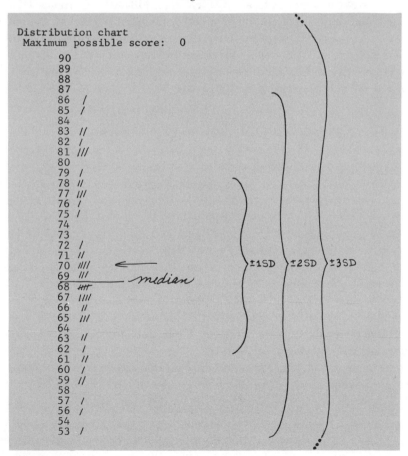

Distribution chart
Maximum possible score: 0

Score	
90	
89	
88	
87	
86	/
85	/
84	
83	//
82	/
81	///
80	
79	/
78	//
77	///
76	/
75	/
74	
73	
72	/
71	//
70	////
69	///
68	////
67	////
66	//
65	///
64	
63	//
62	/
61	//
60	/
59	//
58	
57	/
56	/
54	
53	/

← ——— median

±1SD ±2SD ±3SD

4.2.2c MEDIAN

The *median* refers to the score obtained by the middle paper of the whole group of tests. On this test the median fell between 68 and 69 because 25 papers scored 68 and lower and 26 papers scored 69 and higher.

4.2.2d MEAN

The *mean* score of the test is the average score. To calculate the mean, all the scores are added and the sum is divided by the number of papers:

$$(M)\text{mean} = \frac{\text{sum of the scores}}{\text{number of papers}} = \frac{\sum S}{n}$$

In the hypothetical test of 90 items, the mean was calculated to be 70:

$$M = \frac{3570}{51} = 70$$

4.2.2e STANDARD DEVIATION AND THE NORMAL CURVE

The *standard deviation* (*SD*) is a measure of the spread of the scores on a test. The larger the standard deviation, the greater the range of the scores.

The standard deviation may best be understood in terms of the *normal curve* (which is also referred to as the normal probability curve or the normal distribution curve). The normal curve is a symmetrical bell-shaped curve capable of being divided into standard deviation units, each of which contains a fixed percentage of the test scores. As indicated in Figure 12, 34 percent of the scores fall between the mean and +1 SD, 14 percent of the scores between +1 SD and +2 SD, and 2 percent of the scores between +2 SD and +3 SD. The percentages are identical in the intervals below the mean.[2]

Figure 12

NORMAL CURVE

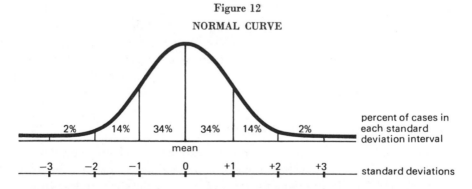

² These figures have been rounded off for convenience. More precisely, 68.26 percent of the scores fall between ± 1 SD; 95.44 percent of the scores between ± 2 SD, and 99.74 percent between ± 3 SD. The remaining .26 percent of the scores are beyond three standard deviation units from the mean.

If the scores on a classroom test follow a roughly normal distribution, about $\frac{2}{3}$ of the papers will fall between ± 1 SD, about 95 percent between ± 2 SD, and over 99 percent ± 3 SD.

The standard deviation is derived through a rather complex mathematical formula. However, the classroom teacher can rapidly calculate the approximate standard deviation for a test as follows:[3]

$$SD = \frac{\text{sum of high sixth} - \text{sum of low sixth}}{\text{half the number of students}}$$

For the sample test (Figure 11), we would proceed in this manner:

One sixth of 51 students is $8\frac{1}{2}$.

The sum of the top $8\frac{1}{2}$ papers (scores of the top 8 papers plus $\frac{1}{2}$ score of the ninth paper) is 701.

The sum of the bottom $8\frac{1}{2}$ scores is 497.

Half the number of students is $\frac{51}{2}$, or $25\frac{1}{2}$.

Hence, $\frac{701 - 497}{25.5} = 8$. The standard deviation of the test is 8.

The mean of this test was 70. Therefore, $\frac{2}{3}$ of the papers should fall between -1 SD (70 $-$ 8, or 62) and $+1$ SD (70 $+$ 8, or 78). Ninety-five percent of the papers should fall between -2 SD (70 $-$ 16, or 54) and $+2$ SD (70 $+$ 16, or 86). And 99 percent of the papers should fall between -3 SD (70 $-$ 24, or 46) and $+3$ SD (70 $+$ 24, or 94, which is off the top of the scale). Figure 11 shows that 34 students (about $\frac{2}{3}$ of 51, the total number of papers) have scores between 62 and 78. There are 50 students, or somewhat over 95 percent, who have scores falling between 54 and 86. Remember that the larger the sample of papers, the more accurate the statistical treatment of the scores.

An understanding of the meaning of the standard deviation can help the teacher interpret the statistics given in handbooks that accompany standard tests. Furthermore, the teacher is better able to compare the performances of his or her students to those in the norm sample, or the group of students on whose performances the statistics were calculated.

4.2.2f RELIABILITY COEFFICIENT

The correlation coefficient (see Section 4.1.3) may also be employed in the statistical evaluation of the reliability of an examination. Two sets of scores are compared, just as was done for the two parts of the German test (Figure

---

[3] Paul Diederich, *Short-Cut Statistics for Teacher-Made Tests*, Evaluation and Service Series, No. 5 (Princeton: Educational Testing Service, 1960), p. 23. This is a free booklet distributed by ETS (hereafter cited as *Short-Cut Statistics*).

10, p. 48). However, since the *reliability coefficient* refers to an entire test, statisticians employ various methods to obtain two sets of scores. They may compare the results of one group of students taking the examination twice, or of two similar groups of students taking the same examination, or of two groups taking equivalent version of the examination. Another way that usually proves more feasible is to compare each student's performance on the even-numbered questions with his or her performance on the odd-numbered questions (split-half reliability).

For a standardized test, publishers try to attain a minimum reliability of .90. However, not only are classroom tests shorter than most standardized tests; the teacher has little opportunity to pretest items in order to select those that are best. The reliability of a good classroom test generally falls between .60 and .80.[4]

An estimate of classroom-test reliability may be obtained with the following Kuder-Richardson formula:

$$\text{reliability} = 1 - \frac{M(n - M)}{nSD^2}$$

Here M is the mean, n the number of items, and SD the standard deviation. Let us refer once again to the sample test scores described above to calculate the reliability of that test.

$$M \text{ (mean)} = 70$$
$$n \text{ (number of items)} = 90$$
$$SD \text{ (standard deviation)} = 8$$

Hence,

$$\text{reliability} = 1 - \frac{70(90 - 70)}{90 \cdot 8^2}$$
$$= 1 - \frac{70 \cdot 20}{90 \cdot 64}$$
$$= 1 - .243$$
$$= .76$$

4.2.2g STANDARD ERROR

The *standard error* (*SE*) of a score is a statistical estimate of the variation to be expected in the scores of a test. If the hypothetical test were given a second time, student scores would fluctuate; even if the test were given over and over, the scores would shift somewhat each time.

[4] For a table showing the approximate reliability of tests, see Diederich, *Short-Cut Statistics*, pp. 30–31.

Perhaps an example from the area of music will help clarify the concept of standard error. Robert has been studying piano for several years. When he plays easy pieces he knows well, he plays them almost perfectly every time: the fluctuation from one performance to the next is almost zero at the top of the scale. When he plays a difficult piece that he can barely decipher, he does very poorly every time: again the fluctuation from one performance to the next is almost zero at the bottom of the scale. When Robert is at a lesson and plays a piece that he has been working on for the teacher, the results vary: sometimes his performance in this situation is much worse than the way he has been playing the piece all week; at other times, his playing is much better than he expected; and most of the time his performance is about what it has been all week. Thus at the middle of the range, there is a certain fluctuation, and a single performance is not always a true reflection of the student's ability at a given moment. This anticipated fluctuation in the performances is reflected in the standard error.

The following table may be used to obtain a rough estimate of standard error:[5]

Figure 13

n number of items	SE standard error	Exceptions: regardless of the length of the test, the standard error is:
< 24	2	
24-47	3	0 when the score is zero or perfect
48-89	4	1 when 1-2 points from 0 or 100%
90-109	5	2 when 3-7 points from 0 or 100%
110-129	6	3 when 8-15 points from 0 or 100%
130-150	7	

Mathematically, the standard error functions like the standard deviation unit. If we apply the table in Figure 13 to our sample test data, we find that the standard error for a 90-item objective test is 5. Now let us consider the student who scored 72. If the student were to take the test repeatedly under similar conditions (and not learn anything by repetition), we could expect to find 68 percent of his or her scores within 1 SE, that is, between 67 and 77 (72 $\pm$ 5). Moreover, 95 percent of the scores would fall within 2 SE—between 62 and 82 (72 $\pm$ 10). Thus we would have a 95 percent change of being correct in assuming that he or she was inferior in performance to the top

[5] Diederich, *Short-Cut Statistics*, pp. 30–31.

four students in the class and better than the bottom eight. We would have a 68 percent chance of being correct in assuming that the student would do less well than the top eleven students and better than the bottom sixteen students were the test given again. We are much less certain about how this student would perform in comparison with those students who made scores close to his or hers.

An awareness of standard error will help the teacher realize that the performance on a single test is not a totally reliable estimate of student ability, unless the score is at the top or the bottom of the scale. However, as the teacher gives a sequence of tests and uses a variety of evaluation procedures throughout the school term, he or she will find the average of these performances providing an increasingly reliable measure of student ability.

4.2.3   Interpreting the scores on a classroom test

The manner in which the scores on a test are translated into grades depends on the type of test and the way in which the language course is set up.

4.2.3a   GRADES ASSIGNED ON A CURVE

On a longer test, letter grades are often assigned on a curve that ideally reflects the features of the normal curve (Figure 12). A small percentage of students receive an "A," a somewhat larger percentage receive a "B," the majority receive "C," and then there are fewer with "D," and less with "F." Before assigning letter grades on a test, the teacher waits to see the distribution of the scores. Sometimes the scores seem to cluster around certain areas and divide themselves conveniently into letter groups. In any case, the teacher will study the distribution chart and consider the difficulty of the test.

For our hypothetical test, we have indicated three possible ways of assigning letter grades (Figure 14); the actual choice would depend on the teacher's opinion about the difficulty of the test.

Recently there has been a trend to skew the curve to the upper end of the scale: teachers are awarding more and more grades of "A" and "B," and "C" has become almost unacceptable. The grades of "D" and "F" are increasingly rare. Many educators have expressed concern over this type of "grade inflation."

Grading on the curve tends to classify students with reference to a specific class: the resulting letter grades have no absolute value. For instance, the student with a "B" in an honors class might have mastered more German than the student with an "A" in the regular course. Furthermore,

Figure 14

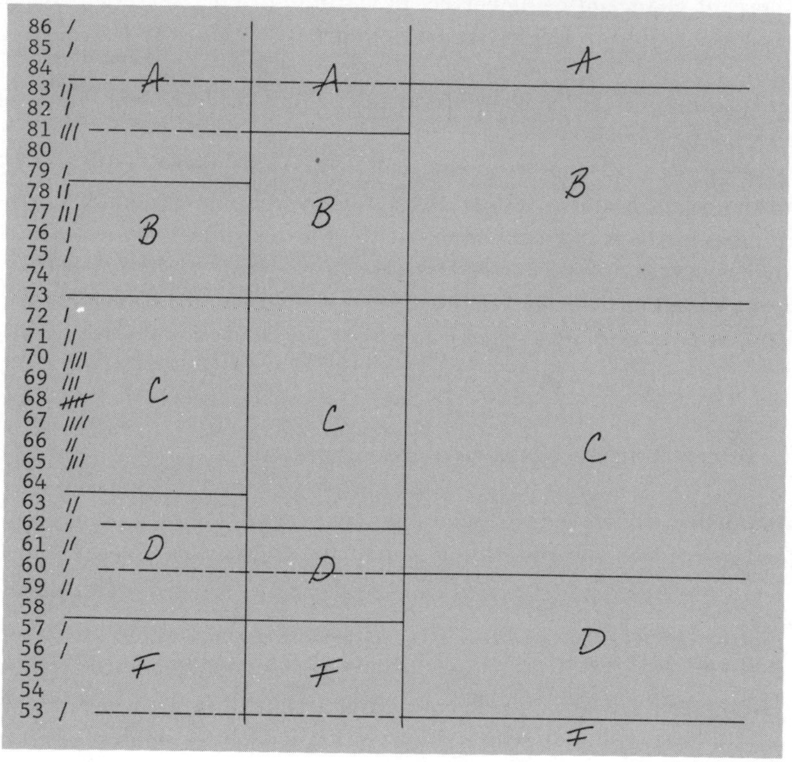

the "A" from one teacher might not correspond to the "A" assigned by another teacher.

4.2.3b GRADES ASSIGNED ON A PERCENT BASIS

In some schools letter grades are assigned on a percent basis. It is assumed that the examinations are good reflections of course objectives, and that an "A," for instance, should be awarded to all students who responded correctly to 91 percent or more of the items. Similarly, an "F" is given to all those who scored below 60 percent. In this situation, it is possible for some letter grades not to be awarded at all. It is also possible for almost all students to receive an "A" on a test.

The percent basis is also used for assigning grades in terms of "pass-fail." A certain cutoff point is established, and students who fall above that mark pass the course. In some college courses, the cutoff point is set very low: students may opt for a "pass-fail" grade if they feel that the corresponding letter grade would be detrimental to their grade point average.

In many individualized courses, the pass-fail cutoff point is set rather high. For instance, on an individualized phonetics test, students may be expected to attain a score of 90 percent in order to pass. The opportunity is provided for tests to be taken over one or more times. The result of the high pass-fail point is that students are encouraged to put in extra effort to attain a demanding goal. The pass-fail grades may be reported as "A" (high pass), "B" (pass), and "F."

4.2.3c GRADES ASSIGNED ON A MODIFIED CURVE

If a teacher finds that the results on a classroom test graded on the percent basis are very poor (for instance, that half the class is below 60 percent), he or she may resort to a modified curve system. With the modified curve the distribution does not follow the normal pattern of the standard curve, but rather gives passing grades to the students at the lower end of the percent scale.

It is also possible, although this is less frequently the case, to apply a modified curve when the grades cluster near the top of the percent scale. For instance, if two-thirds of the class obtain scores above 91 percent, the teacher may decide that 91 percent and 92 percent will correspond to a "B" rather than an "A."

4.2.3d CLASS STANDING

Fifty years ago, most classroom teachers ranked the students within each class, from first to last. Now the schools have turned away from ranking, except for selecting the class valedictorian.

If a teacher wishes to rank the students on a test, the papers or scoring sheets are placed in sequence from the best to the poorest. On the hypothetical class test whose scores are depicted in Figure 14, the student who scored 82 would be ranked fifth in a class of 51.

4.2.4 Interpreting the scores on a standardized test

On *standardized tests*, the raw scores are transformed into standard scores, which report the student's performance in terms of a much larger sample or *norm group*. The tables that accompany standardized tests often present several interpretations for a specific raw score, depending on the student's age, the number of years of study, and other factors. Figure 15 shows the relationship between the normal curve and the more common standard scores: the College Board scale and stanines.

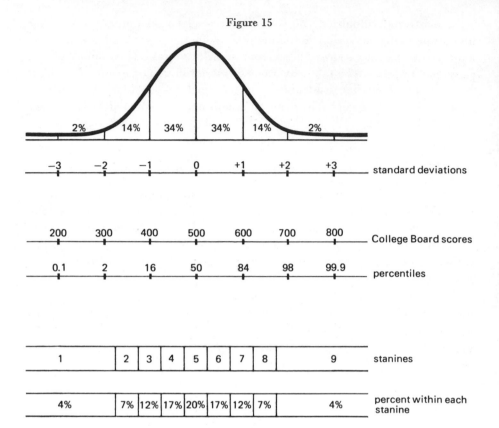

Figure 15

4.2.4a COLLEGE BOARD SCALE

In the College Board scale, the mean is equated with 500 and the standard deviation with 100. Thus a score of 550 indicates that the student's performance is one-half of a standard deviation above the mean. A score of 700 lies two standard deviations above the mean.

If one compares the College Board score with the corresponding percentile scale, it is evident that a score of 700 places the student in the 98th percentile or among the upper 2 percent of the group of students with whom the norms were established. A score of 600 corresponds to the 84th percentile, and so on.

4.2.4b STANINES

Some commercial test scores are converted to stanines. The name reflects the fact that the raw scores are divided into nine segments (standard nines). Stanine 5 is located at the center of the normal curve, and extends one-fourth of a standard deviation to either side of the mean. With the exception of stanine 1 and stanine 9, which are open ended, each stanine interval corresponds to a distance of one-half of a standard deviation. The lowest line of Figure 15 shows about how many students, expressed in percents, are included within each stanine.

4.3   ITEM ANALYSIS: THE NORM-REFERENCED TEST

An analysis of the responses to the individual items of a test will prove helpful for two reasons. First, the teacher can discover if there are certain points that a sizable number of the students have failed to master. Remedial work may be indicated before proceeding to the next unit. Second, the teacher can verify how well certain items have performed in relation to the test as a whole. This information will be useful in constructing new tests.

Several terms should be clarified. Item *difficulty* is determined by observing what percentage of the students answer the item correctly. The more difficult the item is, the fewer will be the students who select the correct option. *Discriminatory power* tells how well the item performs in separating the better students from the poorer students. If the upper third of the students get the item correct and the lower two-thirds generally get the item wrong, then it is a good discriminator between these two groups. Very difficult items should discriminate between the very good students and all of the others; relatively easy items should discriminate between the majority of the students in the class and the few poor ones.

4.3.1   Tallying errors

For short tests and for tests with two options, the teacher can do a very rapid item analysis by tallying the errors. If errors are marked in red pencil during grading, the teacher can easily find them for transfer to the analysis sheet. Here is a sample tally chart:

Figure 16

| Subject _Russian I_ | Test number _8_ |
| Class _A_ | Number of papers _31_ |
Item number or description	Number of errors
1	////
2	─HH //
3	//

When the results have been tallied, the teacher can see which items proved particularly difficult. A review of the item should be made to determine whether the item itself was faulty (ambiguous wording? poor recording?) or whether the point being tested had not been properly assimilated by the students.

4.3.2 Full item analysis: the entire sample

On a multiple-choice objective test administered with answer sheets, the teacher may wish to analyze the performance of the various options. The answer sheets are reviewed one by one, and the student's selected response for each item is transferred to the analysis chart. Here is a sample item-analysis chart:

Figure 17

| Subject _Spanish I_ | Test number _12_ |
| Class _9ᵗʰ grade_ | Number of papers _30_ |

Item number	Options				Total
	A	B	C	D	
1	⦅₳₳ ₳₳ ₳₳ //⦆	//	₳₳	₳₳	30
2	////	⦅₳₳ ₳₳ ₳₳⦆	₳₳ /	₳₳	30
3	⦅₳₳ ₳₳ /⦆	///	₳₳ ₳₳ /	₳₳	30
4	////	₳₳ ₳₳ ₳₳ //	//	⦅₳₳ /⦆	29
5	₳₳	₳₳	⦅₳₳ ₳₳ ////⦆	₳₳ /	30
6	⦅₳₳ ₳₳ ₳₳ ₳₳ ₳₳ ₳₳⦆				30
7	//	///	///	⦅₳₳ ₳₳ ₳₳ ₳₳ //⦆	30

Once all the tallies have been entered, the correct answer for each item is circled for rapid identification.

In Figure 17, Items 1, 2, 5, and 7 performed well. The majority of the students selected the correct response, and the remaining tallies are distributed rather evenly over the remaining three options. Item 3 should be reviewed because most of the responses were evenly divided between A and C; perhaps the wording of the item was faulty, or perhaps the item was very difficult and the distractor C represented a common error for American students (indicating the need for more intense drill in class). On Item 4 the majority of the students selected the wrong answer. Was the answer key at fault? Was the item poorly stated? Was an especially tricky point being tested? For Item 6 all the students selected the correct response; this item does not help in discriminating between students and on a subsequent test should be rejected or used as an initial item.

4.3.3 Full item analysis: divided sample

When two or more classes have taken the same test, a more informative type of item analysis may be made. First, the answer sheets are arranged in rank order from the highest score to the lowest.

4.3.3a DIVISION BY THIRDS

The papers are divided into three piles: the top third, middle third, and bottom third. As each paper is reviewed, the student responses are entered in the appropriate column on the analysis chart. Here is a sample analysis chart:

Figure 18

Subject *Italian* Test number *8*
Class *Sections A, B, C* Number of papers *44*

Item number	Top third (N = 15)				Middle third (N = 15)				Bottom third (N = 14)			
	A	B	C	D	A	B	C	D	A	B	C	D
1	(𝍸 𝍸 /)		//	//	(𝍸 //)		////	////	(𝍸)		𝍸	////
2	(𝍸 𝍸 𝍸)				(𝍸 𝍸 ///)	/		/	(𝍸 𝍸)	/	/	//
3	/	/	/	(𝍸 𝍸 //)	///	//.	/	(𝍸 ////)	///	///	////	(////)
4	//	(𝍸 //)	/	𝍸	///	(𝍸)	//	𝍸	//	(𝍸 ////)	/	//
5		/	(𝍸 𝍸 ///)	/	///	////	(𝍸)	///	𝍸	///	(//)	////

In a good item the top third should show more correct choices than the middle third, and the middle third should show more than the bottom third. An easy item (Item 2) can be answered by all three groups; if used on another test, it should be the first item. Item 3 discriminates between the middle group and the bottom group. Item 5 is another good item, though more difficult than Item 3; it discriminates between the top group and the middle group. Item 4 should be revised or discarded since it performed negatively: more students in the lowest group answered it correctly than students in the top group. Option B in Item 1 should be revised: it was so obviously a wrong response that it was not an effective distractor.

4.3.3b UPPER 27 PERCENT AND LOWER 27 PERCENT

In a formal statistical item analysis, the upper and lower 27 percent of the papers are selected and the performances of the two groups compared. A good item discriminates positively between the two groups; for the lower group all the distractors appear relatively attractive. In a formal item analysis the difficulty, the reliability, and the discriminatory power of the test items will be calculated in statistical terms. For the classroom teacher, a visual comparison will immediately provide usable results. Here is a simplified item-analysis chart:

Figure 19

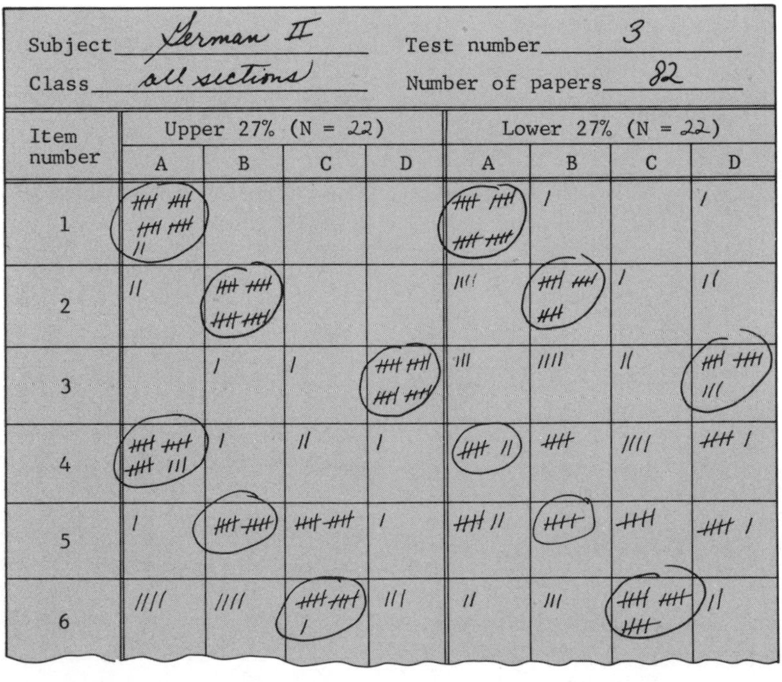

Items 1 through 4 are found to have been arranged in order of increasing difficulty; all performed well though Item 1 (answered correctly by all but two students) was particularly easy. Items 5 and 6 should be reviewed for possible faulty wording or ambiguity.

4.3.4   Item analysis by show of hands

Realizing that the tallying of student scores represents quite an investment in teacher time, Paul Diederich developed the system described in the following sections for carrying out simple item analyses in the classroom.[6]

4.3.4a   COUNTING ERRORS

The scored test papers are either returned to their owners or distributed randomly. As the teacher calls out each item number, those students holding a paper with a *wrong* answer raise their hands. For each item the teacher counts the show of hands and enters the figure on his or her copy of the test. If a sizable percentage of the students answered an item wrong, that item may be discussed later in class. After the first few weeks of instruction, the analysis may be carried out in the target language.

4.3.4b   HIGH-LOW ANALYSIS

After scoring the papers, the teacher arranges them in rank order from high to low. The top half of the papers is distributed to one side of the class, the bottom half to the other. If there is an odd number of papers, the responses on the middle paper are not counted in the analysis. The student who holds this middle (or odd) paper is appointed scorekeeper; he or she records the figures for analysis on the blackboard. He or she also writes the figures on the odd paper.

This time, as the item number is read, the students will raise their hands only if their paper got the item *right*. One student counts hands for the low group and another counts hands for the high group. As the items analysis proceeds, four figures are recorded for each item:

H   number of highs who answered correctly
L   number of lows who answered correctly
H + L   total number who answered correctly (success)
H − L   how many more highs than lows answered correctly (discrimination)

[6] Diederich, *Short-Cut Statistics*, pp. 6–12.

The teacher or scorekeeper first writes the high and low on the board (as these figures are called out by the two student counters), then mentally calculates and notes H + L and H − L on the board. The students copy these figures on the test they have before them; the teacher marks them on his or her copy, and the scorekeeper marks them on the odd test paper.

For example, on Item 1 the numbers might read:

$$13 \quad 7 \quad 20 \quad 6$$

This would mean that 13 in the high group and 7 in the low group answered Item 1 correctly. In all, 20 got the item right (success), and the difference between the groups (discrimination) is 6.

In order to interpret success and discrimination the teacher must take into account the number of students in the class. In the above sample, 28 papers were used. Generally, the most appropriate and most effective items are those answered correctly by 60 to 70 percent of the class, but on classroom tests this might range from 30 to 90 percent. A figure under 30 percent indicates an item is probably too difficult; one over 90 percent, that it is too easy. On the above test, from 8 to 25 students should have selected the right answer on each item. Discrimination should be above 10 percent—preferably 15 percent—of the class; this would mean more than 3 or 4 in the above test. Note: These are statistical evaluations of the item's *performance*. The foreign-language teacher must always remember the importance of the item *content;* only when satisfied that the proper content is being tested should the teacher strive to improve the performance of the item.

When students get their own papers back, they can see how well they did on each item in relation to the rest of the class. Students are usually eager to point out poor distractors, ambiguities, and other faults, thus helping the teacher improve the items. In addition, such a classroom item analysis conducted in the target language gives the students excellent practice in handling numbers and carrying out simple arithmetic operations.

Independently, the teacher should look into those items that proved too easy or too difficult and perform a full item analysis on those items with a poor discrimination index.

4.4 DIAGNOSTIC INFORMATION: THE CRITERION-REFERENCED TEST

The *criterion-referenced test* provides the students with an evaluation of their performance with reference to specific objectives. The most common type of criterion-referenced test is the quiz or the segment of a chapter test that is based on specific grammatical structures or a thematic vocabulary. The passing grade is predetermined: for example, 90 percent or 7 out of 8 questions correct. In marking the test, the teacher indicates whether the student passed or not, and in the latter case suggests remedial work. It is also possible to let students mark their own papers.

Here is a French example of a criterion-referenced quiz evaluating the use of direct object pronouns.[7]

Express Philippe's opinions about the persons indicated in parentheses by completing the sentences below with the appropriate pronouns.

Modèle: (Nicole) Philippe __la__ trouve jolie.

(Nicole) Philippe finds her pretty.

1. (Henri) Philippe _____ déteste.
   (Henri) Philippe dislikes him.
2. (Monique) Il _____ déteste aussi.
   (Monique) He dislikes her too.
3. (ce garçon) Il _____ trouve idiot.
   (that boy) He finds him stupid.
4. (Jeannette et Sophie) Il _____ trouve adorables.
   (Jeannette and Sophie) He finds them adorable.
5. (ses cousins) Il _____ trouve stupides.
   (his cousins) He finds them stupid.
6. (ses cousines) Il _____ trouve idiotes.
   (his [girl] cousins) He finds them dumb.
7. (ce professeur) Il _____ aime bien.
   (his teacher) He likes him.
8. (sa tante Joséphine) Il ne _____ aime pas.
   (his aunt Joséphine) He doesn't like her.
9. (ces deux garçons) Il va _____ inviter.
   (those two boys) He's going to invite them.
10. (Jacqueline) Il va _____ inviter aussi.
    (Jacqueline) He is going to invite her too.

Scoring: 1. le, 2. la, 3. le, 4. les, 5. les, 6. les, 7. l', 8. l', 9. les, 10. l'

Interpretation:

If you have nine or ten correct answers: you pass.
If you have eight correct answers or less, review Sections 5.2B and 5.4B. (If you failed to use the elision form *l'* in item 7, 8 or 10, remember that *le* and *la* become *l'* before a vowel sound.)

The student who has not passed the test is encouraged to carry out the required review work and then asked to take a similar test to show that he or she learned the material in question. The teacher's interpretation of the

---

[7] Taken from Jean-Paul Valette and Rebecca M. Valette, *French for Mastery: Book One* (Lexington, Mass.: D. C. Heath, 1975), pp. 208 and 432.

test results may refer the student to specially prepared worksheets in addition to textbook references.

Criterion-referenced tests are also very useful for courses in remedial phonetics. The teacher corrects the recorded tape, and lists the major pronunciation mistakes made by the students. The student works on his or her weaknesses, and then takes the phonetic test again as often as needed in order to obtain a "passing" evaluation.

4.5 ERROR ANALYSIS: THE COMMUNICATION TEST

In the *communication test*, the students are demonstrating their language skills. In oral self-expression (speaking) and written self-expression (writing), the students use whatever language components they can to communicate. Standard item analysis techniques or the preparation of diagnostic answer keys are not appropriate, for the teacher cannot predict which sentences the students will produce. An interpretation of performance on a communication test may employ error analysis techniques.

At present error analysis is primarily used by psychologists and linguists in their study of language acquisition.[8] One of the goals of error analysis is to reveal learners' strategies and to help in the preparation of more effective learning materials. Another goal is to classify the types of errors and identify those which hinder communication, as well as those which native speakers find difficult to tolerate.

4.5.1 Corder's three-way classification of error types

Pit Corder proposes a three-way classification of errors, based on the student's ability to correct the errors and to explain them (Figure 20).[9]
The postsystematic errors, that is, those mistakes that the students are able to correct and explain when their attention is drawn to them, are less serious pedagogically than the systematic errors—mistakes that the students cannot immediately correct but for which they can provide the explanation once the problem is pointed out. And both postsystematic and systematic errors present less of a pedagogical problem than the presystematic errors—those which the students cannot even explain. Let us look at a French example: Three students, in talking about a nice place for a picnic, say: "C'est une jolie place," instead of "C'est un joli endroit." (It's a nice place.)

[8] For a review of the field, see Albert Valdman, "Learner systems and error analysis," in Gilbert A. Jarvis, ed., *Perspective: A New Freedom*, The ACTFL Review of Foreign Language Education, vol. 7 (Skokie: Ill.: National Textbook Company, 1975), pp. 219–58 (hereafter cited as *Perspective*).

[9] Adapted from the presentation by Valdman, *Perspective*, p. 241.

Figure 20

	Can the student correct the error?	Can the student explain the error?
presystematic errors	no	no
systematic errors	no	yes
postsystematic errors	yes	yes

Student A: The teacher adopts a quizzical look and the student replies: "Pardon, c'est un joli endroit." When asked, the student can describe the difference between "place" and "endroit". (postsystematic error)

Student B: The student does not understand what is wrong with the statement. The teacher provides the cue "Place ou endroit?" The student replies: "C'est un joli endroit" and can provide the reason for the correct form of the sentence. (systematic error)

Student C: The student does not understand what is wrong with the sentence. If the teacher asks "Place ou endroit?", the student might choose the appropriate word, simply because he or she realizes that "place" must be wrong. But the student does not know why the correction is necessary. (presystematic error)

Obviously, Student A has the strongest command of French, while Student C is the weakest in this particular instance.

4.5.2   LoCoco's categorization of source of error

Veronica LoCoco, in her work with college students of Spanish and German, has developed six categories that reflect the source of language errors. Figure 21 briefly describes these error types and gives an example of each. [10]

[10] A fuller explanation of these categories and the related research is found in Veronica Gonzalez-Mena LoCoco, "An Analysis of Errors in the Learning of Spanish and of German as Second Languages" (Ph.D. diss., Stanford University, 1975). See also her article "An Analysis of Spanish and German Learners' Errors," *Working Papers on Bilingualism*, no. 7 (September 1975), pp. 96–124. (Publication of the Ontario Institute for Studies in Education, 252 Bloor Street West, Toronto, Ontario M5S 1V6.)

Figure 21

Type of error	L1 Native language	L2 Target language	L2 error	Sample error (Spanish L2, English L1)	Explanation
interlingual	rule exists	no rule exists	L1 rule is applied	Está cantando mañana.	English can use present progressive to express futurity. Spanish cannot.
intralingual	no rule exists	rule exists	wrong L2 rule is applied	Yo canta, él canto.	Spanish marks finite verbs for person and number. English does not. Student uses wrong endings.
dual	no rule exists	rule exists	no rule is applied	Veo María.	Spanish uses the personal *a*. Student has omitted it.
lack of transfer	rule exists	rule exists	no rule is applied	Ella visto.	Both English and Spanish use an auxiliary in compound tenses. Student has omitted *ha*.
or:	no rule exists	no rule exists	non-applicable rule is applied	Ayer cantas.	Neither English nor Spanish use the present to express past events. Student uses the present tense.
communicative	—	—	Student attempts to use a form or structure not yet taught.	Me gusto leer.	The student has not learned: Me gusta leer.
overlap	—	—	Error is related to two or more sources.	Queremos a ir.	The student overgeneralized the use of *a* with *to*. Correct form is: Queremos ir.

(Note: In the chart, L1 refers to the first or native language, while L2 refers to the second or target language.)

The frequency of some types of errors seems to vary for the target languages. For example, American students of German made many more interlingual errors than American students of Spanish, and most of the German interlingual errors related to word order. For both languages, however, the most common errors were the intralingual ones, that is, they resulted from the misapplication of target language rules (e.g., wrong adjective endings).

4.5.3 Level of error tolerance

Error analysis also permits the teacher to distinguish between errors that interfere with the communication of the message and errors that do not. Speakers of English, for instance, will pay little attention to mispronounced vowel or consonant sounds, but are often unable to understand words in which the accent is placed on the wrong syllable. For instance, eentelleegent is understood as "intelligent," but intelligent is usually misunderstood. French speakers are much more tolerant of glided vowels (final /e/ and /o/) than they are of nasalized vowels before nasal consonants. For instance, "allez" pronounced with a final glide [eⁱ] is less grating than "donne-le-moi" spoken with a nasal vowel [ɔ̃n]. The results of such error analysis could help the teacher develop a scoring system for communication tests that would reflect the relative importance of specific types of errors.[11]

Although much of current error analysis focuses on language production (speaking and writing), similar techniques would also be helpful in interpreting listening and reading comprehension problems.

[11] See Valdman, *Perspective*, p. 245.

Methods of Evaluation

outline

five

The Listening Test

Because of the increased emphasis today on direct communication in the foreign language, the skill of listening has become the object of growing attention. It is, in fact, possible for two persons of different linguistic backgrounds to carry on a productive conversation in which each speaks his or her own language while understanding what the other is saying in the second language. In service occupations such as medicine, law enforcement, or social work, a person can become much more effective if he or she readily understands the language or languages of the local minority groups, even if that person's speaking command is less developed than his or her listening comprehension. Once the listening skill is considered a course objective, it becomes necessary to assess student achievement in that area.

5.1 GENERAL CONSIDERATIONS

What is listening? When Americans comment that French and Italian are musical languages or that German and Arabic sound guttural, they almost certainly do not speak those languages. When people merely "hear" a language spoken, they receive a vague overall impression of new sounds and intonations. These same persons would probably be embarrassed when asked to characterize English succinctly because they are unable to "hear" their native tongue with detachment. Instinctively they are "listening"— attaching meaning to the sounds and patterns that strike their ear.

In learning a second language, students must acquire the skill of listening. Americans, for instance, must learn to differentiate between the sound systems of English and the target language and to discriminate among the unfamiliar sounds of the latter. It is only when they perceive the

73

distinguishing features of the new phonetic system that they can begin to speak the target language accurately. They must rely on their ear both to understand what is being said and to verify their own pronunciation.

The skill of listening requires proficiency in three areas: discrimination of sounds, understanding of specific elements, and overall comprehension. Although the native speaker will find listening a natural single operation, the beginning second-language student may have to develop proficiency separately in each of the three areas. The teacher may wish to measure the student's proficiency in each area or in combined areas.

Native speakers of English automatically make the necessary sound distinctions in their language. They can recognize those elements or sounds that connote meaning even though they have had no training in phonetics and can give no phonetic analysis of the speech of others. When learning a new language, the American student tries to apply English phonemic[1] differences to the target language. The greatest difficulties arise when the target language uses different sounds, or uses sounds that occur occasionally in English but pass unnoticed because they are not phonemic. German, for example, makes a phonemic distinction between long and short vowels, between a pair of words like *Stadt* and *Staat;* an American can lengthen his or her vowels voluntarily but needs practice before learning to automatically discriminate vowels phonemically according to length.

In describing phonemic differences of a language, linguists try to find minimal pairs of utterances, that is, ones in which the difference in meaning depends on only one pronunciation feature. In English, *beat* and *bit* (or *he bit him, he beat him*) form a minimal pair that Americans can easily identify but that offers difficulty to speakers of Spanish, French, and other languages which do not possess this distinction. French speakers tend to differentiate between the two words according to vowel length because *beat* is usually longer than *bit;* when the vowel of the latter is consciously lengthened, the American can still distinguish the two words, whereas the French person may become confused. The ability to discriminate the sounds of a foreign language may initially be equated with the ability to distinguish the minimal pairs of the language. Once students broaden their knowledge of structure and vocabulary, they will be able to rely on context to help them discriminate troublesome phonemes.

The main object of a listening test is to evaluate comprehension. The students' degree of comprehension will depend on their ability to discriminate phonemes, to recognize stress and intonation patterns, and to retain

---

[1] A *phonemic* contrast is a sound contrast that changes meaning. A *phoneme* is a class of sounds that functions as a unit in the language under study and can be distinguished from other such units. The linguist can show the existence of a given phoneme in a specific language by discovering a *minimal pair*, i.e., two utterances with different meanings but pronunciations in which only one sound feature is varied.

what they have heard. In conversation, however, understanding the target language obviously also requires a knowledge of vocabulary and grammar. A foundation in vocabulary and grammar may be acquired orally, through reading, or through a combination of these methods. A person learning English as a second language and who is familiar with vocabulary and structure but who possesses only the most rudimentary ideas about pronunciation will easily be able to distinguish between *taking a bus* and *taking a taxi* since *bus* and *taxi* sound considerably different. But this same foreigner may not be able to understand the difference between *Dad is washing the dog outside* and *Dad is watching the dog outside*. If a teacher asks students to distinguish between *bus* and *taxi* in a listening test, he or she is using an aural testing method to evaluate the students' knowledge of English vocabulary. If the teacher asks them to distinguish between *washing* and *watching*, he or she is measuring the students' competency in listening discrimination. Listening discrimination will be more reliably evaluated if the students' knowledge of the two key words has been previously verified by other means, such as a written vocabulary item.

The phenomenon of listening comprehension is quite complex. In conversation native speakers do not consciously make all the possible phonemic discriminations typical of their language. They are so familiar with certain patterns and contexts that they can understand what is being said even if they do not pay precise attention to every word. To demonstrate this, try the following experiment. Read this paragraph aloud at rapid conversational speed:

> Mr. Jones is driving his car up the driveway. I see he is getting out the hose and a pail of water. And his wife is bringing the rags and sponges and the cleanser for the white sidewalls. But it looks like he's not just going to watch his car; he's planning on waxing it too. A real spring cleanup!

The context in the paragraph is so suggestive that almost all native speakers would assume that you said *wash* rather than *watch*.

Native speakers of a language are able to listen to lengthy questions in that language and answer with ease. When learning a second language, however, these same people can retain only a part of what they have just heard. How often has the teacher seen a student begin to answer a question and then stop to say he or she has forgotten the final part of the answer or to ask that the question be repeated? Experiments evaluating student ability to remember lists of nonsense words or syllables have shown that those students who impose a certain pattern on the words or syllables increase their retention span. In other words, once students have given a certain meaning to the words, they can remember them more easily. Thus, in the target language, once students find themselves at ease in the language and understand it with little difficulty, they can retain longer sentences.

Retention, which is a serious problem for beginners, seems to present less of an obstacle for the intermediate and advanced students.

A marked comprehension problem for the language student arises from the difference between natural and stylized speech. Newscasters, in particular, employ a highly stylized delivery. Movies and television programs in the target language are often hard to understand. In intermediate and advanced classes taped radio broadcasts and foreign-language films can provide a basis for listening-comprehension tests.

More advanced students can be tested on their comprehension of different types of conversational speech. American students may understand the carefully enunciated French of their teacher and the somewhat deformed French of classmates. They may even understand when native Frenchmen are talking with them, but conversation between two Frenchmen sounds to them like gibberish. An effort should be made therefore to familiarize advanced students with the variations of the conversational language. For example, in English *jeetjet* looks like nonsense when seen on the printed page, but when read aloud with a rising intonation any American would understand *Did you eat yet?* All languages have a rapid form of speech, used even by cultivated people, that often seems incomprehensible to the non-native. Excerpts of such speech can serve as the basis of valid comprehension tests.

The native speaker can understand messages under poor acoustic conditions: unclear telephone calls, distant radio stations with heavy static, conversations overheard across a noisy room. The student has acquired a high level of proficiency in listening comprehension when he or she can understand the target language under equally difficult circumstances.

Ongoing research is exploring the role of listening comprehension in the development of the other language skills. The articles collected by Edward Sittler as background reading for the seminar on "Language Acquisition via Listening" (Fourth International Conference of AILA—Association Internationale de Linguistique Appliquée—held in Stuttgart, Germany, in August 1975) underscore the primacy of listening comprehension in the language learning process.[2] As more and more teachers stress the listening skill, they will find listening tests increasingly useful.

5.2 THE SOUND SYSTEM

An essential step in the learning of a new language is acquiring a familiarity with the sound system of that language. At its most rudimentary level, this means being able to distinguish the target language from other "foreign"

---

[2] Edward Sittler, *Die Logik des Hörens: Besser Hören = Besser Lernen*, ed. Manfred Vogler and Rudolf Fröhlingsdorf (Pädagogisches Institut der Landeshauptstadt Düsseldorf Schriftenreihe, Heft 26), Juni 1975.

languages. At the *Mechanical Skills* stage of the taxonomy, the students should be able to differentiate and discriminate among the phonemes, the phonetic features, the intonation curves and the stress and accent patterns of the target language. At the *Knowledge* and *Transfer* stages of the taxonomy, the students attach meaning to these differences in sounds.

In most language courses, the sound system is introduced in meaningful, situational context. Subsequently, students may practice abstract sound discrimination exercises, especially in remedial phonetics courses. In the following pages, the Mechanical Skills sound discrimination tests are presented first (Section 5.2.2), but many teachers may prefer to use only tests in which sound differences are related to meaning (Sections 5.2.3 and 5.2.4).

5.2.1   Identifying the target language

For the beginning student, German, Danish, and Dutch may sound similar, or Spanish may be confused with Portuguese. To develop a sensitivity to the target language, the teacher may play recordings of people speaking various languages and train the class to identify the recordings of the target language.

SAMPLE ITEM TYPE *1*   LANGUAGE DISCRIMINATION

You will hear ten short recordings. Listen carefully to each one. If the selection is French (the target language), mark A. If it is not French, mark B.

5.2.2   Discrimination of sounds in isolation

In acquiring proficiency in the target language, students learn to discriminate among the phonemes of the target language and to differentiate between the distinctive phonetic features of the native language and those of the target language. This ability may be assessed most rapidly through the use of multiple-choice objective tests.

The items described below measure sound discrimination in isolation. Such techniques, while providing an excellent means of judging progress in phonetics classes, are not always suitable for beginning students.

5.2.2a   NATIVE LANGUAGE VS. TARGET LANGUAGE

Not all sounds in the target language need to be tested. Those sounds nearly identical in pronunciation and distribution in both the target and the native language present no great learning problem. Some of the general areas of probable interference between English as the native language and commonly taught second languages are the following:[3]

> vowel substitution: English MAN /mæn/
> > German man /man/
>
> vowel glide: English SAY /sei/
> > Spanish sé /se/
>
> consonant articulation: English MET /mɛt/ (alveolar [t], often un-released)
> > French mette /mɛt/ (dental [t], strong release)

In order to determine the students' sensitivity to these areas of possible interference, the students are asked either implicitly or explicitly to compare their native English with the target language. When told to pick out the English words, some students begin considering the wide variety of American dialects and realize that they can understand English spoken with a broad range of foreign accents. Thus, if the students are requested to pick out which words of a series belong to one of the languages, it appears preferable to ask them to select the words that they consider typical of the target language. In implicit contrast items, students are asked to indicate whether the words they hear are identical or different.[4]

SAMPLE ITEM TYPE *2*   SAME VS. DIFFERENT: TWO WORDS

You will hear two words. Listen to determine whether the two words are the same or different. Indicate your answer as follows: A = same, B = different.

Here is a sample item for Italian:

il   EEL

Correct response: B

SAMPLE ITEM TYPE *3*   SAME VS. DIFFERENT: THREE WORDS

You will hear three words. Indicate which word in the group is different.

Here is a sample item for French:

A. gai   B. gai   C. GAY

Correct response: C

---

[3] English words will be printed in capital letters.

[4] In his work with same-different Spanish tests, Eugène Brière found that items in which the words to be compared were different proved twice as effective as those in which all words were the same (paper read at the annual MLA meeting, Chicago, December 1965).

SAMPLE ITEM TYPE *4*   SAME VS. DIFFERENT: DIRECTED COMPARISON

You will hear one word. After a slight pause you will hear three more words. Indicate which of the three words is exactly the same as the initial word.

Here is a sample item for German:

Dach   A. DOCK   B. DOCK   C. Dach

Correct response: C

SAMPLE ITEM TYPE *5*   TARGET LANGUAGE VS. NATIVE ENGLISH: PAIRS

You will hear two words. Indicate which word of the pair is German (the target language).

Here is a sample item:

A. Vieh   B. FEE

Correct response: A

SAMPLE ITEM TYPE *6*   TARGET LANGUAGE VS. NATIVE ENGLISH: COUNTING

You will hear a series of three similar-sounding words. Some may be French (target language); some may be English. Count how many of the words are French. Indicate your answer as follows:

A. Only one (1) is French.

B. Only two (2) are French.

C. All three (3) are French.

D. None are French.

l
2
3
0

Here is a sample item:

TWO   tout   tout

Correct response: B

5.2.2b   PHONEMES IN THE TARGET LANGUAGE

Generally, the target language makes phonemic contrasts that do not exist in the native language. The target language often possesses phonemes that have no counterpart at all in the native language. Recognition of these phonemic differences must precede, or at least accompany, the assigning of lexical or grammatical meaning to these sounds.

Pure discrimination tests are usually content-free; that is, the student can select the correct answer without understanding the meanings of the words used. The items are constructed around minimal pairs, utterances in which only the element under study changes. Vowels and final consonant contrasts may be effectively incorporated into an item that requires the student to select perfect rhymes. The ability to make finer contrasts, or contrasts that do not occur in stressed position, is best evaluated through same-different items.

SAMPLE ITEM TYPE 7   RHYME: TWO WORDS

You will hear two words. Listen to determine whether the two words rhyme perfectly with each other. Indicate your answer as follows: A = rhyme, B = no rhyme.

Here is a sample item in German:

fuhr   für

Correct response: B

SAMPLE ITEM TYPE 8   RHYME: THREE WORDS

You will hear three words. Listen to determine which word does *not* rhyme with the others and mark the corresponding letter.

Here is a sample item in German:

A. Vater   B. Vetter   C. Kater

Correct response: B

SAMPLE ITEM TYPE 9   THREE-SYLLABLE WORDS OR PHRASES

You will hear a word or phrase of three syllables. Listen carefully to determine which, if any, of the three vowel sounds are the same. Indicate your answer as follows:

A. In syllables 1 and 2 the vowel sounds are the same. | 1+2 |

B. In syllables 1 and 3 the vowel sounds are the same. | 1+3 |

C. In syllables 2 and 3 the vowel sounds are the same. | 2+3 |

D. In syllables 1, 2, and 3 the vowel sounds are the same. | 1,2,3 |

E. The vowel sounds of the three syllables are all different. | 0 |

Here are two sample items in French:

pas du tout

Correct response: E

   tout d'un coup

Correct response: B

In testing the discriminatory ability of more advanced students, the teacher should use unfamiliar words or phrases. If common phrases are used, the students might well arrive at the proper answer by recalling the spellings of the words.

5.2.3   Discrimination of sounds: lexical meaning

For intermediate and advanced students sound-discrimination tests may incorporate known vocabulary. The contrast in sound between a pair of utterances distinguishes the meaning of those utterances. Vocabulary-discrimination tests offer a learning incentive because students realize that the ability to differentiate between minimal pairs may be crucial in understanding the target language. For such tests the students should be quite familiar with the words being contrasted so that the only element determining their choice is one of sound discrimination.

SAMPLE ITEM TYPE *10*   KEY WORD PLUS PICTURE

You will hear two (or three) words. On your answer sheet indicate which word corresponds to the picture in your booklet (on the board, etc.).

Here is a sample item in French:

A. poison
B. poisson

poison
fish

Correct response: B

To place the word being tested in a more natural context, such utterances may be used as:

A. Voici un poison.
B. Voici un poisson.

Here is a poison.
Here is a fish.

or:

A. L'enfant mange un poison. ·
B. L'enfant mange un poisson.
          The child is eating a poison.
          The child is eating fish.

SAMPLE ITEM TYPE *11* KEY WORD PLUS PICTURES

You will hear a word or sentence. Look at the pictures in your test booklet (on the board, etc.) and select the one corresponding to the utterance you have just heard.

Here is a sample item in German (based on the minimal pair *Kirche* and *Kirsche*):

Ich sehe die Kirsche.

or

Das ist die Kirsche.

I see the cherry.

That is the cherry.

A   B

Correct response: B

SAMPLE ITEM TYPE *12* COMPLETION ITEMS: EXPLICIT DISCRIMINATION

You will hear a single sentence, followed by sentences A and B (and C). Choose the sentence that best completes the idea expressed in the initial sentence.

Here is a sample item in French. (The explicit contrast is between *monte* and *mente*.)

Il doit toujours dire la vérité.

A. Je ne veux pas qu'il monte.
B. Je ne veux pas qu'il mente.

He should always tell the truth.

I don't want him to go upstairs.
I don't want him to lie.

Correct response: B

SAMPLE ITEM TYPE *13* COMPLETION ITEMS: IMPLICIT DISCRIMINATION

You will hear a single sentence, followed by sentences A and B (and C). Choose the sentence that best completes the idea expressed in the initial sentence.

Here is a sample item in French. (The implicit contrast is between *au-dessus* and *au-dessous*.)

Nous habitons au troisième et les Dupont habitent au-dessus.

A. Alors l'appartement des Dupont est au second.
B. Alors l'appartement des Dupont est au quatrième.

We live on the "third" floor and the Duponts live above us.

So, the Duponts' apartment is on the "second" floor.
So the Duponts' apartment is on the "fourth" floor.

Correct response: B

5.2.4   Discrimination of sounds: structural meaning

In most languages, certain phonemic distinctions are of morphological importance. The change in a single sound may change the meaning of the grammatical structure. The particular areas tested in a sound-discrimination test will vary from language to language. In this section the sample items will be in French.

SAMPLE ITEM TYPE *14*   VERB FORMS

You will hear a sentence once. Listen carefully to determine whether the subject and verb are singular or plural. Indicate your answer as follows:

A. singular
B. plural
C. could be singular or plural

Alternate instructions for a situational context:

You will hear Jean-Jacques talking about several of his friends. Is he talking about one person or several people? If he could only be talking about one person, mark A for singular. If he could only be talking about two or more people, mark B for plural. If it is not clear whether he is talking about one person or several people, mark C for singular or plural.

Here are some sample items:

1. Il vient maintenant.   *He is coming now.*
2. Ils acceptent notre offre.   *They accept our offer.*
3. Elle(s) le cherche(nt).   *She is looking for it./They are look-*
                                          ing for it.

Correct responses: A, B, C

SAMPLE ITEM TYPE *15*   ARTICLES

You will hear a sentence. Listen carefully to determine whether the last word is masculine singular, feminine singular, or plural. Indicate your answer as follows:

A. masculine singular
B. feminine singular
C. plural

Alternate instructions for a situational context:

Marie-Ange is visiting a department store and making comments about furniture she sees. Can you tell whether the objects she is talking about are masculine singular, feminine singular, or plural? If you hear *le*, the object is masculine singular: mark space A. If you hear *la*, the object is feminine singular: mark space B. If you hear *les*, she is talking about several objects: mark space C for plural.

Here are some sample items:

1. J'aime la table.	*I like the table.*
2. Je n'aime pas les chaises.	*I don't like the chairs.*
3. Je prends le fauteuil.	*I'm taking the armchair.*

Correct responses: B, C, A

Items of this type might well employ vocabulary not yet studied; then sound discrimination and not familiarity with a given word would form the basis of choice. The vocabulary element may even be eliminated entirely by asking the student to identify the gender and number of direct object pronouns.

You will hear a sentence once. Listen carefully to determine whether the object is masculine singular, feminine singular, or plural. Indicate your answers as follows:

A. masculine singular
B. feminine singular
C. plural

Alternate instructions for a situational context:

Pierre is a music lover. Can you tell whether he is talking about his record player (son électrophone), his guitar (sa guitare) or his cassette tapes (ses cassettes)? Listen carefully. If you hear *le*, mark column A for l'électrophone. If you hear *la*, mark column B for la guitare. If you hear *les*, mark column C for les cassettes.

Here are some sample items:

1. Je la vends.	*I'm selling it.*
2. Je le prends.	*I'm taking it.*
3. Je les veux.	*I want them.*

Correct responses: B, A, C

SAMPLE ITEM TYPE *16* VERB TENSES

You will hear a sentence once. Listen carefully to determine whether the verb is used in the present or the imperfect tense. (Or: Listen carefully to determine whether the action described occurred in the past or is taking place at present.) Indicate your answer as follows:

A. present
B. imperfect (past)

Alternate instructions for a situational context:

Imagine you are sitting in a Paris café and are overhearing snatches of conversations. Can you tell whether the speakers are talking about present or past events? Listen carefully for the verb. If it is in the present tense, mark column A. If it is in the imperfect, mark column B.

Here are some sample items:

1. Cherche-t-il?   *Is he looking?*
2. Nous finissions le devoir.   *We were finishing the exercise.*
3. Vous alliez là-bas.   *You were going over there.*

Correct responses: A, B, B

NOTE: All the examples above incorporate minimal-pair contrasts. This explains the use of the interrogative form in the first sentence: *cherche-t-il* /ʃɛrʃətil/ and *cherchait-il* /ʃɛrʃetil/ both have the same number of syllables, whereas *je cherche* /ʒəʃɛrʃ/ and *je cherchais* /ʒəʃɛrʃe, ʒəʃɛrʃɛ/ do not.

5.2.5 Intonation tests

Since English uses a rich variety of intonation patterns, most American students learning a foreign language are sensitive to such distinctions. For example, in English the declarative sentence *You're coming* may be transformed into the question *You're coming?* when spoken with a rising intonation. Consequently, most American students can easily identify the same pattern in French: *Tu viens?* In many instances, however, the target language uses intonation patterns that have no English counterpart or that have a different effect than they have when used in English. An intonation pattern suggesting cheerfulness in English may have a cool or impolite tone in Italian.

The students' ability to pick out these differences in intonation without specific reference to meaning can be assessed through tests incorporating items such as Sample Item Types 2 to 6 suggested earlier. In such items, students will find it easier to compare the intonations of two identical sentences than of sentences using different words.

Two additional item types are suggested below: the first tests intonation in isolation; the second attaches meaning to the intonation patterns.

SAMPLE ITEM TYPE *17*   LINEAR REPRESENTATION OF INTONATION

You will hear a sentence. Choose the linear pattern that most closely depicts the intonation curve of the sentence.

Here is a sample item in French:

Qui est là?

A. ⌒

B. ⌒

C. ⌒

Correct response: A

SAMPLE ITEM TYPE *18*   MEANING OF INTONATION

Your will hear a sentence. Read the choices given in your answer booklet and choose the most accurate interpretation of the sentence you have just heard.

Here is a sample item in Italian:

Buon giorno. (spoken: ⌒ ↓)

A. Good morning! (cheerful)
B. Good morning! (Well, you finally got up!)

Correct response: B

NOTE: In this type of item the reading and vocabulary factors can most easily be eliminated by having the options appear in the students' native language, in this case English.

5.2.6   Stress and accent tests

Since in English stress is usually indicated by loudness and a rise in pitch, American students experience little difficulty in recognizing stressed syllables if the target language handles them in the same way. Conflict occurs when the target language uses stress to signal distinctions not made in English. When the target language employs very few stress patterns, American students must unlearn the habits of their native language; these habits are primarily an obstacle to speaking, however, rather than to listening.

In teaching a foreign language, the teacher will want to evaluate the students' ability to discriminate between stress patterns. Sample Item Types 2 to 6 may be adapted by asking students to distinguish between minimal pairs, such as CONvert and conVERT in English or *portabagagli* (baggage carrier) and *porta bagagli* (he carries baggage) in Italian.

SAMPLE ITEM TYPE *19*   WRITTEN REPRESENTATION OF
STRESS AND ACCENT

You will hear a sentence once. In your answer booklet you will see the sentence transcribed two (or three or four) ways. Capital letters are used to indicate the stressed syllable. Select the transcription that describes the sentence you have just heard and mark the corresponding space on your answer sheet.

Here is a sample item in German:

Er kauft NUR einen Hund.   *He is* only *buying a dog.*

A. Er kauft NUR einen Hund.   *He is* only *buying a dog.*
B. Er kauft nur EINen Hund.   *He is buying* only *one dog.*

Correct response: A

SAMPLE ITEM TYPE *20*   MEANING OF STRESS AND ACCENT

You will hear a sentence once. In your answer booklet you will see two (or three or four) interpretations of the sentence. Select the phrase which best describes the sentence you have just heard and mark the corresponding space on your answer sheet.

Here is a sample item in Spanish:

Sí, ésta.

A. Yes, this one.
B. Yes, he is.

Correct response: A

The options may be given in the target language if the teacher is certain that no comprehension problem exists for the students.

5.3   UNDERSTANDING VOCABULARY

The ability to understand the target language greatly depends on one's knowledge of vocabulary—vocabulary in the broadest sense. Many commercial listening tests may be termed modified vocabulary tests since the correct response to most of the items hinges on one or two cue-words which, if understood, elicit the correct answer. Such listening tests, however, are much superior to traditional written or oral "vocabulary tests" because the lexical items are presented naturally; the student must pay careful attention in order to determine which are the key words and how they are being used.

Since classroom tests should contribute to the learning process, no incorrect forms should appear in listening items. The student's ear should become accustomed to correct, natural speech. Consequently, vocabulary to be tested should be introduced in a natural conversational framework. A wide variety of oral quizzes may be adapted so that they assess primarily the students' comprehension of key lexical terms.

5.3.1 Body-movement tests

Listening comprehension may be assessed by asking the students to carry out specific instructions, such as raising their left hands or opening their books. Body-movement tests are more practical in the freer, more mobile atmosphere of the elementary school. Such tests do have their limitations. If the entire class is asked to perform a task, such as standing up, the poorer students will imitate the better ones. If each student is given a different order to carry out, the test is not extremely reliable because each student is tested on different vocabulary items and on only one or two tasks. Reliability can be improved by treating body-movement tests as quizzes and by keeping a cumulative record of student performance across the semester or marking period.

The following may be used as games or as informal tests. In the latter case, the teacher discreetly evaluates the performance of each student. It is generally advisable not to eliminate students, since those who make mistakes are the ones in greatest need of practice.

SAMPLE ITEM TYPE *21* SIMPLE COMMANDS

Each student is told to perform an action. In French, for example, the teacher might suggest:

Robert, lève la main droite.	*Robert, raise your right hand.*
Marie, va au tableau.	*Marie, go to the blackboard.*

SAMPLE ITEM TYPE *22* DISCRIMINATION OF COMMANDS

The students individually or in groups are told to perform an action. When the teacher fails to use a command form, the students are not to respond. Those who react inappropriately to a sentence are sent to the back of the group. They continue playing and benefit from observing the students in front of them. The winner is the student standing at the front of the group at the end of the test. In Spanish the teacher might suggest:

Levántese Ud.	*Stand up.*
Siéntese Ud.	*Sit down.*
Abran Uds. los libros.	*Open your books.*
Tengo un lápiz.	*I have a pencil.*

SAMPLE ITEM TYPE *23* "SIMON SAYS"

This game may be adapted to the language classroom. Only actions preceded by "Simon says" (*Pierrot dit, Siegfried sagt, Pablo dice,* etc.) are to be performed. Students who react inappropriately are sent to the back of the group. The winner is the student left standing in front. In French the game might proceed as follows:

Pierrot dit: Levez la main gauche.	*Raise your left hand.*
Pierrot dit: Touchez votre nez.	*Touch your nose.*
Pierrot dit: Mettez les mains sur les genoux. Levez la main droite.	*Put your hands on your knees. Raise your right hand.*
Pierrot dit: Fermez les yeux.	*Close your eyes.*

SAMPLE ITEM TYPE *24* COMMANDS WITH VISUALS

The range of vocabulary and grammar tested in body-movement tests can be increased through the use of pictures or poster cards. For instance, if the students have been learning the names of buildings, and if pictures of these vocabulary items have been mounted on cardboard, a listening quiz could be set up as follows. Place all the cards on the chalk tray. Then tell each student how to manipulate one or more cards.

Mary, give the church and the hotel to Paul.

Dick, take the school and place it between the hospital and the post office.

To encourage careful listening, the teacher should give the commands at normal to fast conversational speed.

Body-movement tests may be scored on a five-point scale:

4 points = The student carried out the command correctly after hearing it only once.

3 points = The student carried out the command correctly after having it repeated.

2 points = The student carried out the wrong command, but was able to correct himself/herself without hearing it repeated again.

1 point = The student carried out the wrong command, but was able to correct himself/herself upon hearing it repeated again.

0 points = The student carried out the wrong command on the second try.

5.3.2 Drawing tests

Elementary-school students enjoy drawing tests. Students may use pencils or crayons if color is used in the instructions. A short quiz might be composed of four or five pictures. Here are samples in French.

SAMPLE ITEM TYPE *25*   DRAWING SIMPLE VERSION

Dessinez une fleur (rose).   *Draw a flower = pink.*

Dessinez un cercle (bleu).   *Draw a circle = blue.*

SAMPLE ITEM TYPE *26*   DRAWING COMPLEX VERSION

Dessinez une fleur rose si vous êtes *Draw a pink flower if you are a*
une fille, une fleur pourpre si vous *girl, a purple flower if you are a*
êtes un garçon. *boy.*

Dessinez un cercle bleu si votre *Draw a blue circle if your name*
nom commence avec une voyelle, *begins with a vowel, a yellow*
un cercle jaune si votre nom *circle if your name begins with a*
commence avec une consonne. *consonant.*

Dessinez une étoile verte si vous *Draw a green star if you are*
portez des chaussettes blanches, *wearing white socks, an orange*
une étoile orange si vos *star if your socks are not white.*
chaussettes ne sont pas blanches.

With older students, pencil-and-paper tests are usually limited to the following item types (which are also effective with FLES classes): telling time by drawing in the hands of a clock, indicating dates on a blank calendar, writing down dates and times, and carrying out arithmetical operations of varying degrees of complexity. (Since the writing of digits cannot really be considered part of the writing skill, such items have been classified as "drawing" tests.)

5.3.3   Picture tests

The potential of picture tests in language classes has not yet been fully exploited; the possibilities are many, even for the teacher who does not feel artistically gifted. Magazine pictures, cut out and mounted on cardboard, can be shown to the class while the items are being read. Overhead transparencies are also easy to prepare. Care, of course, must be taken in their selection in order to avoid ambiguous interpretations.

SAMPLE ITEM TYPE *27*   SINGLE ITEM PICTURES: TRUE-FALSE FORMAT

Look at the pictures in your test booklet (on the screen, that I hold up). For each picture, indicate whether the statement you hear is true or false.

This is a tree.

Correct response: true

SAMPLE ITEM TYPE *28*   SINGLE ITEM PICTURES: MULTIPLE-CHOICE
                         FORMAT

In this type of item, several pictures are prepared for each sentence.
Look at the pictures in your test booklet. Indicate which picture corresponds to the statement you hear.

The boy is running.

Correct response: A   A   B   C

SAMPLE ITEM TYPE *29*   SINGLE ITEM PICTURES: MATCHING FORMAT

The teacher prepares ten pictures corresponding to new vocabulary items:
these could be ten flash cards or mounted magazine pictures that are lined
up on the chalkboard, or lightweight pictures that can be fastened to the
board with magnets (if the board is magnetized) or to a feltboard. Ten
simple line drawings could be prepared on an overhead transparency. Each
of the ten pictures is labeled sequentially from A to J. (If the chalkboard is
used, the letters can simply be written in chalk next to each of the pictures.)

You will hear ten sentences about foods. For each sentence, write the
letter that corresponds to the food that is mentioned.

1. My mother loves ice cream.
2. I never have soup for breakfast.

NOTE: The sentences in this type of test can be read rather rapidly, and if
desired, some of the words in the sentences may be unfamiliar to the students.
The object of the test is to determine whether students understand specific
vocabulary items. The test may be made more difficult by having more
pictures than sentences: for instance, twelve pictures for ten sentences.

SAMPLE ITEM TYPE *30*   MULTIPLE ITEM PICTURES: TRUE-FALSE
                         FORMAT

One picture that may be used for a sequence of items saves the teacher
much time in preparing visuals. Commercial posters or transparencies that
accompany the basic language program can be used for this type of test.
(Old posters stored in the language department closet can find new use in
this type of testing.) The teacher may wish to use a pointer to accompany
the reading of the sentences.

You will hear a series of sentences about this picture. Decide whether each sentence is true or false according to the picture. Indicate your answer as follows: A = true, B = false.

Here is a sample series in German:

Hier ist eine Uhr.	*Here is a clock.*
Sie ist blau.	*It is blue.*
Es ist jetzt neun Uhr.	*It is now nine o'clock.*
Ein Kind kommt in das Zimmer.	*A child enters the room.*
Es ist ein Mädchen.	*It is a girl.*

SAMPLE ITEM TYPE *31*   MULTIPLE ITEM PICTURES: FILL-IN FORMAT

The teacher prepares a drawing on a ditto master with arrows pointing to the vocabulary items to be tested.

You will hear Mary's mother telling her to set the table. Write the number of each statement in the circle corresponding to the item she mentions.

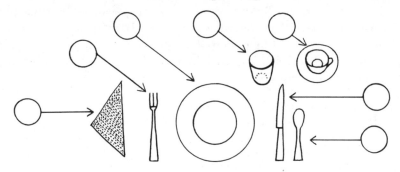

1. Take the large plates.
2. We will use the red napkins today.
3. Each person should have one fork.

In an alternate form of this item type, the teacher can use a single poster or transparency or drawing on the chalkboard. In this case, each circle would contain a letter of the alphabet. The students would write their answers on a plain sheet of paper: 1 = A, 2 = C, etc.

SAMPLE ITEM TYPE *32*   MULTIPLE ITEM PICTURES: ABCD FORMAT

In this type of item, four pictures are selected to represent different scenes or situations.

Here is an example in French that uses an ABCD answer sheet.[5]

---

[5] Adapted from Jean-Paul Valette and Rebecca M. Valette, *French for Mastery Testing Program: Book One* (Lexington, Mass.: D. C. Heath, 1976), Ach. Test 2/1.

You will hear a series of questions or statements in French. Listen carefully and decide which picture each statement refers to. Mark the corresponding letter, A, B, C, or D, on your answer sheet.

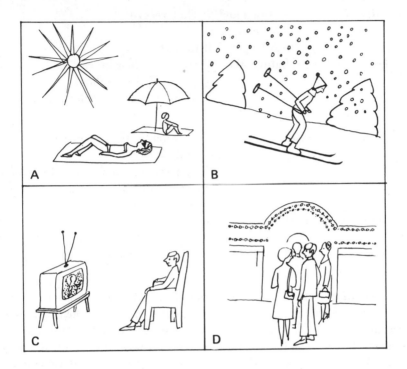

1. Il neige.   *It's snowing.*
2. Ils vont au cinéma.   *They are going to the movies.*
3. Jacques est chez lui.   *Jacques is at home.*
4. Il fait très chaud.   *It is very hot.*
5. Regardez-vous souvent la télé?   *Do you often watch TV?*

Correct responses: B, D, C, A, C

In a somewhat different presentation, this type of item forms the basis of the Common Concepts Test (see Appendix).

5.3.4 Conversation-type tests

In items of this type, both the stimulus or the cue and the options are spoken. In order to answer the item correctly, the students must isolate the key word or key words in a short dialog or conversation. If the key word is used in its usual context, and if the understanding of this key word means that the student will definitely select the correct option, such items are vocabulary items. However, if the student must understand more than just a key word, the item is a general comprehension item.

Vocabulary item: —How much is that record?
                       —Five dollars.
                       —All right, I'll take it.
This conversation probably takes place   A. in a store
                                           B. in a school
                                           C. in a restaurant

Correct response: A

General comprehension item: —How much is that record Bob?
                                  —Five dollars.
                                  —That's too much for me. I'll just come
                                    over to your house when I want to listen
                                    to it.
This conversation probably takes place   A. in a store
                                           B. in a school
                                           C. at Bob's home

Correct response: A

Conversation items should be prepared in advance and later reviewed in order to eliminate ambiguities. They are most effective when recorded with different voices, so as to simulate the conversational context. Since the preparation and recording of these items takes time and requires, for optimum effectiveness, good recording conditions and native voices, they are more often found on commercial tests than on teacher-made tests.

SAMPLE ITEM TYPE *33*   BRIEF DIALOG

You will hear a brief dialog. Decide whether the last response is appropriate or inappropriate. Indicate your answer as follows: A = appropriate, B = inappropriate.

Here is a sample item in Italian:

—Dimmi, ti piace giocare al tennis?   *Say, do you like to play tennis?*
—Mi piace, sì; ma preferisco giocare   *Yes, I do; but I prefer playing*
    al baseball.   *baseball.*

Correct response: A

SAMPLE ITEM TYPE *34*   SITUATION

You will hear a short dialog followed by a descriptive statement. Choose the appropriate response.

Here is a sample item in German:

„Was möchten Sie?"	*What would you like?*
„Eine Bratwurst, bitte, und ein Glas Bier."	*A sausage, please, and a glass of beer.*
„Ein Moment, bitte."	*Just a moment, please.*
Die Dame ist wahrscheinlich	*The lady is probably*
A. im Bus.	*in a bus.*
B. im Konzert.	*at a concert.*
C. im Restaurant.	*in a restaurant.*

Correct response: C

SAMPLE ITEM TYPE 35   QUESTION-ANSWER

You will hear a question followed by a series of answers. Select the most appropriate answer to the question and mark the corresponding space on your answer sheet.

Here is a sample item in German:

Wann essen Sie?	*When do you eat?*
A. Um sechs.	*At six.*
B. Auf der Straße.	*In the street.*
C. Mit meiner Familie.	*With my family.*

Correct response: A

SAMPLE ITEM TYPE 36   STATEMENT-REJOINDER

You will hear a sentence spoken; after a slight pause you will hear three (or four) additional sentences. From the three (or four) sentences select the one that would continue the conversation along the same lines.

Here is a sample item in German:

Ich studiere Geschichte.	*I'm studying history.*
A. Das möchte ich auch.	*I'd like to do that too.*
B. Ich kenne sie nicht.	*I don't know her.*
C. Ich wasche mich auch.	*I'm also washing up.*

Correct response: A

SAMPLE ITEM TYPE 37   COMPLETION OF THOUGHT

You will hear a sentence followed by a series of sentences (or part of a sentence followed by a series of phrases). Select the sentence (or phrase) that most appropriately complements the stem (the original sentence or phrase).

Here is a sample item in English:

I would like to eat now.   A. I'm very hungry.
                            B. The movie sounds terrific.
                            C. Jimmy likes her, too.

Correct response: A

Here is a sample item in German:

Der Briefträger bringt uns   *The mailman brings us*

A. die Post.   *mail.*
B. die Haare.   *hair.*
C. kleine Kinder.   *small children.*

Correct response: A

Items of this type may also be used to test false cognates, that is, words with similar forms in the native language and the target language but with different meanings. In a test based on cognates, both true and false cognates should be included so that the student will not assume that all items appearing to be cognates are false ones and automatically discard them in his selection of responses.

Here is a sample item in French:

Mon frère ne pouvait pas finir ses   *My brother wasn't able to finish*
    devoirs de français hier soir, et   *his French homework last night,*
    alors   *and so*

A. j'y assistais.   *I was there.*
B. je l'ai attendu.   *I waited for him.*
C. je l'ai aidé.   *I helped him.*

Correct response: C

NOTE: For Item Types 34 to 37, the option should all be of about the same length. If the test is given in the classroom, students should be told not to mark their answer sheets until they have heard all the options. If the better students identify A, for example, as the correct response before having heard the remaining options and if they begin to mark their papers, this movement of hands will indicate to the weaker students that A must be the appropriate answer.

It should also be noted that Item Types 34 to 37 are artificial rather than realistic. In a true conversation, one does not hear three responses or consider three thought completions and then select the appropriate one. If classroom emphasis has been placed on interaction and communication, the teacher might not wish to use many items of this sort.

5.3.5   Comprehension ease

One of the goals of language teaching is enabling the students to "think" in the target language, to understand what is said without having to make a mental translation into their native language. Listening-comprehension items can be employed to measure the ease with which a student understands vocabulary, especially numbers and times, in the target language. The items are read quite rapidly and are not repeated. Because of the speed element, students for whom the lexical items have acquired a meaning independent of their native-language equivalents will perform better on this type of test than students less familiar with the vocabulary. On these tests, items should be arranged in order of increasing difficulty in order not to discourage weaker students from the outset.

SAMPLE ITEM TYPE *38*   RAPID TRUE-FALSE TEST

In the rapid true-false test, each item is read only once, and very little time is allowed for students to think about the answers.

Here is an example in Italian that tests knowledge of colors.

You will hear a series of sentences read only once. Decide whether each sentence is true or false. Indicate your answer as follows: A = true, B = false.

1. La neve è bianca.   *The snow is white.*
2. I colori della bandiera americana   *The colors of the American flag*
   sono rosso, bianco, e verde.   *are red, white, and green.*

Correct responses: A, B

SAMPLE ITEM TYPE *39*   RAPID RIGHT-WRONG TEST

This test is like the rapid true-false test, except that the statements are made about a visual. It is usually convenient to mount the cues on large index cards, showing them to the class one at a time while reading the corresponding statement. (In the language laboratory, the visuals can be prepared on overhead transparencies, and the oral cues prepared on a tape or cassette.)

You will see a card and hear a statement. If the statement corresponds to the card, mark A = right, B = wrong.

Here is a math example in English using arithmetic flashcards.

1. Card: $2 \times 4 = ?$ Two plus four equals six.
2. Card: $3 - 2 = ?$ Three minus two equals one.

Correct responses: B, A.

Similarly a clock face may be used as the cue. The times are read rapidly.

Here is an example in Spanish:

1. Clock: 2:00   Son las doce.
2. Clock: 10:30   Son las diez y media.

Correct responses: B, A

SAMPLE ITEM TYPE 40   RAPID DICTATION OF NUMBERS

Intermediate and advanced language students often have difficulty understanding times and numbers given at normal conversational speed. A quick way of developing proficiency in oral comprehension is to give daily dictation quizzes (without entering the students' grades, except at the end of a marking period). To prepare for such quizzes, the teacher distributes five index cards to each student, and asks the class to write out five different three- or four-digit numbers (or five different prices or times) in large dark print. The teacher collects the cards, shuffles them, and takes the top ten.

Write down the numbers (prices, times) as you hear them.

1. Card (which is not shown to the class): 7215
        seven thousand two hundred fifteen
    or: There were seven thousand two hundred fifteen spectators.
2. Card: $21.19
        Twenty-one dollars and nineteen cents
    or: At the sale I earned twenty-one dollars and nineteen cents.
3. Card: 2:35 p.m.
        two thirty-five
    or: It's twenty-five minutes to three in the afternoon.
    or: (for languages using a twenty-four hour clock, such as French)
        Le train part à quatorze heures trente-cinq.

After the teacher has read through the ten cards, the numbers (prices, times) are read once more and the card is shown to the class so that the students can quickly correct their papers. The same stack of cards can be used for several weeks of quizzes.

5.4 UNDERSTANDING STRUCTURES

In order to understand the target language, the students must be able to recognize the patterns of that language. Although the ability to identify the syntax and the grammar of a language does not of itself imply the ability to use these elements in speaking, it is nonetheless true that unless the students can recognize patterns, they will not be able to employ them with assurance and accuracy. In beginning classes it is essential that students hear the differences in the forms of the target language and that they understand the role played by different elements in the sentence.

Only items that are grammatically correct should be employed. Elementary and intermediate students should never be asked whether a certain sentence is correct or not; such items should only be used in teacher-preparation classes, and even in such instances, students profit most from continual contact with correct forms.

5.4.1 Picture tests

Picture items can be developed to test whether the student understands the syntax and structure of the target language. However, these should first be tried out on another teacher, since pictures can often be interpreted in various ways.

SAMPLE ITEM TYPE *41*   SINGLE ITEM PICTURES

You will hear two sentences for each picture. Indicate which sentence described the picture most accurately.

Here is a sample item in French:

A. Marie court vite mais
   Georges court plus vite
   qu'elle.

   *Marie runs fast, but
   Georges runs faster
   than she does.*

B. Marie court vite mais
   Georges court moins vite
   qu'elle.

   *Marie runs fast, but
   Georges runs less quickly
   than she does.*

Correct response: A

Here is a sample item in German:

A. Der Mutter gibt das
   Kind das Buch.
B. Die Mutter gibt dem
   Kind das Buch.

The child gives the
   mother the book.
The mother gives the child
   the book.

Correct response: A

5.4.2 Identification of forms

The teacher often wishes to determine whether the student can easily recognize specific grammatical forms of the target language. Such items may be incorporated into diagnostic quizzes; for, until all students can identify given forms, it is futile to engage in more complex discussions, explanations, or drills utilizing these forms. Brief quizzes incorporating the following item types may be given frequently in elementary classes. (These items differ from those given in Section 5.2.4.; here gross distinctions rather than minimal-pair differences are tested.)

SAMPLE ITEM TYPE *42*   MULTIPLE CHOICE WITHOUT CONTEXT

For items of this type, the students are given ABCD answer sheets, and are told which distinctions to listen for. Common problem areas include identification of tenses, of number, and of gender.

You will hear a series of short sentences. Listen carefully and decide whether the verb is present or imperfect. Indicate your answer as follows: A = present, B = imperfect.

Here are some sample items in French:

1. Jean était ici.   *Jean was here.*
2. Marie finissait sa leçon.   *Marie was finishing her lesson.*
3. Vous finissez votre leçon.   *You are finishing your lesson.*

Correct responses: B, B, A

The specific tenses and the key would be modified according to the specific material being covered.

You will hear a series of short sentences. Decide whether the subject in each sentence is singular or plural. Indicate your answer as follows: A = singular, B = plural (if appropriate: C = either singular or plural).

Here are some sample items in German:

1. Die Häuser sind grau.   *The houses are gray.*
2. Die Frau kommt gleich.   *The lady is coming right away.*
3. Unser Hund schläft.   *Our dog is sleeping.*

Correct responses: B, A, A

The directions may be modified so that the student is asked to describe the direct object, the last word in the sentence, the noun (in sentences having only one), the pronoun, etc.

You will hear a series of short sentences. Decide whether the last word of the sentence is masculine, feminine, or neuter. Indicate your answer as follows: A = masculine, B = feminine, C = neuter.

Here are some sample items in German:

1. Ich kaufe den Tisch.   *I'm buying the table.*
2. Paul nimmt die Lampe.   *Paul is taking the lamp.*
3. Wir verkaufen das Bett.   *We are selling the bed.*

Correct responses: A, B, C

SAMPLE ITEM TYPE *43*   MULTIPLE CHOICE WITH SITUATIONAL CONTEXT

Beginning students are often more receptive to structure comprehension tests if the items are presented in a situational context. The following sample items also test awareness of verb tenses, number and gender, but in a less abstract fashion.

Madame Dupont is talking about various things she is doing today and is going to do tomorrow. Can you tell them apart? Listen carefully. If the verb is in the present tense, she is doing them today: mark column A = today. If the verb is in the future tense, she is doing them tomorrow: mark column B = tomorrow.

1. Je vais au bureau.   *I am going to the office.*
2. J'irai au cinéma.   *I will go to the movies.*

Correct responses: A, B

There are four children in the Hernández family: José, María, and the twins Pablo and Mora. Can you tell which ones the relatives are talking about? If you hear the pronoun "him," mark column A for José. If you hear the pronoun "her," mark column B for María. If you hear "them," mark column C for Pablo and Mora.

1. I don't see him.
2. Uncle Pepe is with them.
3. Grandmother just adores her.

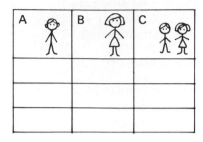

Correct responses: A, C, B

5.5   LISTENING COMPREHENSION: COMMUNICATION

Listening comprehension as a communication skill falls into stage four of the taxonomy: Communication. Tests at this level evaluate the students' communicative competence, that is, the students' ability to understand what is being said by native speakers of the target language when they are using the language in a natural manner.[6] The key concern of the evaluator is to determine whether the students have received the message that was intended, and not on whether they made certain sound discriminations or identified specific structural signals. To use Wilga Rivers' distinction, the items described in previous sections are primarily tests of "skill-getting," whereas the communication items are tests of "skill-using."

5.5.1   Getting the gist of the message

The first step in listening comprehension is getting the gist of the message. In order to do this, the learner of the target language, much like the child acquiring a first language, focuses on content words, especially nouns, verbs, and adjectives. Therefore, many of the items in Section 5.3, "Understanding vocabulary," can be adapted to evaluate whether the students are beginning to grasp what is being said. The vocabulary items, however, usually consist of one sentence, whereas in a natural language situation students frequently hear much longer segments of the target language. The following items suggest ways of using longer passages to test whether students have a general idea of what is being said.

[6] For a full discussion of communicative competence, see the review article: Renate A. Schulz and Walter H. Bartz, "Free to communicate" in Gilbert A. Jarvis, ed., *Perspective: A New Freedom*, ACTFL Review of Foreign Language Education, vol. 7 (Skokie, Ill.: National Textbook Company, 1975), pp. 47–92.

SAMPLE ITEM TYPE *44*   RECOGNIZING PROPER NAMES

This type of item is effective with beginners. A segment of a news broad-cast is played, and the students are told that in the broadcast they will hear the name of a world leader (or country or city, etc.). They write out the name in their native language. (This type of item is valid with languages where the names are pronounced somewhat differently.)

Here is a sample in German:

> Cue: Gestern in der Sowjetunion haben die Arbeiter . . . (broadcast
>   continues)
> Response: Soviet Union

SAMPLE ITEM TYPE *45*   IDENTIFYING A FAMILIAR STORY

This type of item is effective at the elementary school, but may also be used with older students. The teacher tells a familiar story, such as "Little Red Riding Hood," and asks the students to identify it by giving the corres-ponding title in the native language.

SAMPLE ITEM TYPE *46*   ORAL DESCRIPTION

The teacher describes a place, person, object, film, or event that all students are familiar with, and asks the students to write down what is being described. (Beginning students will give their answers in their native language; more advanced students can use the target language in their responses.) For example, the teacher may describe a popular television program, and the students write down the name of the show.

With intermediate and advanced classes, the students themselves can take turns giving the oral descriptions while their classmates write down the answers. At the end of the testing activity, each student turns in his or her list of identifications and receives a listening grade based on the number of correct answers. (For suggestions on grading the speaker, see Section 6.5.2.)

SAMPLE ITEM TYPE *47*   BRIEF RECORDINGS: IDENTIFICATION FORMAT

For items of this type, the teacher prepares a short tape recording of a segment of a radio program. The students are asked to identify the type of program: newscast, commercial, etc.

Similar items may be prepared for specialized language courses. For example, in a Spanish for Medical Personnel course, a listening test might consist of a group of recordings by Spanish-speaking patients arriving at the emergency ward. The students are asked to identify the emergency: for instance, the baby swallowed a bottleful of aspirin, the boy broke his arm playing football, the girl has a high fever.

SAMPLE ITEM TYPE *48*   BRIEF RECORDINGS: MULTIPLE-CHOICE FORMAT

The teacher prepares a tape that contains a sequence of excerpts from a radio newscast. Each excerpt is numbered.

You will hear a series of radio newscasts. Listen carefully to each recording, and try to determine whether it is a news item, a sports item, or a weather report. Mark your answer sheet as follows: A = news, B = sports, C = weather, D = I don't know.

5.5.2   Passage comprehension

Standardized listening comprehension tests usually include passage comprehension items. The recorded passage is usually a contrived dialog read by native speakers or a monolog or talk read by one native speaker. The questions follow a multiple-choice format.

Since the aim of such a test is to evaluate the student's ability to follow a long passage or conversation, the questions must be framed in an unambiguous and easily comprehensible format. In other words, a student should not do poorly on a passage-comprehension test because, although he did understand the passage, he was misled by the wording of the questions. If the problem lies in the phrasing of the question itself, then it is a waste of time to have the students listen to the passage.

Usually the recorded passage is played through once or twice, and then the students respond to questions. To minimize the role of recall, the following format may be preferred. The passage is played once in its entirety. Then it is played a second time in segments. Questions are asked after each segment.

Preparing comprehension tests from scratch is a difficult and time-consuming operation: The passage must be written and checked for authenticity. Then it must be recorded by native speakers, preferably speakers with some acting ability. Furthermore, the test questions must be written (and often recorded). The teacher can make up valid passage comprehension tests by using, as a point of departure, the dialogs and conversations of the tape program that accompanied a basic program no longer in use. (When schools change books, they generally keep a few copies of the old text and the accompanying tapes. These can be "cannibalized" to provide the basis of teacher-made comprehension tests.)

Here is a sample conversation from an English text for adults that will form the basis of the sample items that follow:

Joan: Oh Bob, I have to go shopping this morning.
Bob: What time will you be back?
Joan: About twelve-thirty.
Bob: That means one o'clock, then!
Joan: I have to go to five different stores.
Bob: But that won't take two and a half hours, will it?
Joan: Yes. They're always terribly busy on Saturday mornings.[7]

SAMPLE ITEM TYPE *49*   PASSAGE COMPREHENSION—TRUE-FALSE
FORMAT

You will hear the passage once. Then you will hear a series of sentences, each read only once. Listen carefully to each sentence and determine whether, according to the passage, it is true or false. Indicate your answer as follows: A = true, B = false.

1. This conversation takes place on Saturday morning.
2. Bob and Joan are going shopping.

Correct Responses: A, B

NOTE: If students read the target language easily, the items may be printed rather than recorded. However, if reading presents difficulty for the students, it is advisable to present the true-false questions orally.

SAMPLE ITEM TYPE *50*   PASSAGE COMPREHENSION—MULTIPLE-CHOICE
FORMAT

You will hear the passage once. After the completion of the passage, you will hear a series of questions concerning the passage. Each question will be followed by three (or four) suggested responses, A, B, and C (and D). On your answer sheet, blacken the space corresponding to the appropriate response.

1. Who is going shopping?   A. Joan
                             B. Bob
                             C. Joan and Bob

Correct response: A

NOTE: If students read the target language easily, two alternate presentations are possible. The entire item could be printed, so that students see both the cue and the options. Or the options alone could be printed, with the cues

[7] Taken from Ronald Mackin, *A Short Course in Spoken English* (Portland, Oregon: English Language Services; New York: Oxford University Press, 1975), p. 103.

recorded. When the entire item is recorded or when the question cue is recorded, students will not be able to answer until they have heard the entire passage. Furthermore, the recorded versions allow the teacher to determine the speed at which the students answer the items and guarantee that all students are on the same question at a given moment.

If the teacher prefers using the printed cue and printed options, and yet also wishes to have the students answer the questions only *after* having heard the passage, the students could be told to keep their test booklets closed until the passage has been played. An even more effective way of assuring that all students are answering the same item at the desired time is to prepare a set of overhead transparencies, one per item. After the passage has been played, the items are projected on the screen, one at a time.

SAMPLE ITEM TYPE *51*   PASSAGE COMPREHENSION—SHORT-ANSWER QUESTIONS

While standardized listening tests use either the true-false format or the multiple-choice format for comprehension questions, the classroom teacher might find it easier to prepare a few short-answer questions for the class.

1. Where is Joan going this morning?
2. How long will she be away?

For beginning students, these questions might be in the native language. For intermediate and advanced students, the questions are usually in the target language; however, the teacher grades the responses for content only, and not for spelling or grammar.

5.5.3   Obtaining Information

Obtaining information from a speaker of the target language is a much more realistic situation for most students than trying to "overhear" conversations, which is the primary ability typically tested by passage comprehension items (Section 5.5.2.). If the students do spend time in a country where the target language is spoken, they might frequently find themselves in situations where is is essential to ask others for information, or where they must understand amplified announcements.

SAMPLE ITEM TYPE *52*   MAP TESTS

The students are given maps of a place where the target language is spoken. These could be copies of road maps, city maps, subway maps, etc.

A starting point is indicated on the map. The students are then told, by the teacher or by a recording, how to get to a specific place (for example, a new restaurant they just heard of).

Pass-fail scoring: The student marks where the destination is on the map. The correct location passes (or earns five points). All incorrect locations fail (or earn zero points).

Partial scoring: The student draws out the path to be followed and marks the destination on the map:

one quarter of the way correct	= 1 point
half the way correct	= 2 points
three quarters of the way correct	= 3 points
all the way correct	= 4 points

In order to validate this type of test with a specific group of students, it might be good to give a similar test in the native language. Such a test is a valid test of listening comprehension only if the students are able to perform perfectly on such an exercise in the native language. If students have trouble with map reading in the native language, then such items are inappropriate.

SAMPLE ITEM TYPE *53* OBTAINING SPECIFIC INFORMATION: FILL-IN FORMAT

The students are placed in an imaginary situation where they are to obtain specific information that is to be entered into a prepared sheet: the post position of certain horses at a race, the numbers of certain baseball players on a team and their batting averages, the weather forecast for certain regions.

Here is an example in French:[8]

Imagine that you have decided to register at an interpreters' school in Paris where you will be studying several languages. This is the first day and the director is giving you your weekly schedule. Fill in your schedule with the appropriate courses.

Tape: Mesdames, Mesdemoiselles, Messieurs, bonjour! Ce matin je vais annoncer le programme des cours de langues. Faites attention.
Français: lundi, mercredi et jeudi à 9 heures.
Espagnol: lundi à 10 heures, mardi à 8 heures et jeudi à 13 heures.
Anglais: lundi à 11 heures, mardi à 14 heures et vendredi à 9 heures.
Italien: lundi à 14 heures, mercredi à 10 heures et vendredi à 13 heures.

[8] Adapted from Jean-Paul Valette and Rebecca M. Valette, *French for Mastery Testing Program: Book One* (Lexington, Mass.: D. C. Heath, 1976), Ach. Test 2/2.

Student answer sheet:

	lundi	mardi	mercredi	jeudi	vendredi
8h00					
9h00					
10h00					
11h00					
12h00					
13h00					
14h00					

Scoring: 1 point for each course correctly entered in the schedule. Do not count spelling errors.

English equivalent of text:

> Good morning, ladies and gentlemen. I am going to announce the schedule of your language courses. Please pay attention.
> French: Monday, Wednesday, and Thursday at nine.
> Spanish: Monday at ten, Tuesday at eight, and Thursday at one.
> English: Monday at eleven, Tuesday at two, and Friday at nine.
> Italian: Monday at two, Wednesday at ten, and Friday at one.

SAMPLE ITEM TYPE *54*   INTERPRETING SPECIFIC INFORMATION: FILL-IN FORMAT

In items of this type, the students are placed in an imaginary situation and are asked to draw conclusions regarding the information they hear: which of several trains will get them to their destination on time, which attractions they can see at the fair on a specific afternoon, and which ones they will have to miss.

Here is a sample item in English:

> Imagine that tonight you and your friends want to go to the movies. Cinemas One and Two are playing *Jaws*, *Lucky Lady*, *Cabaret*, and *The Towering Inferno*. It is 6:30 and from where you are it takes thirty minutes to get to the movie house.

If you go to the movies right away and eat later,

what film could you see? _____

what time does it start? _____

If you eat first—supper would take about an hour—and then go to the movie house,

what film could you see? _____

what time does it start? _____

You dial the movie house and hear the following recorded announcement:

Tape: Thank you for calling Cinemas One and Two. Today in Cinema One, we are playing *Jaws* and *The Towering Inferno.* Show times for *Jaws* are 2:30 and 7:15. *The Towering Inferno* will be screened at 5 and at 9:20. In Cinema Two we are playing two movies starring Liza Minelli: *Cabaret* and *Lucky Lady. Cabaret* will be shown at 3:45 and 8:05. *Lucky Lady* will begin at 6:10 and 10:15. Thank you for calling Cinemas One and Two.

SAMPLE ITEM TYPE 55 SELECTIVE LISTENING

Here the student is given an imaginary identity. For instance, the student is told that he is in a train in the Frankfurt railway station. His destination is Bonn. The student then hears a series of announcements over the loudspeaker in the train station. One of these announcements tells all Bonn passengers to change trains. The student must identify this relevant piece of information and note it in writing.

5.5.4 Relaying oral messages

Sometimes learners of a second language find themselves in positions where they are asked to relay a message to someone. In situations of this type, it is important to transmit as many bits of information as possible. When testing the students' ability to relay an oral message, the examiner may assign one point for every bit of information contained in the initial message, and calculate the students' scores accordingly.[9]

SAMPLE ITEM TYPE 56 TELEPHONE MESSAGES

Imagine you are visiting an American family where the parents understand your native language. You are at home alone when the phone rings. The person on the line insists on giving you a message. Take notes as the

[9] See Schulz and Bartz, "Free to communicate," pp. 85–86.

person talks to you, and then write up the message for your host in your native language.

Tape: This is Bob Jones. I'm a cousin of Harry's. Tell him that I am in Boston and have a flat tire. That means I'll be at least half an hour late for dinner and they should start without me.

Scoring: 1 point for each bit of information reported.

5.5.5 Taking notes

More advanced students may be asked to take notes in outline form. Such a test is no longer a pure listening test, but one that evaluates the student's note-taking and organizational ability as well as his command of the written language.

The notes may be assigned three grades: comprehension (content), organization, and correctness (spelling and structure).

5.5.6 Taking dictations

The dictation is a precise measure of the students' listening comprehension. The student must understand the meaning of the passage as a whole, while also understanding each word and the relationships between the words. Since the response is made in writing, the dictation is only effective as a listening comprehension test with students who can handle the written language.

In the dictation test, the passage is paused and read slowly so that students can write down the sentences in small segments. The transcription test is more demanding than the dictation, for here the student is presented with an authentic recording: a song, a speech, a segment of a conversation. It is the student who creates the pauses by manipulating the tape or the cassette.

For suggestions on giving and scoring dictations, see Section 8.5 in the chapter on writing.

5.6 LISTENING COMPREHENSION: RETENTION

Occasionally the teacher will want to assess the students' second-language retention. Since retention ability has not yet been proven directly proportional to comprehension, the retention test is often considered diagnostic from the teacher's point of view.

It is best to arrange retention-test items in order of increasing difficulty; here difficulty is proportionate to sentence length and to the position of the changing element. Short sentences are naturally easier to remember than long ones; in sentences of equal length, most students have less difficulty spotting a variation toward the beginning of the sentence than near the end. Since retention, rather than sound discrimination, should be evaluated, the choices offered should be based on more than minimal-pair distinctions.

As a control, the teacher might wish to make up a similar retention test in the native language. A comparison of results would show the differences in retention ability among students with respect to their native language and would permit correlation between their performances in that native language and those in the target language.

In both native- and target-language tests, the sentences in the items should be read with identical intonation and stress.

SAMPLE ITEM TYPE 57   SAME VS. DIFFERENT: PAIRS

You will hear two sentences. Listen carefully to determine whether the sentences are the same or different. Indicate your answer as follows: A = same, B = different.

If the test is given for diagnostic purposes, the directions may be modified to include "not sure." The presence of such an option will reduce the guess factor. The test will discriminate between those who thought they remembered (but were wrong) and those who realized that they did not remember.

Here are some sample items in French:

1. Je viens demain. — *I am coming tomorrow.*
   Il vient demain. — *He is coming tomorrow.*
2. Jean part à deux heures. — *Jean is leaving at two.*
   Jean part à trois heures. — *Jean is leaving at three.*
3. Si j'avais mille dollars, je m'achèterais une voiture. — *If I had $1000, I would buy myself a car.*
   Si j'avais mille dollars, je m'achèterais une moto. — *If I had $1000, I would buy myself a motorcycle.*
4. J'espère faire la connaissance de mon cousin français cet hiver. — *I hope to meet my French cousin this winter.*
   J'espère faire la connaissance de mon cousin français cet hiver. — *I hope to meet my French cousin this winter.*

Correct responses: B, B, B, A

SAMPLE ITEM TYPE 58   RETENTION DICTATION

This hybrid item type uses sentences of increasing length that contain only very familiar structures and vocabulary. Each sentence is read only once at a normal to fast conversational speed. At the end of the sentence there is a pause during which the students write out as much of the sentence as they can remember. Since the focus is on retention ability, there is no penalty for poor spelling. Students receive points for the number of elements they remembered and wrote down.

SAMPLE ITEM TYPE 59   MEMORY SPAN DICTATION

This item is similar to the retention, except that all the sentences are paired. The first sentence of the pair uses a simple sentence construction while the second one contains a dependent clause.[10]

You will hear each sentence read only once. Try to remember the entire sentence and write it down.

1. Jane was a history teacher at the university last year.
2. If you're not too busy, let's walk to the store.

Two scoring methods are possible, and provide similar results:

Scoring for content accuracy
Each sentence is marked as follows:

5 points = Accurate throughout. Very minor changes are permitted.
3 points = Student finished the sentence but distorted the meaning somewhat; for example: If we'll not to be busy, let's go to the store.
1 point = Unacceptable performance, including incomplete sentences.

The values of 4 and 2 are used for sentences that fall between the ratings 5 and 3 and 1.

Scoring for grammatical accuracy

5 points = Grammatical throughout. The meaning of the sentence may have changed and grammatically unimportant elements may have been dropped.
3 points = Sentence contains one grammatical error, including the omission of a grammatically essential element such as a subject or verb.
1 point = Sentence contains two or more grammatical errors, or student response is too short to be a real sample.

---

[10] The sample sentences and suggested scoring are described by David P. Harris in "Report on an Experimental Group-Administered Memory Span Test," in Leslie Palmer and Bernard Spolsky, eds., *Papers on Language Testing: 1967–76* (Washington: Teachers of English to Speakers of Other Languages, 1975), pp. 6–17.

The values of 4 and 2 are used for sentences that fall between the ratings 5 and 3 and 1.

5.7   LISTENING COMPREHENSION UNDER ADVERSE CONDITIONS

Second-language learners who can understand clearly enunciated speech often encounter difficulty when they hear the language under adverse conditions. Telephone calls in the target language present problems because the equipment does not transmit the high frequencies with fidelity, thus making it more difficult to distinguish between consonants like /f/, /s/, /ʃ/, and /θ/. Similarly dialectal variations, rapid speech, and conversations in noisy locations all make it more difficult for the second-language learner to understand what is being said.

Native speakers can usually understand their language under difficult conditions, for they rely on the redundancy of language to provide sufficient clues to allow them to reconstitute the elements they did not quite hear. For instance, the phrase "they (noise) coming" could be interpreted in several ways: "they are coming," "they were coming," "they will be coming," "they would be coming," "they might be coming," etc. However, if the noise segment is so short that it only covers one consonant sound, and if the phrase is in a sentence "They (noise) coming tonight at seven," the native speaker will quickly reconstitute the phrase as "they're coming." This ability to use language redundancy to understand unclear messages distinguishes the native or near-native speaker from the advanced and intermediate students.

Native speakers also understand their own language readily because of what John Oller calls their "expectancy grammar."[11] The listener anticipates elements in a sentence to occur in sequence. In fact, the listener may even be a step ahead of the speaker, and when the latter fumbles for a word, the former can provide it. At a structural level, the native speaker who hears "they're come . . . " will automatically expect the next syllable to be "ing": "they're coming." Semantically, also, the native speaker expects certain words to occur within specific contexts. If a speaker of English hears "They are coming tonight to our . . . ," he or she could anticipate "party" or "house" or "play," but not "dog" or "homework" or "chair." If the last word of the sentence were muffled so that one heard only "par . . . ," the native speaker would interpret the word as "party" and not "parson" or "part" or "parsnip."

[11] For a more complete discussion of this concept, see John W. Oller, Jr., "Expectancy for Successive Elements: Key Ingredient to Language Use." *Foreign Language Annals* 7, no. 4 (May 1974), pp. 443–52.

5.7.1 Rapid speech

Often the language student who can understand the second language when spoken slowly is unable to follow the same text spoken more rapidly. For advanced students, there is the gap between understanding rapid but clearly enunciated speech: "I'm going to get you at nine," and rapid telescoped speech: "Ahmuhnuh getchut nine."

Most of the item types suggested in Section 5.5. can be adapted to rapid conversation tests by increasing the rate of speech. To reinforce the correct responses and to verify the students' comprehension of more measured speech, the same taped cue could be recorded a second time with the participants enunciating more slowly. The same questions could be asked twice and the results compared.

The following item types may also be used:

SAMPLE ITEM TYPE *60* RAPID SPEECH—ORAL TRANSPOSITION

The students hear a short selection in rapid speech. Then they hear the tape again, one sentence at a time. In the pause provided they record the slower and more clearly enunciated equivalent of what has been heard.

Here is a French example:

—M'enfin ... où est Paul ?   *Well, where's Paul?*
—Ché pas.   *I dunno.*
—On va pas l'attend' comme ça.   *We're not going to wait for 'm like this.*

Correct responses: Mais enfin, où est Paul ? Je ne sais pas. On ne va pas l'attendre comme cela.

SAMPLE ITEM TYPE *61* RAPID SPEECH—WRITTEN TRANSCRIPTION

This item type is similar to number 60. The student writes out the standard equivalent rather than speaking it. Since the key concern is comprehension rather than writing, spelling mistakes should not be counted unless they reflect a lack of understanding of the text.

5.7.2 Levels of language

Students who can understand the standard language of educated speakers often have trouble understanding familiar and popular levels of speech. Dialects may also present a problem, depending on the degree to which they differ from standard speech. Usually the very formal level of language used by a talented orator is more readily understood because of its closeness to the written language and its clear delivery.

Comprehension of levels of language can be tested by using the techniques suggested in section 5.7.1. Students are requested to provide the standard language equivalent of selections they hear on tape.

Indirectly, comprehension of levels of language can be tested in a written test based on selections by authors who try to transcribe different types of speech.

SAMPLE ITEM TYPE *62* INTERPRETING WRITTEN TRANSCRIPTIONS OF SPEECH

Rewrite the following sentences from Raymond Queneau, *Zazie dans le métro*, in standard French:

1. "C'est hun cacocalo que jveux et pas autt chose."
2. "Meussieu Charles, qu'elle dit, vzêtes zun mélancolique."
3. " ... Mais un vrai sale type. Faut sméfier, faut sméfier, faut sméfier. Mais quoi, les bloudjinnzes ... "[12]

Correct responses:

1. C'est un Coca-Cola que je veux   *It's a Coke I want, and not*
   et non pas autre chose.   *anything else.*
2. Monsieur Charles, dit-elle, vous   *Mister Charles, she said, you're*
   êtes un mélancolique.   *a melancholy guy.*
3. ... Mais un vrai sale type.   *But a real dirty guy.*
   Il faut se méfier, il faut se   *You have to watch out.*
   méfier, il faut se méfier.   *But what does it matter,*
   Mais quoi, les blue-jeans ...   *the blue-jeans . . .*

Awareness of the cultural parameters of different speech styles can be assessed by asking the students to identify and analyze selections they hear.

SAMPLE ITEM TYPE *63* LEVELS OF LANGUAGE—ANALYSIS

The student hears a short selection of recorded speech and identifies the conditions under which the language was used and the probable relationship between the speaker and listener: e.g., schoolyard slang, coarse speech, campaign rhetoric, etc.

[12] Raymond Queneau, *Zazie dans le métro* (Paris: Gallimard, Livre de poche, 1959), pp. 16, 18, 46.

5.7.3 Distorted speech

Recent research has been done on listening comprehension tests where redundancy is reduced by adding white noise or static to recorded sentences. Under these adverse conditions, native speakers are better able to understand the sentences than second-language learners. Thus the noise tests may function as an indirect measure of language proficiency and may perhaps prove useful as an efficient means of placing incoming students in an advanced language program, e.g., placing foreign students on an American campus into the appropriate English courses.[13]

SAMPLE ITEM TYPE *64* NOISE TEST—DICTATION

The student hears a series of recorded sentences that have been distinctly enunciated, but to which white noise has been added. The student writes out each sentence.

SAMPLE ITEM TYPE *65* NOISE TEST—MULTIPLE CHOICE

The student hears a recorded series of sentences that have been distinctly enunciated, but to which white noise has been added. The student selects the sentence, among those suggested, that matches the sentence on the tape.

Tape: Tell them where she is leaving it.

- A. Tell them where she is living at.
- B. Tell him where she is living.
- C. Tell them when she is leaving.
- D. Tell them where she is leaving it.

NOTE: The options for this type of test may be prepared by first administering the dictation-type noise test to a group of students. Their wrong answers will provide the material for the distractors.

It may be that sentences—like the preceding example—that incorporate minimal differences ("leaving" vs. "living") may prove to be too tricky. In this case the sentences could be revised to eliminate unnecessary ambiguity: "Tell me where she is leaving the book."

---

[13] For a complete discussion of this topic, see Harry L. Gradman and Bernard Spolsky, "Reduced Redundancy Testing: A Progress Report," in Randall L. Jones and Bernard Spolsky, eds., *Testing Language Proficiency* (Arlington, Va.: Center for Applied Linguistics, 1975), pp. 59–70.

outline

six

The Speaking Test

Over the past twenty years, one of the major reasons that students have been enrolling in language classes is to acquire the ability to communicate with people of a different linguistic background. Behind the development of new instructional programs and the dissemination of audio-visual materials is one aim: teaching the students to speak the language.

Yet all too frequently the speaking skill is more or less ignored when tests are being planned. While many teachers claim that they can assign overall grades for speaking ability according to class performance, such scores are to a certain extent subjective. In addition, if all formal tests are of the pencil-and-paper variety, students will quickly realize that their preparation is most profitably spent on reading and writing. The acquisition of fluent speech habits is relegated to the status of a pleasant luxury; students no longer consider it an essential goal of the course. An oral production test at the end of the term or semester will affirm the importance of the speaking skill.

Some students may be timid and even nervous about speaking tests. Others who read and write with difficulty can speak with confidence. For these reasons speaking tests are sometimes termed "unfair." Yet if the speaking skill is to be learned, there must be a testing program.

6.1 GENERAL CONSIDERATIONS

Speaking is a social skill. Whereas one can read and write in private or listen to the radio or watch television alone, a person rarely speaks without an audience of some sort. Communication being the goal of the second-language program, emphasis is placed on the development of correct speech habits.

Even for those students who intend only to read the language, the acquisition of near-native pronunciation and intonation in the early stages of language learning provides a useful foundation. Many persons subconsciously use their speech muscles and vocal cords when reading, even though their lips do not move. Thus indirectly the time spent on reading a foreign language reinforces the student's speech habits.

Speaking, however, is more than pronunciation and intonation. At the functional level, speaking is making oneself understood. At a more refined level, speaking requires the correct and idiomatic use of the target language. The newcomer in a foreign country learns to express himself in order to obtain the essentials of life; first he or she uses gestures, then gradually picks up words and phrases. But with no formal training and without the incentive for perfection, he or she retains a marked accent and uses simplified, and often inaccurate, structures.

In the classroom the language student is expected to learn correct pronunciation and speech patterns. The classroom setup usually offers less incentive for communication than the true-life situation; nevertheless, when communication is a class objective, the testing program should measure not only accurate expression but also ease and fluency in communication.

It is necessary to distinguish between acquiring control of elements of language (pronunciation, vocabulary, grammatical patterns) via speaking on the one hand, and communicating one's ideas via speaking on the other. To use Wilga Rivers' distinction, we must distinguish between skill-getting and skill-using. In this chapter, sections 6.2, 6.3, and 6.4 fall into the former category, while 6.5 and 6.6 focus on speaking for communication.

6.1.1　Problems of administration

The classroom teacher is often unable to give speaking tests like those used in the standardized language test batteries; the standardized tests are administered in the language laboratory and evaluated by teams of trained scorers. Many schools do not have laboratories in which all students can be accommodated at "record" positions. Even if the speaking test can be administered in the laboratory, the teacher often discovers during the scoring that some tape recorders recorded poorly or not at all. Thus, some students must be called back for a second testing. Furthermore, listening to student tapes is a time-consuming task. Not only must the actual playing time be taken into account, but also the time needed to rewind the tape, take it off the machine, and thread the next tape. Cartridges or cassettes can be manipulated more rapidly. If tapes are used, however, it is sometimes possible to have a student assistant duplicate all the student tapes on one long tape that the teacher has to thread only once.

How can the busy teacher best evaluate student proficiency in speaking? Fortunately it has been found that formal speaking tests need not be given often: once a semester will suffice in high-school and college classes. Moreover, if the items are carefully chosen, the test itself can be quite short; much can be said in five minutes, much even in three. For this formal test the teacher can schedule each student individually.

During the year the teacher may give frequent informal speaking tests. The recitation of dialogs or the performance of pattern drills, for example, may be evaluated. Here, too, the teacher should prepare a scoring system so that every student is graded on specific aspects of his or her speech. In the elementary schools, such informal testing is very effective.

Many communication tests can be administered as full-class or group activities. These activities often resemble games in that the students "play" in order to transmit information correctly. The students who are quickest to succeed may be allowed to earn extra credit points.

6.1.2   Problems of objectivity

Poorly planned speaking tests are usually unreliable instruments for assessing student proficiency. Since most classroom teachers do not record student responses on tape, but rather evaluate the performance as it occurs, it is essential that a careful scoring system be established in advance and applied rigorously to each student performance.

In each of the following sections, specific scoring suggestions are provided. In selecting item types, the teacher will also determine how student performance is to be evaluated. As the test is given, each response should be scored immediately and that score entered onto a scoring sheet or into the record book.

6.2   THE SOUND SYSTEM

One aspect of learning to speak a second language is mastering a different sound system. Once the student controls the intonation, rhythm, and stress patterns of the new language, he or she can usually be fairly well understood by native speakers of the language. The accurate pronunciation of individual vowel and consonant sounds is also important, but in many languages a mispronounced sound is less likely to interfere with comprehension than a wrongly stressed syllable. It is possible to speak a second language effectively with a near-native control of vocabulary and grammar, and still retain a noticeable "foreign accent."

The test items suggested in this section, therefore, should be seen within this general perspective: perfect or near-perfect control of the sound system of the target language is a desirable goal, but not the most important aspect of the speaking skill.

6.2.1   Analyzing the problems of pronunciation and intonation

Pronunciation and intonation problems may be traced to differences between the native language and the target language; thus, there are not simply problems for students of French, but, more precisely, certain problems for English-speaking students of French, others for Spanish-speaking students of French, etc.

What are the problem areas that must be tested? In Section 5.2, two aspects of sound discrimination were discussed. Every student must learn to distinguish among the phonemes of the target language and to differentiate the distinctive phonetic features of the target language and the native language. Unless students can discriminate the sounds accurately, they can only hope to produce them in a haphazard fashion: their own ears must control the sound production. However, learning to identify the phonemes of a new language does not of itself imply the ability to produce those sounds, hence the need for sound-production tests to determine the quality of student pronunciation and intonation.

All the problems of sound discrimination that arise—for example, when English-speaking students are learning Spanish—must be incorporated into sound-production tests.

In addition to these areas of listening discrimination, the speaking tests must also include all cases where students tend to transfer native language speech habits to the target language. One persistent habit that American students erroneously tend to transfer to Spanish, French, German, and other languages is the reduction of unstressed vowels. For most Americans, the following underlined vowels are all pronounced the same: "palatable," "benefit," "civilize," "phonograph," "suppression."

Another problem arises when the target language possesses only one vowel sound in instances where the native language has two or more sounds. For example, American students have little or no difficulty in distinguishing the sound /a/ in French or Spanish, because a similar phoneme exists in English. However, in speaking French or Spanish, American students frequently transfer other English pronunciations of the letter *a* to the target language, and the French *panne* or Spanish *pan* becomes not /pan/ but /pæn/.

More difficult are the cases in which similar phonemes exist in both languages but in different combinations. Linguists term this a problem of *distribution*. The English word "sank" has a nasal vowel, a consonant /ŋ/, and a final /k/ and is pronounced (sɛ̃ŋk/; the French *cinq* is similar but the /k/ immediately follows the vowel: /sɛ̃k/. The English student experiences great difficulty in trying to eliminate the consonant /ŋ/ from his production of the French word. In a more general sense, the fact that English nasal vowels are always followed by nasal consonants explains why so many students of French tend to nasalize vowels before *n* and *m*, contrary to French pronunciation habits, and to introduce an *n* or *m* between a nasal vowel and the following consonant.

The rhythm, stress, and intonation of the target language play an important role in communication. American students have difficulty imitating the even rhythm of French. Students learning English as a target language must learn where to place the stress in each word, distinguishing for example between ge<u>o</u>graphy and geo<u>gra</u>phical, between m<u>o</u>ment and mom<u>en</u>tous.

In preparing tests to measure the students' control of the sound system, the teacher should establish a list of the problems the target language poses to speakers of the given native language.

6.2.2   Pronunciation tests

In the pronunciation items, the teacher will be evaluating the production of the segmental phonemes—vowels and consonants—of the target language. Since the pronunciation test should simulate the natural use of the language, the phonemes to be considered are incorporated into typical sentences.

To maintain the objectivity essential for arriving at a reliable score, the teacher should listen for only *one* aspect of each sentence or phrase. In order to take into consideration the fact that students will sometimes pronounce a sound correctly on one occasion and incorrectly on another, it is suggested that the key sound appear at least twice in the test items. Although the students obviously realize that their speaking performance is being scored, they should not be aware which particular element is coming under the teacher's scrutiny. A variety of stimuli or cues may be employed to induce the students to utter the phrase or sentence desired.

SAMPLE ITEM TYPE *1*   MIMICRY

Repeat the sentences you hear.

Here are some sample items in French:

Bonjour J<u>ea</u>nne, comment ç<u>a</u> v<u>a</u>?   /a/

In the preceding sentence, the teacher would grade only the production of the phoneme /a/.

Très bien, merci, et toi?   /R/

Here the teacher listens only for the uvular *r*.

The student recites from memory a poem or passage, or two students recite a dialog. In order to grade each student's performance reliably, the teacher will have prepared a control version of the material as a scoring guide.

Here are some sample items in French:

Les sanglots longs	1.	/e/	no diphthong
Des violons	2.	/ɔ̃/	as distinguished from /ã/; no *n*-sound after
De l'automne			the vowel
Blessent mon cœur	3.	/l/	no "dark" *l*
D'une langueur	4.	/œ/	accuracy of production
Monotone.	5.	/ɔ/	accuracy of production; no nasalization on
			the third *o*

Teachers finding it difficult to grade five features simultaneously would do well to concentrate on three sounds. Some may wish to reduce the scoring to three categories as follows (in such cases it is assumed that the key sound appears twice in the recitation):

1. both renditions poor
2. one good, one poor
3. both renditions good

In scoring a dialog the teacher must establish parallel grading systems. Both students should be graded on the same sounds, even though these sounds will probably appear in a different sequence in the two parts of the dialog.

Exercises may be used as pronunciation tests. In order not to disadvantage the poor students, these exercises should be very familiar. Since the teacher wishes to assess to what extent the student has mastered and assimilated the pronunciation features of the target language in his or her normal performance, it is preferable that such quizzes not be designated formal pronunciation tests.

Here is a sample item in French:

>Cue: Jean finit-il son travail? *Is Jean finishing his work?*
>Response: Oui, Jean (il) fi̱ni̱t son *Yes, he is finishing his work.*
>travail. /i/

(Both sounds should be identical.
Avoid /ɪ/.)

SAMPLE ITEM TYPE 4 ORAL CUE—COMPLETION

Well-worded completion items lead the student to pronounce a word that does not appear in the stem. Such an item eliminates simple imitation. Completion items must be carefully prepared in advance so that all students will furnish the desired word or phrase.

Here is a sample item in German:

>Cue: Man schneidet Fleisch mit *One cuts meat with a ... knife.*
>einem ...
>
>Response: Messe̱r final /ʌ/

SAMPLE ITEM TYPE 5 PICTURES

Pronunciation tests with visual cues should not be confused with vocabulary tests. The former are most effectively used to bring the student to say a word that offers a particular pronunciation problem. It is often helpful to accompany the picture with a spoken or written cue.

Here is a sample item in French:

>Cue: Voilà des nombres entiers. 1, 2, 3 *Those are whole numbers.*
>Et voici des... $\frac{1}{2}, \frac{1}{4}$ *And here are...*
>Response: fractions *fractions.*

In this item the teacher should check /ksjɔ̃/; a common error is /kʃjɔ̃/.

SAMPLE ITEM TYPE 6 READING ALOUD—FAMILIAR MATERIAL

For students who have acquired the reading skill, the pronunciation test may consist of a series of sentences to be read aloud. If the phrases are familiar, such a test will produce a fairly natural speech sample.

There are two ways of scoring such a test. On the one hand, the teacher could prepare a special version of the text in which specific elements to be scored are clearly indicated. On the other hand, the teacher could use a plain version of the text as a scoring sheet, and mark all the poor pro-nunciations. The test could be graded on a pass/fail basis (for example, no more than four mistakes on a test of fifteen sentences), and students could be given the opportunity to take the test over until they have passed it.

SAMPLE ITEM TYPE 7   READING ALOUD—UNFAMILIAR MATERIAL

The pronunciation test based on new material not only measures the students' production of certain specific sounds but also indicates the accuracy and the rapidity with which they associate the sounds of the target language with the printed word. Many intermediate students, who have mastered the sounds of the new language, will perform unevenly on this type of test. Here, too, the teacher could carefully predetermine which sounds or com-binations will be scored. Words that present the greatest difficulty are English cognates that are pronounced differently in the target language.

If preferred, an individualized scoring system could be established. On a pretest, the students would each read ten unfamiliar sentences containing most of the pronunciation problems of the target language. The teacher would correct each recording and list three errors that the student should try to correct. On the final test, each student's grade would be a function of how well that student corrected his or her three weaknesses. Such a person-alized system encourages all students to improve their pronunciation, for each student has an equal chance to get a good grade, regardless of his or her background in the language.

6.2.3   Intonation tests

Each language has its own intonation patterns, and often the dialects within a given language are in part characterized by their own intonation patterns. When learning a new language, the student tends to transfer the intonations of his or her native language to the target language. Cases in which this transfer can validly be made present no learning problem. In classroom testing the teacher need be principally concerned with two major types of intonation: those that distinguish the target language from the native language of the students and those that connote special meaning in the target language.

For intonation tests, items that permit the evaluation of one or two specific aspects of intonation should be prepared. The students' performance is graded as acceptable or unacceptable on each point.

With beginning students, the teacher may wish to test intonation with mimicry or memorization items (see Sample Item Types 1 and 2). The following items may also be used:

SAMPLE ITEM TYPE *8*   ORAL CUE

A response is elicited either by a question or through a direction. Since the student tends to concentrate on the content of his response, the teacher can readily judge whether the intonation patterns of the target language have become habits or whether the student reverts to the patterns of his or her native language when under stress.

Here are two sample items in French:

Cue: Demandez à Pierre l'âge   *Ask Pierre how old he is.*
        qu'il a.
Response: Quel âge avez-vous   *How old are you?*
        (as-tu)?

Check whether the student continually employs a falling pitch.

Cue: Que feriez-vous si vous   *What would you do if you were*
        étiez riche?   *rich?*
Response: Si j'étais riche (1),   *If I were rich, I would go to*
        j'irais en France (or   *France.*
        some other appro-
        priate answer) (2).

Listen for a rising pitch at (1) and a falling pitch at the end of the sentence (2).

SAMPLE ITEM TYPE *9*   VISUAL CUE

Students are asked to tell a story suggested by a series of drawings or to describe a picture. This type of test is less objective because different students will use different sentence structures. However, it is possible to evaluate the students' general intonation pattern on the following points:

1. intonation within word groups
2. intonation at the end of word groups
3. final intonation in declarative sentences

SAMPLE ITEM TYPE *10*   READING ALOUD

Each student is asked to read a passage aloud. This type of test may prove less satisfactory and less valid than the above types since reading intonation is often unnatural, even when students are requested to read aloud in their native language.

6.2.4   Stress tests

Since most polysyllabic English words carry not only a primary stress, but also secondary and weak stresses, English-speaking students can usually hear and reproduce stress easily in other languages. English-speaking students do, however, face certain stress problems.

First, the American student tends to apply the English weak-stress pattern and the consequent vowel reduction to the target language. In a weak-stress position, most English vowels are pronounced identically, regardless of their spelling. Most English-speaking students must learn to overcome the tendency to reduce the unaccented or unstressed vowels of the target language.

Second, in a language with a stress system, special attention must be paid to cognates in which the positions of the stressed syllables do not correspond. For example, consider English *stúdent* and German *Studént*, or English *úniform* and Spanish *unifórme*. Often a misplaced stress will render the word incomprehensible to the native speaker of the language.

Third, in learning a language with no stress system, such as French, students must make a conscious effort not to introduce a primary stress inappropriately into long words.

Fourth, a different problem arises when the distribution of stressed syllables in the target language does not correspond with that in English. For example, the spondee, or succession of two stressed syllables, while rare in English, is frequent in Spanish. Students tend to introduce an inappropriate glottal stop[1] to separate the stressed syllables, for example, *habló alto*.

Similarly, students learning English as a second language will have to learn the English stress system.

SAMPLE ITEM TYPE *11*   ORAL CUE

For a stressed language, a question or completion-type item may be used to elicit the desired word. Often a picture or other visual cue is helpful. Such items should be constructed in advance and carefully reviewed in order to eliminate the possibility of ambiguity.

Here is a sample item in German:

Cue: Der Man, der ein Flugzeug fliegt, ist ein...	*The man who flies an airplane is a ...*
Response: Pilot	*pilot.*

In items of this type, the examiner is limited in the choice of vocabulary to words with which the student is actively familiar. Such items are conse-

---

[1] The *glottal stop* is a consonant sound formed by a momentary closing of the vocal cords.

quently of limited usefulness. They fail to discriminate well between students who have acquired a feeling for the stress patterns of the target language and those who can mimic accurately but revert to English habits when faced with less familiar vocabulary.

SAMPLE ITEM TYPE *12*   READING ALOUD

A printed text to be read aloud affords the most reliable stress test. The teacher, uncritical of intonation or fluency, judges whether the students accentuate the proper syllables. Cognates not previously used in class may be included if their pronunciation reflects the regular patterns of the target language.

6.2.5   Written tests of the sound system

There are certain written tests that are helpful in evaluating the students' knowledge of how the language is spoken. Such tests have two advantages: they can be scored rapidly, and they can be administered to the class as a group. English, because of its varied spellings, irregular stress patterns, and complex intonation, lends itself particularly well to this type of written testing.[2] The following written tests should be used sparingly, however, because students can learn pronunciation rules and still not pronounce well.

6.2.5a   COMPARING SOUNDS

For varied presentations of comparison items using three, four, and five options, see Section 5.2.

SAMPLE ITEM TYPE *13*   SAME VS. DIFFERENT—TWO WORDS

Compare the underlined letters. If they represent the same sound, mark A; if they represent different sounds, mark B.

Here are two sample items in Spanish:

1. baso   vaso
2. duda

Correct responses: A, B

[2] See Robert Lado, *Language Testing* (New York: McGraw-Hill, 1964), pp. 95–104, 113–15, 137–39.

SAMPLE ITEM TYPE *14* SAME VS. DIFFERENT—THREE WORDS

Compare the sounds of the underlined letters. On your answer sheet indicate which two words contain underlined letters with the same sound.

Here are two sample items in French:

1. A. soi   B. sot   C. seau
2. Son chien (A)   était bien (B)   patient (C).

Correct responses: B, C; A, B

SAMPLE ITEM TYPE *15* RHYMES—TWO WORDS

Compare the two words and indicate whether they rhyme with each other; do not consider a "visual" rhyme, but only the sounds of the words. Mark A if they rhyme; mark B if they do not rhyme.

Here are two sample items in French:

1. ville, fille
2. faim, fin

Correct responses: B, A

SAMPLE ITEM TYPE *16* RHYMES—THREE WORDS

Compare the sounds of the three words. On your answer sheet indicate which two words of the group rhyme with each other.

Here are two sample items in German:

1. A. schöne   B. Söhne   C. rönne
2. A. den   B. wenn   C. zehn

Correct responses: A, B; A, C

NOTE: This technique of comparing sounds is effective with advanced students. When used for languages with fairly well-defined spelling systems, such items can measure the student's knowledge of the exceptions to the general patterns of pronunciation.

6.2.5b COMPARING SOUNDS: OMITTED LETTERS

In word-completion items, the sounds to be compared are left blank. Consequently, the key word must be presented in an unambiguous context so that the problem of guessing does not interfere with student performance.

SAMPLE ITEM TYPE *17*   OMITTED LETTERS—SIMPLE VERSION

On your answer sheet indicate in which words the omitted letters represent identical sounds.

Here is a sample item in French:

A. r__ponse   B. r__construction   C. r__connaître

Correct response: B, C

In some cases pictures may be included for the sake of clarity.

SAMPLE ITEM TYPE *18*   OMITTED LETTERS—COMPLEX VERSION

On your answer sheet indicate which word or words contain underlined letters that sound the same as the letters omitted in the original sentence.

Here is a sample item in French.

Les Américains ont gagné leur indépend__ce.
A. pend<u>en</u>t   B. bi<u>en</u>   C. c<u>am</u>p   D. p<u>an</u>ne

Correct response: C

6.2.5c   TESTING STRESS AND INTONATION

In paper and pencil tests, the students are asked to identify the accented syllables or to compare words or sentences.

SAMPLE ITEM TYPE *19*   LOCATING STRESS

On your answer sheet indicate which syllable receives the greatest (primary) stress.

Here are some sample items in German:

1. A B C
   arbeitslos
2. A B C D
   Toilettentisch
3. A B C D E
   Lockenperücke

Correct responses: A, B, A

NOTE: Alternate forms of the above item type are possible. For instance, students could be asked to circle or to underline the accented syllables.

SAMPLE ITEM TYPE *20* COMPARING STRESS

On your answer sheet mark the letters of the two words which have the same stress pattern.

Here are two sample items in German:

1. A. Frühling   B. Bücher   C. Geschäft
2. A. heiraten   B. begreifen   C. rasieren

Correct responses: A, B; B, C

SAMPLE ITEM TYPE *21* COMPARING INTONATION

Decide whether the intonation patterns of the two sentences are the same or different. On your answer sheet, indicate your answer as follows: A = same, B = different.

Here is a sample item in Spanish:

¿Tienes tiempo?   ¿De dónde viene?

Correct response: B

Intonation tests of this type present two drawbacks. First, it is difficult to formulate a sentence open to only one type of intonation. Second, students who are acquainted with the basic elements of intonation will often be able to select the correct response on paper even though they may lapse into English intonation patterns when speaking.

6.3 TESTING VOCABULARY VIA SPEAKING

Vocabulary acquisition is an important aspect of the speaking skill. Simple, direct communication can take place in the target country on the "Me Tarzan, you Jane" level, where the student uses primarily stressed pronouns, uninflected nouns and adjectives, and verbs in the infinitive form.

In testing vocabulary in the classroom, the teacher should always encourage the students to speak in natural utterances. Thus, when asked to identify a color in English, the student could say "red," because such a one-word answer is used by native speakers. But when asked to identify an object, the student should say "a book" or "That's a book," for the native speaker would not give the one-word answer "book."

6.3.1 Visual cues

Visual cues are very helpful in testing spoken vocabulary, especially at the elementary and intermediate levels. Generally the visual cue is accompanied by a direct question which elicits the desired lexical items.

SAMPLE ITEM TYPE *22*   TELLING TIME—CLOCK

With the aid of a large clock with movable hands, the teacher asks each student to give the time orally.

SAMPLE ITEM TYPE *23*   TELLING TIME—TIMETABLE

If a large timetable is available (or a regular timetable enlarged with an opaque projector), questions may be asked that concern arrivals and departures of trains or planes, the length of trips, the length of stops in various cities on the route, etc.

SAMPLE ITEM TYPE *24*   READING NUMBERS ALOUD

Using available realia, the teacher asks students to read numbers aloud. With a menu, the teacher can ask the prices of various dishes. With a gift catalog, the teacher can ask the prices of the items listed. With a classroom display emphasizing important dates in the target culture, the students can be asked to read these dates aloud. With posters showing conversion tables (Fahrenheit ↔ Centigrade; quarts ↔ liters; miles ↔ kilometers), the teacher can ask for equivalents.

SAMPLE ITEM TYPE *25*   NUMBERS—ORAL COMPUTATION

Ease in handling numbers may be tested orally, usually by means of a straight question-answer technique.

Here is a sample item in German:

Cue: Wieviel ist fünf und acht?   *How much is five and eight?*
Response: Fünf und acht ist   *Five and eight is thirteen.*
dreizehn.

If flash cards are used, the calculation to be performed is presented in figures and the student describes the calculation and the answer in the target language (the response would be similar to the preceding sample).

NOTE: The realia suggested in Sample Item Type 24 can also form the point of departure for oral computation questions.

"Look at the menu. You want a hamburger, French fries, and a small Coke. How much would that cost?"

SAMPLE ITEM TYPE *26*   IDENTIFYING REALIA

The teacher asks each student to identify a specific object. These may be classroom objects (pens, pencils, chairs); toys; plastic fruit; doll clothing and doll furniture; place settings; small tools, etc.

Cue: What is this? (holding up an object)
Response: That's a hammer.

NOTE: In languages where the gender of nouns presents a learning problem, the objects may be presented in such a way that their gender is obvious. For instance, in a German class, the teacher may write *der*, *die* and *das* across the blackboard. When holding up an object of feminine gender, the teacher would stand next to the article *die*.

Variation: Students may be asked to identify attributes of the realia.
> Cue: What color is this fruit? (holding up a red apple)
Response: It's red. *or* Red.

SAMPLE ITEM TYPE *27*   IDENTIFYING PICTURES

The teacher asks students to identify objects depicted on pictures: commercial posters, student drawings, magazine pictures. See Item Type 26, above. It is advisable to select the same pictures for testing that have already been used for teaching the spoken vocabulary: in this way, all students will give a drawing the same interpretation. Stylized drawings may be used to elicit adjectives and adverbs.

> Cue: How is Pierre today?
Response: (a) He is happy.
> (b) He is sad.

a   b

NOTE: With a composite picture, the teacher can point to various objects and ask individual students to identify and/or describe them.

SAMPLE ITEM TYPE *28*   DESCRIBING SLIDES

The visual cue for a spoken vocabulary test can also be provided by slides of the target country and of its contributions to world civilization (such as paintings, sculpture, drama). The slide is projected on the screen and the teacher uses a long pointer to indicate specific aspects of the photograph. This type of vocabulary test has the additional advantage of increasing the students' familiarity with various aspects of the target culture.

Here are some sample items in French:

> Cue: Voici un tableau célèbre de l'artiste russe Marc Chagall, qui habite en France.
> Qu'est-ce que c'est? (pointing at horse)
Response: C'est un cheval.
> Cue: De quelle couleur est ce cheval?
Response: Bleu. *or* Il est bleu.

Here is a famous painting by the Russian artist Marc Chagall, who lives in France.

What's this?

It's a horse.

What color is this horse?

Blue. or *It's blue.*

6.3.2   Oral cues in the target language

Oral cues may also be used to elicit spoken vocabulary. In an informal classroom test, the teacher will ask the questions, trying to give the students items of equivalent difficulty. On a more formal test, the teacher will record the questions or read them aloud from the console in the language laboratory or electronic classroom, and the students will record their responses.

SAMPLE ITEM TYPE *29*   SYNONYMS AND ANTONYMS

Give a synonym and an antonym for the words you hear.

Cue: quickly
Response: rapidly (slowly)

Here is the same type of item in a situational context:

Contrary-minded. Mr. Brown is asking you questions about how often you do things. Just to frustrate him, you answer every question in the negative, using antonyms.

Cue: Do you often play baseball?
Response: No, I never play baseball.
Cue: Do you usually chew gum?
Response: No, I rarely chew gum.

On items of this type, the teacher would grade only the production of the appropriate adverb and ignore the other elements in the response.

SAMPLE ITEM TYPE *30*   SEQUENCES

Continue the suggested sequence.

Cue: Monday, Tuesday, Wednesday
Response: Thursday, Friday, Saturday, Sunday
Variation: Name the month that comes before (after) August.

SAMPLE ITEM TYPE *31*   TARGET LANGUAGE DEFINITIONS

The student hears a definition and provides the key word.

Cue: Name the object you would use to remove the lid from a can of soup.
Response: A can opener.

SAMPLE ITEM TYPE *32* QUESTIONS

The student answers questions in the target language.

Here is an item in French:

Cue:	Quel est l'animal qui dit	*Which is the animal that says*
	"coin coin"?	*"quack, quack"?*
Response:	le canard	*the duck*

SAMPLE ITEM TYPE *33* WORD ASSOCIATION

The student is given a word in the target language and is asked to respond by giving as many related words as possible within a 60-second interval.

Cue: house

Response: big—white—home—bedroom—kitchen—living room—fire-place—etc.

NOTE: This type of item is effective with more advanced students. It may be used as a measure of bilingual dominance by having students respond to some cues in their native language and others in the target language.[3]

6.3.3 Oral cues in the native language

Depending on course objectives, the teacher may or may not wish to use native language cues to elicit spoken vocabulary. It should be noted, however, that the first type of item closely parallels the kind of situation that might occur in a real communication context.

SAMPLE ITEM TYPE *34* ASKING FOR EQUIVALENTS

Here is an item in French:

Cue:	Comment dit-on	*How do you say "raincoat" in*
	"raincoat" en français?	*French?*
Response:	On dit "imperméable".	*You say "imperméable."*

SAMPLE ITEM TYPE *35* ORAL TRANSLATION

In oral translation, or lightning translation, the student provides a target language equivalent of a sentence in the native language. Since the emphasis is on vocabulary, the syntax is kept simple. The students' responses should be scored for their rapidity and fluency as well as their accuracy. If most

---

[3] For the range of possible interpretations of word associations in measuring bilingualism, see Leon A. Jakobovitz, *Foreign Language Learning: A Psycholinguistic Analysis of the Issues* (Rowley, Mass: Newbury House, 1970), pp. 181–82.

responses are sluggish and unnatural, such tests should be postponed to a later date or simplified so that a quick pace is maintained.

Here are some sample items in French:

> Cue: I'm hungry.
> Response: J'ai faim.
> Cue: I'm sleepy
> Response: J'ai sommeil.

Oral translation tests may be scored as follows:

> 2 points = The student gives the correct equivalent on the first try.
> 1 point = The student gives a wrong answer, but gives the correct equivalent on the second try.

6.4   TESTING GRAMMAR VIA SPEAKING

Oral grammar test items measure the ease and accuracy with which the student handles the patterns of the target language. Since the range of correct responses is narrowly defined, the student's performance may be judged with high objectivity. Only the aspect under evaluation, that is, the use of structure and syntax, should be evaluated. Pronunciation enters into the judging only if it is crucial to the meaning of the response.

6.4.1   Visual cues

If visual cues have been used to teach new structures, these same visual cues may be incorporated into spoken grammar tests. (Visual cues are sometimes ambiguous and open to several interpretations. Therefore, if the students are familiar with the visual cues through previous practice, there will be no question of misinterpretation during the actual test situation.)

SAMPLE ITEM TYPE *36*   DESCRIBING ACTIONS IN THE CLASSROOM

The student describes what the teacher or a classmate is doing.

Mary is entering the room.
She is going to her desk.
She is sitting down.

Variation: The actions can be described in other tenses or constructions. For instance:

Mary entered the room. She went to her desk. She sat down.
As I looked up, Mary was entering the room. Etc.
That's Mary who is entering the room. Etc.

SAMPLE ITEM TYPE *37*   DESCRIBING A SEQUENCE OF ACTIVITIES

With a poster, a blackboard drawing or an overhead transparency, the teacher sets a scene. The students describe the actions of a stick figure superimposed on the scene.

(French: map)

Jean-Pierre est sur les Champs-Elysées. Il va tout droit.

Jean-Pierre is on the Champs-Elysées. He goes straight ahead.

(German: street scene)

Cue: Wo ist Inge?
(picture: in front of store)

Where is Inge?

Response: Sie ist vor der Bäckerei.

She is in front of the bakery.

Cue: Wohin geht sie?
(picture: goes into store)

Where is she going?

Response: Sie geht in die Bäckerei.

She's going into the bakery.

The scoring system will reflect the intent of the test. For instance, in the French example, the students may receive 1 point for the correct verb form, and 1 point for general fluency. In the German test, the students may receive 1 point for the correct preposition and 1 point for the correct case ending (der Bäckerei; die Bäckerei).

Variation: The students may be asked to respond in other tenses or by using more complex sentence structure.

SAMPLE ITEM TYPE *38*   CHANGING PRONOUNS

The teacher places a pronoun chart at the front of the room:

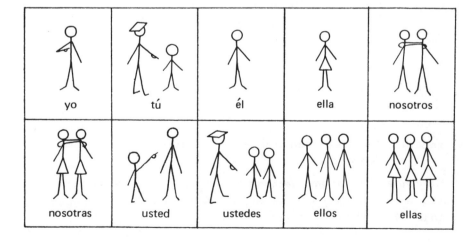

Students are asked to transform sentences by substituting the pronoun that the teacher points to.

(subject)	Hablo español. (points to *ellos*)	*I speak Spanish.*
	Response: Hablan español.	*They speak Spanish.*
(object)	Te lo da. (points to *nosotros*)	*He gives it to you.*
	Response: Nos lo da.	*He gives it to us.*

6.4.2 Oral cues in the target language

Generally most of the exercises used in class may be adapted with good results to informal speaking tests. Usually the teacher reads the instructions, gives the model, and then reads the cue to the student. Informal tests of this sort can be scored as follows:

4 points = The student provided the correct response without hesitation.

3 points = The student provided the correct response after much hesitation, or after having the cue repeated.

2 points = The student first gave the wrong answer, and then corrected it without hesitation when the first answer was not accepted.

1 point = The student first gave the wrong answer, and then provided the correct answer after much hesitation or after having the cue repeated.

0 points = Even on the second try, the student gave the wrong answer or no answer.

SAMPLE ITEM TYPE *39* CORRELATION

The student replaces one element in the sentence with another and is consequently obliged to effect other changes.

Here is a sample item in German that requires modification of the definite article:

Cue: Ich nehme das Buch. (Bleistift)	*I am taking the book. (Pencil.)*
Response: Ich nehme den Bleistift.	*I am taking the pencil.*

Similar items may be constructed to evaluate student proficiency in handling the indefinite and partitive articles; descriptive, demonstrative, and possessive adjective forms; pronouns, reflexives, verb forms, and sequence of tenses.

SAMPLE ITEM TYPE *40* MODIFIED SUBSTITUTION

The student must modify the new element before substituting it in the key sentence.

Here is a sample item in Spanish:

| Cue: Tengo un libro. (ver) | *I have a book. (see)* |
| Response: Veo un libro. | *I see a book.* |

Similar items can be used to test noun forms, adjective forms, comparison of adjectives and adverbs, cardinal and ordinal numbers.

SAMPLE ITEM TYPE *41* PRONOUNS

The student replaces a noun or phrase with the appropriate pronoun.

Here is a sample item in French:

| Cue: Les étudiants vont à Nice. | *The students are going to Nice.* |
| Response: Ils vont à Nice. | *They are going to Nice.* |

Similar items can be used to evaluate student proficiency in handling personal, demonstrative, and possessive pronouns and the position of pronouns.

SAMPLE ITEM TYPE *42* TRANSFORMATION

In items of this type the student changes a sentence according to precise instructions. Although the suggested items are single sentences, the teacher may wish to arrange sentences of this type into a situational context. Sample situational directions are given in parentheses for each example.

(French: *number*)

Change the following sentences from the singular to the plural.
(Rich farmer: Monsieur Lepauvre and Monsieur Leriche are looking for their animals. But where Monsieur Lepauvre only has one of each kind of animal, Monsieur Leriche has several. After you hear Monsieur Lepauvre's questions, give Monsieur Leriche's corresponding question.)

| Cue: Où est mon cheval? | *Where is my horse?* |
| Response: Où sont mes chevaux? | *Where are my horses?* |

In this sentence there are three plural changes to be made by the speaker. In isolation or in combination the following elements can be used in this type of item: articles, adjectives, nouns, pronouns, verb forms. Changes may be made from singular to plural or from plural to singular.

(German: *negation*)

Change the following sentences to the negative. (Opposites: You will hear Helga say what she did. Say that you did not do these things.)

Cue: Ich habe es verkauft.	*I sold it.*
Response: Ich habe es nicht verkauft.	*I didn't sell it.*

(French: *interrogative*)

Change the following statements into questions using the inverted form. Begin your questions with *pourquoi* (*why*). (Curiosity: Jean-François is talking about his cousin Monique. Every time he makes a statement, his sister asks why. Play the role of the sister, beginning your questions with *pourquoi* and using inversion.)

Cue: Elle cherche son père.	*She is looking for her father.*
Response: Pourquoi cherche-t-elle son père?	*Why is she looking for her father?*

(Spanish: *tense*)

Change the following sentences to the future, using the negative form. (Weekend: Pedro is busy today, but on the weekend he relaxes. Say that he will not be doing the following things on Saturday.)

Cue: Pedro trabaja.	*Pedro is working.*
Response: No trabajará el sábado.	*He won't work on Saturday.*

SAMPLE ITEM TYPE *43*   FOLLOWING COMMANDS

This type of item parallels the classroom directed dialog.

Here is a sample item in French:

Cue: Dites à Madame Lebrun de s'asseoir.	*Tell Mrs. Lebrun to sit down.*
Response: Asseyez-vous, Madame.	*Sit down, Mrs. Lebrun.*

Such items may be used to evaluate the student's command of first and second person verb forms in a variety of modes and tenses in addition to his or her mastery of pronoun forms and word order. It should be noted, however, that only the commands "ask" and "tell" reflect common use of the language.

The items would be scored on correctness of word order and of forms. Since such a test measures student command of the grammatical patterns of the language, comprehension problems should be avoided unless knowledge of difficult verb forms or noun forms is being tested.

SAMPLE ITEM TYPE 44 JOINING SENTENCES

The students' ability to use conjunctions and relative pronouns, as well as their understanding of verb tenses, modes, and word order, may be evaluated with the following item type: Given two independent statements, the students are asked to join them into one complex or compound sentence.

Here is a sample item in Spanish:

> Cue: La casa es muy cómoda.   *The house is very comfortable.*
> Habitamos en la casa.   *We live in the house.*
> Response: La casa en que habita-   *The house we live in is very*
> mos es muy cómoda.   *comfortable.*

SAMPLE ITEM TYPE 45 DIRECTED QUESTIONS AND ANSWERS

In the question-answer speaking test, the students are told what kind of response to give. Although students are not completely free to choose their answers in such a directed test, they often enjoy such items because they so closely approximate a real conversational situation.

Here is a sample item in French:

> Cue: Croyez-vous qu'il sache   *Do you think he knows how to sing?*
> chanter? (oui)   *(yes.)*
> Response: Oui, je crois qu'il sait   *Yes, I think he knows how to sing.*
> chanter.

NOTE: In this particular example the student must modify two verb forms.

In a variation of this item type, the student is given the answer (perhaps on a sheet of paper) and asked to supply the appropriate question.

Here is a sample item in German:

> Cue: Ich will das blaue Buch   *I want to buy the blue book.*
> kaufen.
> Response: Welches Buch wollen Sie   *Which book to you want to buy?*
> (willst du) kaufen?

Such items may test verb forms, word order, the use of pronouns, and question words.

SAMPLE ITEM TYPE 46 DIRECTED INTERVIEW USING PICTURES

In this type of test, the teacher and student talk about a set of pictures. The teacher asks questions to which the student replies, or, if desired, the student is requested to ask pertinent questions.

Here is an example in German:

Visual: a series of pictures, each with a clock, depicting . . .

a. 7 a.m., girl getting up
b. 7:15 a.m., girl having breakfast
c. 7:40 a.m., girl waiting for school bus

Cue: Das ist Gisela. Was macht sie? (teacher points to picture a)	*This is Gisela. What is she doing?*
Response: Sie steht auf.	*She's getting up.*
Cue: Wann steht sie auf?	*When does she get up?*
Response: Um sieben.	*At seven.*
Cue: Wie spät ist es hier? (teacher points to picture b)	*What time is it here?*
Response: Es ist Viertel acht.	*It is quarter after seven.*

By adding more indications to the picture sequences, such as "gestern" (yesterday), "heute" (today), and "morgen" (tomorrow), the student responses can utilize other tenses.[4]

6.4.3   Oral cues in the native language

In some classes, the teacher may wish to use native language cues to elicit spoken structures. The emphasis here is on providing an acceptable target language equivalent, and not on word-for-word translation.

SAMPLE ITEM TYPE 47   ASKING FOR EQUIVALENTS

Here is an example in French:

Cue: Comment dit-on "He will come" en français?
Response: On dit "il viendra".

SAMPLE ITEM TYPE 48   ORAL TRANSLATION

Give the French equivalents of the following sentences:

Cue: I have been living here since June.
Response: J'habite ici depuis juin.

---

[4] Donna Ilyin has developed an interview test for English as a Second Language using similar picture cues. The questions are sequenced in order of increased difficulty. See the Appendix for a description of the *Ilyin Oral Interview*.

Oral translation items are particularly effective in testing the students' command of structures that are not parallel in the native and target languages. These items may be scored for fluency as well as for accuracy of structure.

6.5   SPEAKING FOR COMMUNICATION: DIRECTED EXPRESSION

When students are being evaluated on their ability to communicate orally, the main emphasis focuses on the transmission of a message or series of messages. The essential consideration is whether the students are able to make themselves understood. This accent on the meaning of the message, rather than on its grammaticality, characterizes speaking tests of this type. The student is instructed about what to say. The choice of words and structures, however, is not specified and is left up to the student.

In oral communication tests, successful performance depends on personality as well as linguistic competence. The extrovert may often score higher than the qualified introvert, a fact that teachers tend to find disturbing. However, since gestures and intonations do play a sizeable role in interpersonal communication, it is probably fair to reward those who get their ideas across effectively, even if it is at the expense of linguistic precision. Other elements of the course, such as command of vocabulary and grammar, are usually tested separately, and these scores will also enter into the determination of the final grade.

6.5.1   Visual cues: The Upshur scoring systems

Visuals may provide the point of departure for oral communication, especially at the elementary levels.

SAMPLE ITEM TYPE *49*   PICTURE WRITING

Thanks to a system of picture writing developed by TAVOR Aids, it is possible to bypass both the native language and the skills of listening and reading in the target language and still elicit specific spoken responses. Whole ideas are represented through simple line drawings called "ideograms." Obviously the students will have to be familiar with the symbols before taking the test; however, this picture-writing technique is a welcome addition to classroom teaching aids.

In an informal testing situation, the ideograms may be drawn on flash cards; for a formal test, mimeographed copies of the selected ideograms can be distributed.

Let us look at some examples in English.

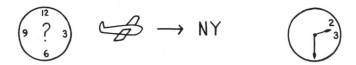

(When is there a plane for New York? *or* When does the plane leave for New York?)
Response: There is one at two-thirty. *or* At two-thirty.

(What is the man planning to do?)
Response: He is going to the bookstore to buy a book. (The balloon con-

tains symbols of the man's intentions. The symbol

represents a roof: thus, 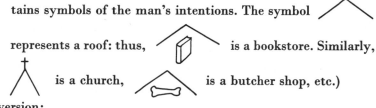 is a bookstore. Similarly,

is a church, is a butcher shop, etc.)

Another version:

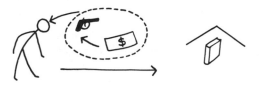

Response: He is going to hold up the bookstore.[5]

On a picture-writing test of directed expression, the students will be given ten to fifteen situations to interpret. Such a test might be scored as follows:

1 point = for each sentence in which the intent of the picture would be correctly conveyed to a native speaker
1 point = for each correct response that sounds fluent and natural

[5] For similar ideograms, see *TAVOR Aids Bulletin*, no. 2 (February 1966), pp. 2–3. TAVOR Aids, P.O. Box 282, Forest Hills, N.Y. 11375.

SAMPLE ITEM TYPE *50*   PICTURE IDENTIFICATION

The student sees a group of four similar pictures, each identified by a letter. The student is then given a letter and must describe the corresponding picture so that the listener can pick it out from among the group of pictures. The student may not point at the picture or refer to its number.

John Upshur has been experimenting with communication tests of this sort, and has developed two types of scoring systems.[6]

Scoring the amount of communication:

The students are given thirty-six sets of pictures and describe one in each set. The total score is the number of pictures described accurately enough so that the listener could guess the correct picture.

Scoring the rate of communication:

The students are given thirty-six sets of pictures and are to describe one in each set. A time limit of two minutes is set. The total score is the number of pictures described accurately in that time span.

The classroom teacher may wish to conduct the picture identification test as a full-class activity. In this case, each set of four pictures is drawn on a poster or prepared on an overhead transparency. After a student has described a picture, the members of the class write down the letter that corresponds to the picture they think was being described. The following grading system could be adopted:

A   =   All the students in the class knew which picture was described
B   =   90–99 percent of the students knew which picture was described
C   =   80–89 percent of the students knew which picture was described
D   =   70–79 percent of the students knew which picture was described
F   =   less than 69 percent knew which picture was described

This type of scoring system encourages active listening on the part of the entire class and helps the students realize that communication requires both speaking and listening.

Speaking in a way that is comprehensible to one's classmates is often easier than speaking in a way that could be easily understood by a native speaker. American students of French, for instance, are more likely to understand the "interlanguage"[7] of their classmates than are native speakers with no knowledge of English.

[6] See John A. Upshur, "Productive Communication Testing: Progress Report," in John W. Oller, Jr. and Jack C. Richards, eds., *Focus on the Learner: Pragmatic Perspectives for the Language Teacher* (Rowley, Mass.: Newbury House, 1973).

[7] "Interlanguage" is the learner's version of the target language, which does not totally fit the norms of the target language as spoken by native speakers. See Larry Selinker, "Interlanguage" in John Schumann and Nancy Stenson, eds., *New Frontiers in Second Language Learning* (Rowley, Mass.: Newbury House, 1974). This article also appeared in *IRAL International Review of Applied Linguistics* 10, no. 3.

6.5.2 Verbal cues: The Jakobovitz-Gordon and Bartz rating scales

Instructions for tests of directed expression may be given orally, either in the native language or the target language. Sometimes a written guide is used.

SAMPLE ITEM TYPE *51* STATEMENT AND REJOINDER

In a statement-rejoinder item, the teacher speaks a sentence and then indicates by a gesture or a facial expression the type of reaction the student is to manifest. Not only the choice of the rejoinder, but also the promptness of the response and the appropriateness of the intonation may be scored. This type of informal classroom test affords the more creative students an opportunity to show their inventiveness and thus encourages the other students to listen to the answers.

Here is a sample item in French:

Cue: Je ne peux pas venir.   *I can't come.*
     (sad reaction)
Response: Ah! quel dommage!   *That's too bad!*

SAMPLE ITEM TYPE *52* EXPRESSING INTENTIONS

In items of this type, the student is asked to transform a sentence so as to express certain intentions. The student is scored on the effectiveness of the transformation.

Sample sentence: She will be going to the lecture.
    Cue: Indicate obligation.
Response: She has to go to the lecture. She is required to go to the lecture. Etc.
    Cue: Indicate permission.
Response: She is allowed to go to the lecture. She may go to the lecture. Etc.
    Cue: Indicate irony.
Response: She's just *delighted* to be going to the lecture! Wouldn't she just *love* to go to the lecture! Etc.

SAMPLE ITEM TYPE *53* FACILITATING COMMUNICATION

The student plays the role of a teacher or leader and phrases a statement in such a way as to facilitate communication.[8] Although exercises of this type have been developed primarily to increase teacher effectiveness, they

---

[8] For further ideas, see Joe Wittmer and Robert D. Myrick, *Facilitative Teaching: Theory and Practice* (Pacific Palisades, Calif.: Goodyear, 1974).

are also appropriate in increasing the students' command of the second language.

Here is an example in English:

Transform the closed question (which only elicits a yes/no answer) into an open question (which encourages the other person to say something more).

Cue: Do you understand this poem?
Response: Which lines of the poem are the most difficult?
Cue: You don't like this play, do you?
Response: What is there about this play that you don't like?

SAMPLE ITEM TYPE 54 DIRECTED CONVERSATION

Two or more students are assigned roles and are given precise directions as to the type of conversation they are to engage in. For elementary classes the directions are best given in the target language, but for more advanced students they may be given in English if the teacher wishes to test fluency of vocabulary and structure. This test should not become an exercise in oral translation; that is, it should not be so difficult that the student must stop and grope for words. Sample directions would be given as follows:

Two roles: Jack Smith, an American, and a waiter in a French restaurant. Jack enters the restaurant and is seated. He and the waiter greet each other. The waiter asks him what he would like. Jack says he is hungry and wants ham and eggs with a glass of milk. The waiter replies that they have no ham and eggs, and gives him a menu. The waiter suggests steak, French fries, and wine. Jack accepts the steak and potatoes, but says he hates wine. The waiter then suggests lemonade and Jack agrees.

The students are given the sample instructions in their native language, and if desired are given the printed text as a memory aid.[9]

Student performance may be rated simply on the basis of the amount of information transmitted. A general scale may be set up as follows:

1. Almost no relevant information was transmitted.
2. About $\frac{1}{4}$ of the relevant information was transmitted.
3. About $\frac{1}{2}$ of the relevant information was transmitted.
4. About $\frac{3}{4}$ of the relevant information was transmitted.
5. All the relevant information was transmitted.

A more reliable scoring sheet would consist of a checklist on which the teacher would mark the pieces of information that were transmitted:

[9] For a wide variety of sample conversations, see Gerald E. Logan, *German Conversational Practice* (Rowley, Mass.: Newbury House, 1973); Gerald E. Logan and Michèle Leroux, *French Conversational Practice* (Rowley, Mass.: Newbury House, 1975); Gerald E. Logan and Hilda Bals, *Spanish Conversational Practice* (Rowley, Mass.: Newbury House, 1976).

Jack Smith: _____		Waiter: _____	
(name of student)		(name of student)	
1 _____	greetings	2 _____	greetings
4 _____	hungry	3 _____	what would he like?
5 _____	ham	6 _____	no ham
7 _____	eggs	9 _____	no eggs
8 _____	milk	10 _____	offers menu
12 _____	steak OK	11 _____	suggests steak
14 _____	French fries OK	13 _____	suggests French fries
16 _____	hates wine	15 _____	suggests wine
18 _____	lemonade OK	17 _____	suggests lemonade
_____	*total*	_____	*total*

SAMPLE ITEM TYPE 55   REPORTING A CONVERSATION

The student listens to a live or recorded conversation between two native speakers of the target language. The student then reports on the content of what was said.

Variation: The student reads a story or article and reports on its contents.

Leon Jakobovits and Barbara Gordon have developed the following rating scale for a free expression test of this sort. The emphasis is on "transactional competence" rather than on correctness of pronunciation and syntax.[10]

Rating Scale: Student's name:

1. Accuracy of Information
   very poor   0 1 2 3 4 5 6 7 8 9 10   fully accurate
2. Amount of Information Related
   very little   0 1 2 3 4 5 6 7 8 9 10   all of it
3. Fluency of Speech
   very hesitant 0 1 2 3 4 5 6 7 8 9 10   ordinary fluency
4. Naturalness of Discourse Organization
   abnormal   0 1 2 3 4 5 6 7 8 9 10   normal
5. Style of Expression
   foreign   0 1 2 3 4 5 6 7 8 9 10   native
6. Clarity of Expression
   unclear   0 1 2 3 4 5 6 7 8 9 10   clear
7. Gestural Fluency or Conversational Naturalness
   odd   0 1 2 3 4 5 6 7 8 9 10   normal
8. Complexity of Transactional Performance[11]
   straight   0 1 2 3 4 5 6 7 8 9 10   skillfully intricate
                                 Total score: _____

[10] See Leon A. Jakobovits and Barbara Gordon, *The Context of Foreign Language Teaching* (Rowley, Mass.: Newbury House, 1974), p. 54.
[11] Student contributed commentary on the reported conversation in his or her reporting of it. (Footnote by Jakobovits and Gordon.)

The classroom teacher may find that this rating scale is too complicated. It is probably advisable to have only 4 to 6 points on each aspect to be evaluated and to develop descriptions of each of these points. Furthermore, the teacher may wish to use only selected aspects from among the eight suggested.

SAMPLE ITEM TYPE 56   GETTING INFORMATION

The student plays the role of an interviewer and tries to obtain certain information from the teacher (or an examiner) who pretends to be a monolingual native speaker of the language under study. The student may use only the target language in conducting the interview and then writes up the information obtained. (Beginning students may write up the information in their native language, and more advanced students might use the target language.)

Here are sample questions prepared for American college students studying German:[12]

Try to find out the following information and *more* if at all possible:

Name of person interviewed
Where he/she comes from
How long he/she will stay in the US
What he/she is doing here
What he/she has seen of the US
Which part of the country he/she likes best
If he/she would like to live here
Why? (Why not?)
What he/she will do when he/she gets back home

Walter Bartz developed the following rating scale for this type of item:

A. Fluency	1	2	3	4	5	6
B. Quality of Communication	1	2	3	4	5	6
C. Amount of Communication	1	2	3	4	5	6
D. Effort to Communicate	1	2	3	4	5	6

The levels of the scales are defined as follows:

A. *Fluency* (similar to the Foreign Service Institute scale; see section 6.6.2a)

[12] Sample test item and scoring system are taken from Walter H. Bartz, "A Study of the Relationship of Certain Learner Factors with the Ability to Communicate in a Second Language (German) for the Development of Measures of Communicative Competence," (Ph.D. diss., Ohio State University, 1974).

B. *Quality of Communication*
1. Speech consists *mostly* of inappropriate isolated words and/or incomplete sentences with just a *few* very short complete sentences.
2. Speech consists of *many* inappropriate isolated words and/or incomplete sentences with *some* very short complete sentences.
3. Speech consists of *some* inappropriate isolated words and/or incomplete sentences with *many* very short complete sentences.
4. Speech consists of *hardly any* isolated words and/or incomplete sentences with *mostly* complete sentences.
5. Speech consists of isolated words only if appropriate and *almost always* complete sentences.
6. Speech consists of isolated words only if appropriate, otherwise *always* "native-like" appropriate complete sentences.

C. *Amount of Communication*
1. *Virtually no* relevant information was conveyed by the student.
2. *Very little* relevant information was conveyed by the student.
3. *Some* relevant information was conveyed by the student.
4. *A fair amount* of relevant information was conveyed by the student.
5. *Most* relevant information was conveyed by the student.
6. *All* relevant information was conveyed by the student.

D. *Effort to Communicate*
1. Student withdraws into long periods of silence, without any apparent effort to complete the task.
2. Student makes *little* effort to communicate, what he does do is "half-hearted," without any enthusiasm.
3. Student makes *some* effort to communicate, but still shows a rather "disinterested" attitude.
4. Student makes an effort to communicate but does not use any non-verbal resources, such as gestures.
5. Student makes a real effort to communicate and uses some non-verbal resources, such as gestures.
6. Student makes a special (unusually high) effort to communicate and uses all possible resources, verbal and non-verbal, to express himself or herself.

As a result of his study, Bartz suggests that classroom teachers need use only the third scale, "Amount of Communication," since this accounted for over 90 percent of the variance in the total score.

6.6 SPEAKING FOR COMMUNICATION: FREE EXPRESSION

In a free expression test, the student determines what to say and how to say it. Although a general topic or conversational direction may be suggested, the teacher cannot predict the actual content of the student's talk. This type of test parallels the student's free use of the target language in a real communication situation.

6.6.1   Selecting the testing situation

Although a free expression test allows the students to demonstrate their linguistic creativity, one cannot simply put the student before a tape recorder or in front of the class and say "speak." A testing framework that will facilitate student talk must be established. The following types of items have proven effective.

SAMPLE ITEM TYPE 57   RECORDED MONOLOG—WITH PICTURES

The recorded monolog is frequently part of standardized speaking tests. In the picture format, the student is told to talk about a depicted scene (in which nouns and descriptive adjectives play a significant role) or to narrate a sequence of events (in which verb forms predominate).

Here is an example in English:

Look at the cartoon sequence which shows what happened when Paul (P), Mark (M), and Sylvia (S) went to the movies yesterday. Explain what happened, using the past tense. Are you ready? Begin.

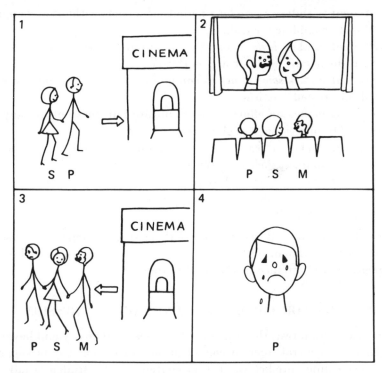

NOTE: The instructions would be in the native language for beginning students, and in English for more advanced students. The important consideration is that all students, even the weakest, are able to understand what they are to do. It is preferable to give the student the printed instructions and also to read them aloud, so that no misinterpretation can occur. This type of test question is usually administered in the language laboratory, and each student is asked to record his or her response.

SAMPLE ITEM TYPE *58*   RECORDED MONOLOG—WITHOUT PICTURES

In the recorded monolog without pictures the students are given precise topics to talk about. It is preferable to provide a series of three or four short topics rather than one long topic. In this way, the teacher has a broader sampling of the student's speaking ability. Moreover, if one topic does not particularly inspire a student, there are other topics that may elicit a more fluent speech sample.

Here are some possible topics in French:[13]

1. Imaginez qu'un ami vous demande de lui prêter votre bicyclette pour la journée. Vous avez peur qu'il la casse et vous ne la lui prêtez pas. Inventez trois excuses. Vous pouvez utiliser les verbes suivants: aller / sortir / partir / faire / rendre visite à.

   Imagine that a friend asks you to loan him your bike for the day. You are afraid that he might break it and you are not going to loan it to him. Invent three excuses. You may use the following verbs: to go / to go out / to leave / to do / to visit.

2. Imaginez que demain vous vous réveillerez beaucoup plus tard que d'habitude. En six phrases, dites ce que vous ferez (ou ce que vous ne ferez pas) pour arriver en classe à l'heure. Mettez tous les verbes au futur si possible. Vous pouvez utiliser les verbes suivants: se laver / se brosser / se dépêcher / se précipiter / se peigner / s'habiller / s'excuser.

   Imagine that tomorrow you wake up much later than usual. In six sentences, say what you will do (or won't do) to get to class on time. Use the future tense if possible. You may use the following verbs: to wash up / to brush one's hair / to hurry / to rush / to comb one's hair / to get dressed / to excuse oneself.

For more advanced students, test topics can be somewhat more general.

Here are some examples in English:

3. You have invited a new friend to come spend the next vacation in your

---

[13] Taken from Jean-Paul Valette and Rebecca M. Valette, *French for Mastery: Book Two* (Lexington, Mass.: D. C. Heath, 1975), pp. 208, 289.

home town. Your friend hesitates. Try to convince your friend to come by explaining the interesting things you can do together.

4. Describe a typical family meal at your house.

SAMPLE ITEM TYPE 59   RECORDED DESCRIPTION

The student is told to describe an object in the foreign language. For intermediate students, the object selected might be a common object: a pencil or a window. For more advanced students, the object might be more complicated: an adding machine, a spaceship, or a wedding invitation. The students may say anything they want about the size, shape, use, location, etc., of the object, but they may not name it nor give a synonym for it.

NOTE: This type of test may also be administered live in the classroom. The reliability of the test is higher, however, when students record their responses, for in this latter instance all students are talking about the same object and the teacher can compare the responses.

SAMPLE ITEM TYPE 60   LIVE MONOLOG

The live monolog is a less formal test than the recorded monolog; however, it introduces the element of face-to-face communication. This test format is most effective when the entire class must participate actively by guessing the topic of each monolog.

Here are some sample topics:

1. Describe a movie you have seen, but do not mention the title. The class must guess the name of the film.
2. Describe a famous person, without mentioning the person's name. The class must guess whom you are talking about.

SAMPLE ITEM TYPE 61   IMPROMPTU ROLE PLAY—OPEN INSTRUCTIONS

In a role play test, several students at once are informally tested. This format is most effective with a circle of no more than ten students. Specific roles are assigned to two or three students, randomly spaced around the circle. Then these students carry out an impromptu conversation.

Here are some sample topics:

1. (spoken instructions) Betty comes home with a kitten she has found. Her mother hates animals. Her father likes cats but doesn't want to anger his wife. Imagine their conversation. (Name three students to play the roles.)
2. (picture cue) Look at this poster (magazine picture, etc.). What are the

people saying? (Name students to take the roles of the persons and/or animals in the picture.)

NOTE: The teacher would prepare a series of topics, so that each student in the class has an opportunity to participate in the test.

SAMPLE ITEM TYPE *62*   IMPROMPTU ROLE PLAY—SECRET INSTRUCTIONS

For more advanced students, the teacher may wish to prepare secret written instructions for the role play test. The format is the same as that of the preceding item.

Here are some sample topics:

1. Betty comes home with a kitten she has found.
   Secret instructions to Betty: The kitten is very hungry and you are insistent on keeping it. You think your parents will understand.
   Secret instructions to mother: You hate cats and are surprised that Betty brought home a kitten.
   Secret instructions to father: You try to find a way to make Betty happy, but you know your wife does not like cats.
2. Peter comes home with a kitten he has found.
   Secret instructions to Peter: You rescued the kitten from a tree. You have a dog at home but hope you can keep the kitten too.
   Secret instructions to mother: You are afraid that the dog and the kitten will not get along. Your dog is a terrier who does not like cats.
   Secret instructions to father: You are a bird lover and have several bird feeders outside. You definitely do not want a cat around.

SAMPLE ITEM TYPE *63*   ACTING AS INTERPRETER

This type of item, which requires two teachers (or testers) for each student, is used on the speaking test of the Foreign Service Institute (FSI). One tester allegedly speaks only the target language, while the other speaks the native language of the student. In a sample situation, one tester is an American tourist in Munich and the other is a German post office clerk. The American wants to mail a package, and the student conveys this message in German to the clerk. The clerk, in turn, asks for additional information, which the student explains to the tourist in English. The situations usually develop as impromptu conversations and are never quite the same from one student to the next.

SAMPLE ITEM TYPE *64*   LIVE CONVERSATION OR INTERVIEW

The most credible, or natural, type of speaking test is a free conversation with the teacher or with another qualified speaker. In the latter case, it is better to have the speaker talk with each student for several minutes. The teacher should try to remain as unobtrusive as possible, perhaps seated behind the student. While the speaker encourages the students to express themselves, the teacher is free to concentrate on scoring the students' performance objectively.

Two teachers might help each other in such a testing session. Generally, it is better to have the visiting teacher speak with the students; this way the host teacher does not feel that his or her own performance is being judged by another. It is also possible to have an advanced student from another class, one who speaks the language easily and is able to put other students at ease, help with the testing session.

The choice of conversation topics depends on the level of the students. With beginning students, personal questions are often used: "What is your name? How old are you? Where do you live? Do you like school? Why or why not?" With intermediate classes, a good starting question is one that asks the students what they would do if they had the money, the time, the opportunity, and so on. Such a question allows the students to orient the conversation. The teacher may then easily follow that response with queries like "Why?" or "Have you considered a different possibility?" "Which one?" "Why did you reject that idea?" etc. The questioner should realize that his or her primary functions are putting the students at ease, encouraging them to speak, and helping them out when necessary.

With advanced students, the conversation may develop around a pre-arranged topic or reading. For instance, after a unit on women in Mexico, the conversation test could revolve around the role of women in Mexico and elicit the students' opinions on the role of women in the United States. After a short story about a Chicano family in New Mexico, the conversation test could include both the literary and sociological implications of the reading.

The teacher should remember that the key concern in the conversation test is to evaluate the student's ability to express himself or herself in the target language and not the intelligence and clarity of the student's insights. Here are some guidelines that should aid the teacher in preparing an effective interview test:

1. Determine which aspects of the students' performance you intend to evaluate. Pronunciation in a free-speaking situation? Appropriate use of tenses? Correct word order? Breadth of vocabulary? Ability to get ideas across? Ability to react to questions and interjections? Fluency?
2. Prepare questions that will elicit those features you have decided to evaluate. For example, if the students are to use the past tense, the questions should relate to past events, and perhaps require the description of what happened on a specific occasion. If you want to determine how well the students react to conversational stimuli, a set of general questions could be listed, such as: "Would you please repeat that? Are

you sure? That's an interesting point: Do your parents think the same way?" If the aim is fluency, ask the students to give an oral resume of something read in class.

3. Prepare a scoring sheet that reflects the elements you will be evaluating and how you intend to score each feature.

4. Prepare a few simple questions and exchanges that will help the student feel at ease at the beginning of the interview. Plan a few words of thanks with which to end the interview.

5. Remember that the main purpose of the interview is to let the students show how much progress they have made. Encourage the students to demonstrate their strengths, and don't probe their weaknesses too deeply. Interview tests will not let you make fine distinctions between students, but will permit you to group them roughly by ability levels. If the students' performance has developed through the course, be sure to congratulate them.

6.6.2   Preparing the scoring system

An essential element of the free expression is the prior preparation of a scoring system. The live speaking test, in particular, must be evaluated immediately upon completion. The easiest system for the busy teacher is to prepare a scoring sheet and duplicate a separate copy for each student. The following suggestions describe systems that have been used to score free expression tests. The teacher may of course, adopt or adapt the system that best fits his or her testing conditions.

6.6.2a   THE FOREIGN SERVICE INSTITUTE RATING PROCEDURE

The FSI oral proficiency rating is an overall judgment about the student's speaking competence.[14] The five levels of proficiency are described as follows:

Level 1: *Able to satisfy routine travel needs and minimum courtesy requirements.* Can ask and answer questions on topics very familiar to him or her; within the scope of his or her very limited language experience can understand simple questions and statements, allowing for slowed speech, repetition or paraphrase; speaking vocabulary inadequate to express anything but the most elementary needs; errors in pronunciation and grammar are frequent, but can be understood by a native speaker used to dealing with foreigners attempting to speak his or her language. While elementary needs vary considerably from individual to individual, any person at level 1 should be

[14] For a discussion of the Foreign Service speaking tests, see Claudia P. Wilds, "The Oral Interview Test," in Randall L. Jones and Bernard Spolsky, eds., *Testing Language Proficiency* (Arlington, Va.: Center for Applied Linguistics, 1975).

able to order a simple meal, ask for shelter or lodging, ask and give simple directions, make purchases, and tell time.

Level 2: *Able to satisfy routine social demands and limited work requirements.* Can handle with confidence but not with facility most social situations including introductions and casual conversations about current events, as well as work, family, and autobiographical information; can handle limited work requirements, needing help in handling any complications or difficulties; can get the gist of most conversations on nontechnical subjects (i.e. topics that require no specialized knowledge) and has a speaking vocabulary sufficient to express himself or herself simply with some circumlocutions; accent, though often quite faulty, is intelligible; can usually handle elementary constructions quite accurately but does not have thorough or confident control of the grammar.

Level 3: *Able to speak the language with sufficient structural accuracy and vocabulary to participate effectively in most formal and informal conversations on practical, social, and professional topics.* Can discuss particular interests and special fields of competence with reasonable ease; comprehension is quite complete for a normal rate of speech; vocabulary is broad enough that he or she rarely has to grope for a word; accent may be obviously foreign; control of grammar good; errors never interfere with understanding and rarely disturb the native speaker.

Level 4: *Able to use the language fluently and accurately on all levels normally pertinent to professional needs.* Can understand and participate in any conversation within the range of his or her experience with a high degree of fluency and precision of vocabulary; would rarely be taken for a native speaker, but can respond appropriately even in unfamiliar situations; errors of pronunciation and grammar quite rare; can handle informal interpreting from and into the language.

Level 5: *Speaking proficiency equivalent to that of an educated native speaker.* Has complete fluency in the language such that his or her speech on all levels is fully accepted by educated native speakers in all of its features, including breadth of vocabulary and idiom, colloquialisms, and pertinent cultural references.

The language proficiency oral interview is carefully structured to allow the examiner to explore the many facets of the student's speaking ability so as to place him or her in one of the above categories. If necessary, the following numerical rating procedure is used to supplement the verbal descriptions of the levels.

The FSI numerical rating procedure evaluates accent, grammar, vocabulary, fluency and comprehension. In each category there are six categories ranging from poor (category 1) to excellent (category 6). These categories do not correspond to the levels of proficiency described above. Here are the numerical ratings:

Accent

1. Pronunciation frequently unintelligible.
2. Frequent gross errors and a very heavy accent make understanding difficult, require frequent repetition.
3. "Foreign accent" requires concentrated listening and mispronunciations lead to occasional misunderstanding and apparent errors in grammar or vocabulary.
4. Marked "foreign accent" and occasional mispronunciations that do not interfere with understanding.
5. No conspicuous mispronunciations, but would not be taken for a native speaker.
6. Native pronunciation, with no trace of "foreign accent."

Grammar

1. Grammar almost entirely inaccurate except in stock phrases.
2. Constant errors showing control of very few major patterns and frequently preventing communication.
3. Frequent errors showing some major patterns uncontrolled and causing occasional irritation and misunderstanding.
4. Occasional errors showing imperfect control of some patterns but no weakness that causes misunderstanding.
5. Few errors, with no patterns of failure.
6. No more than two errors during the interview.

Vocabulary

1. Vocabulary inadequate for even the simplest conversation.
2. Vocabulary limited to basic personal and survival areas (time, food, transportation, family, etc.).
3. Choice of words sometimes inaccurate, limitations of vocabulary prevent discussion of some common professional and social topics.
4. Professional vocabulary adequate to discuss special interests; general vocabulary permits discussion of any nontechnical subject with some circumlocutions.
5. Professional vocabulary broad and precise; general vocabulary adequate to cope with complex practical problems and varied social situations.
6. Vocabulary apparently as accurate and extensive as that of an educated native speaker.

Fluency

1. Speech is so halting and fragmentary that conversation is virtually impossible.
2. Speech is very slow and uneven except for short or routine sentences.
3. Speech is frequently hesitant and jerky; sentences may be left uncompleted.
4. Speech is occasionally hesitant, with some unevenness caused by rephrasing and groping for words.
5. Speech is effortless and smooth, but perceptibly non-native in speed and evenness.
6. Speech on all professional and general topics as effortless and smooth as a native speaker's.

Comprehension

1. Understands too little for the simplest type of conversation.
2. Understands only slow, very simple speech on common social and touristic topics; requires constant repetition and rephrasing.
3. Understands careful, somewhat simplified speech directed to him or her, with considerable repetition and rephrasing.
4. Understands quite well normal educated speech directed to him or her, but requires occasional repetition or rephrasing.
5. Understands everything in normal educated conversation except for very colloquial or low-frequency items or exceptionally rapid or slurred speech.
6. Understands everything in both formal and colloquial speech to be expected of an educated native speaker.

The evaluators use a weighted table that gives heaviest emphasis to grammar, secondary emphasis to vocabulary, and least emphasis to accent. These weightings have been developed through experimentation and permit the numerical total score to correspond to the levels of proficiency. In using the following table, the evaluator would determine the proper description for each category and then circle the number in the corresponding column. After the test, these numbers are entered into the left-hand column and totalled from the Weighting Table.

FSI Weighting Table

Proficiency Description ⟶	①	②	③	④	⑤	⑥	
Accent	0	1	2	2	3	4	_____
Grammar	6	12	18	24	30	36	_____
Vocabulary	4	8	12	16	20	24	_____
Fluency	2	4	6	8	10	12	_____
Comprehension	4	8	12	15	19	23	_____

Total: ☐

The total score is then interpreted with the Conversion Table that follows:

FSI Conversion Table

Total Score	Level	Total Score	Level	Total Score	Level
16–25	0+	43–52	2	73–82	3+
26–32	1	53–62	2+	83–92	4
33–42	1+	63–72	3	93–99	4+

NOTE: The FSI ratings use "plus" scores to indicate a position half-way between two levels. Thus, a person with a score of 2+ falls between Level 2 and Level 3.

6.6.2b THE CLARK FOUR-SCALE SYSTEM

John L. D. Clark has developed a four-scale scoring system that is more appropriate for the classroom teacher who is testing students of approximately the same level of ability.[15]

Pronunciation:
1. Incomprehensible, or no response.
2. Many phonemic errors; very difficult to perceive meaning.
3. Occasional phonemic error, but generally comprehensible.
4. Phonemically accurate pronunciation throughout.

Vocabulary:
1. Vocabulary inaccurate throughout, or no response.
2. Vocabulary usually inaccurate, except for occasional correct word.
3. Minor lexical problems, but vocabulary generally appropriate.
4. Consistent use of appropriate words throughout.

Structure:
1. Virtually no correct structures, or no response.
2. Errors of basic structure, but some phrases rendered correctly.
3. Generally accurate structure, occasional slight error.
4. No errors of morphology or syntax.

Fluency:
1. Long pauses, utterances left unfinished, or no response.
2. Some definite stumbling, but manages to rephrase and continue.
3. Speech is generally natural and continuous. Occasional slight stumblings or pauses at unnatural points in the utterance.
4. Speech is natural and continuous. Any pauses correspond to those which might be made by a native speaker.

The teacher may wish to compare scores using this rating scale with global impressions of each student's performance. The teacher might subsequently wish to develop a weighted table, such as that given in Section 6.6.2a, in which one or two of the aspects are more heavily stressed.

6.6.2c THE SCHULZ COMMUNICATIVE COMPETENCE SCALE

The following scale was developed by Renate Schulz to evaluate free expression tests using questions such as Sample Item Types 57 and 59.

[15] John L. D. Clark, *Foreign Language Testing: Theory & Practice* (Philadelphia: Center for Curriculum Development, 1972), p. 93.

A. Fluency

| 1 | 2 | 3 | 4 | 5 | 6 |

B. Comprehensibility

| 1 | 2 | 3 | 4 | 5 | 6 |

C. Amount of Communication

| 1 | 2 | 3 | 4 | 5 | 6 |

D. Quality of Communication

| 1 | 2 | 3 | 4 | 5 | 6 |

The levels on these scales were defined as follows:

A. *Fluency* (see the Foreign Service Institute scale, Section 6.6.2a)

B. *Comprehensibility*:
  1. No comprehension: The examiner could not understand a thing the student said.
  2. The examiner comprehended small bits and pieces, isolated words.
  3. The examiner comprehended some word clusters and phrases.
  4. The examiner comprehended short simple sentences.
  5. The examiner comprehended most of what the student said.
  6. The examiner comprehended all of what the student said.

C. *Amount of Communication*
  (see the Bartz scale, Section 6.5, Sample Item Type 56)

D. *Quality of Communication*:
  1. No utterances rendered correctly.
  2. Very few utterances rendered structurally correct.
  3. Some utterances rendered correctly, but many structural problems remain.
  4. Many correct utterances, but some problems remain with structures.
  5. Most utterances rendered correctly, only minor problems with structure.
  6. All utterances rendered correctly.

6.6.2d COMPREHENSION SCALE

For an informal classroom test, the teacher may wish to evaluate only the extent to which the student was able to communicate effectively. The following scale may be used with Sample Item Types 60, 61, and 62.

Comprehension by the class:
1. Virtually no one understood what was said.
2. Most of the students got the gist of what was said.
3. Most of the students understood most of what was said.
4. Most of the students understood everything that was said.
5. All the students understood everything that was said.

Comprehension by a native speaker:
1. A native speaker would have understood virtually nothing.
2. A native speaker would have gotten the gist of what was said.

3. A native speaker would have understood half of what was said.

4. A native speaker would have understood most of what was said.

5. A native speaker would have easily understood everything.

If desired, the comprehension scale could be used together with the Bartz effort-to-communicate scale (see Sample Item Type 56).

6.6.2e STUDENT-DEVELOPED SCORING SYSTEMS

In high-intermediate and advanced conversation classes, the development of an oral expression scoring system might be a class project. First the students could discuss, for instance, those aspects of a monolog that determine its effectiveness. Some of the given scales might be presented as a point of departure.

After developing a preliminary scale, the class could evaluate sample monolog recordings made by unidentified students of a different class (another section of the same course, or recordings from a previous year). Once the students have perfected a scale that they feel helps distinguish between the strong monologs and the weaker ones, the teacher could use this new rating system to evaluate the speaking ability of the members of the class.

outline

seven

The Reading Test

Reading used to be the principal aim of most foreign-language courses. Since the study of literature, which for centuries represented the educational goal of the elite, requires only a reading knowledge of foreign languages, the terms "language" and "literature" were formally equated in the curriculum.

In the United States during the 1930s, the Modern Language Association proposed that the primary aim in teaching a foreign language was to enable students to read foreign texts in the original. The rationale behind the Ph.D. language requirement is that doctoral candidates prove their ability to read the literature in their specialty in two foreign languages.

The audio-lingual approach to instruction, which blossomed after World War II and received great impetus after the 1957 Soviet launching of Sputnik, placed the emphasis elsewhere. Language, insisted the New Key proponents, is *spoken* first; the written form frequently is but a transcription of an audio-lingual phenomenon. As for Ph.D. requirements, most linguists will not deny that with a rudimentary grammar book, a good dictionary, and some imagination a candidate will be able to pass the "reading" translation test, but, they add, this experience is not one of reading but of decoding or deciphering. The goal in reading is not verbatim translation, but direct comprehension without recourse to the native language.

In the mid-1970s, reading is once again the object of attention of language teachers. Reading comprehension as a communication skill is gaining in importance in the foreign language curriculum. Students themselves realize that they may find themselves in situations where it is useful to be able to read. In a country where the target language is spoken, they may need to read signs, instructions, menus, programs. They may wish to read target language newspapers or periodicals, or specialized articles in their own area of particular interest. On a less technical level, they may need to read informal correspondence or business letters. In reading for communication, the students' main objective is to understand the written message.

7.1   GENERAL CONSIDERATIONS

Reading, by definition a language skill, requires a familiarity on the part of the reader with the two fundamental building blocks of the particular language under study: structure and vocabulary. The broader the students' knowledge of structure and the greater their vocabulary—regardless of how these two were acquired—the more difficult the texts they will be able to approach.

First of all, reading requires visual perception (except for the blind, who depend on tactile recognition). Just as the young child must first be able to recognize the alphabet of his or her native language when learning to read, so must the student of a second language become familiar with the characters of that language. The alphabets of French, Spanish, and Italian present little difficulty to the literate American; German texts are now generally printed in familiar Roman type. American students *do* require pre-reading instruction in certain languages—Russian, Greek, Arabic, Hebrew, and Chinese, for example.

Once the students are familiar with the writing system of the second language, the written form of the language may be used to test their knowledge of new vocabulary and structure. This is the most frequent use of "reading" items on most classroom tests.

In reading an unfamiliar text for comprehension, students must be able to recognize words and structures in context. Consequently, two general types of test items are necessary to evaluate student reading comprehension potential: word recognition and understanding of syntax.

As Arthur Traxler has pointed out in his studies of native-language reading, reading at a mature level is "an associative process deep within the recesses of the mind. There is no way for an observer to be sure at a given moment whether a subject reading silently is gleaning facts or gathering main ideas or evaluating the writer or gaining esthetic satisfaction or, in fact, whether he is really putting his mind to the printed page at all." [1] Generally reading comprehension is tested indirectly, by having the student read aloud, or by asking the student comprehension questions, or by measuring reading speed.

---

[1] Arthur E. Traxler, "Values and Limitations of Standardized Reading Tests," in Roger Farr, ed., *Measurement and Evaluation of Reading* (New York: Harcourt Brace Jovanovich, 1970), p. 221.

It must be remembered that analytical reading correlates with intelligence, and that not all students are able to read at the same level in their native language. In reading a second language, therefore, students in a class may reflect a broad range of differences that may in part be traced to differences in reading ability in their first language.

Research into second-language acquisition is beginning to explore the validity of "cloze" tests of reading comprehension as general measures of linguistic ability. The student who can restitute words randomly deleted from a text has not only understood the reading passage but exhibits an active command of the second language.

7.2 THE WRITING SYSTEM

If listening and speaking are taught prior to the presentation of reading and writing, then the pre-reading experience will entail the linking of known sounds to written symbols. This experience resembles to some extent the way in which young children learn to read their native language. Similarly, if the characters of the new language are unfamiliar, they, too, must be mastered during a period of pre-reading instruction. For a language with non-Roman characters, such as Russian, or with non-Roman characters and a direction of writing different from English, such as Hebrew or Arabic, the pre-reading period requires a great deal of effort on the part of the student. Classroom quizzes often help break the inevitable monotony of instruction.

7.2.1 Identification of written symbols

Anyone who has learned to read English has developed a sensitivity to seemingly slight differences among printed letters—the difference between *e* and *c* for example. In learning to read a language with a non-Roman alphabet, students must become so familiar with the new alphabet that the identification of letters becomes automatic. In learning non-European languages where single characters represent syllables or whole words, students face a more difficult problem of identification. Facility in handling the new characters can be evaluated by measuring the speed at which the student can identify the characters. Quizzes like those given on page 168 should contain a substantial number of items. When the first student to reach the end of the quiz raises his or her hand, the others are told to stop working. Some teachers may give the test a fixed time limit. In either case, the student's score is based on the number of correct items; the time allowed for the test may also be indicated so that students can evaluate their improvement.

SAMPLE ITEM TYPE *1*   MATCHING LETTERS

Circle the letter (character) that is the same as the first letter (character).

Here is a sample item in Russian:

Ж   Ш Щ Ж Ч Д

SAMPLE ITEM TYPE *2*   MATCHING WORDS OR SENTENCES

Indicate which word (or sentence) is the same as the first word (or sentence).

Here are sample items in Russian:

1. НО́СИМ   A. НО́СИТ
           B. НО́СИМ
           C. НО́СИТЕ
           D. НО́СЯТ
2. ВИ́ДЯТ   A. ВИ́ДИТ
           B. ВИ́ДИМ
           C. ВИ́ДИТЕ
           D. ВИ́ДЯТ

Correct responses: B, D

NOTE: This type of item may be rendered more difficult by writing the options across the page.

3. СТОЮ́   A. СТОЯ́Т
          B. СТО́ЙТЕ
          C. СТО́ЙТ
          D. СТОЮ́

Correct response: D

7.2.2   Sequencing and alphabetizing

In learning an alphabet that differs from the alphabet of the native language, the students must learn in which sequence entries are alphabetized. For instance, the American student learning Spanish must realize that words beginning with "ch" are grouped after all the "c" entries, and that words beginning with "ll" are given after all the "l" entries. Students of Russian must learn how Russian words are alphabetized.

SAMPLE ITEM TYPE *3*   LOCATING DICTIONARY ENTRIES

For each of the following words, write down the dictionary page on which the entry is found.

1. cementaria   ____
2. charro   ____
3. llamar   ____
4. cubrir   ____

Correct responses: corresponding page numbers of dictionary used.

SAMPLE ITEM TYPE 4   USING A PHONE DIRECTORY

Find the telephone numbers of the following people:

NOTE: This type of item is most effective when actual foreign phone directories or pages of directories are used. If entire directories are used, it may be necessary to explain the general layout and any conventions that differ from usage in the native country.

SAMPLE ITEM TYPE 5   ALPHABETIZING

Indicate the proper alphabetical order of the following words by writing the corresponding letters in the appropriate sequence.

a. cena   b. carta   c. chaqueta   d. cuerpo   e. ciencia   f. chocolate
1. ____   2. ____   3. ____   4. ____   5. ____   6. ____

Correct responses: 1b, 2a, 3e, 4d, 5c, 6f

7.2.3   Sound-symbol correspondence

If speaking has been taught before reading, the teacher will want to measure the facility with which students can link the spoken word to its written form. Although this type of pre-reading test (or quiz, since such items are generally used in brief informal tests) resembles many commercial standardized listening-discrimination tests in which the student is asked to match an oral stimulus with the proper printed option, the two tests differ in use and function. The hybrid listening-discrimination test with a printed answer sheet is valid for students whose knowledge of the written language is distinctly superior to their listening ability: it is assumed that the students have no difficulty in linking sounds to spelling and that the crucial factor determining their choice of responses is the power to retain and discriminate among sounds.

The pre-reading test, in which spoken stimuli are matched with printed responses, may be used in two ways: in teaching the graphic forms of languages employing a non-Roman alphabet and in testing spelling ability (via recognition) in languages with a Roman alphabet. Regarding the former case, it may be pointed out that some colleges offer courses in spoken Chinese and spoken Arabic; writing is not introduced until several semesters later. By that time the teacher will have had many opportunities to verify the students' ability in listening discrimination. When work in writing and reading is begun, the problem for these students will be to establish the relationship between spoken word and printed form.

SAMPLE ITEM TYPE 6   SOUND-SYMBOL CORRESPONDENCE—PRINTED OPTIONS

Indicate which word on your answer sheet corresponds to the word you hear.

Here is a sample item in Spanish:

Tape: cuento   A. cuento
                   B. ciento
                   C. quedo

Correct response: A

The voice on the tape could speak short phrases or sentences.

Here is a sample item in French:

Tape: nous savons   A. nous avons
                        B. nous savons
                        C. nos savons

Correct response: B

SAMPLE ITEM TYPE 7   SOUND-SYMBOL CORRESPONDENCE—ORAL OPTIONS

You will hear three (four) words spoken. Indicate which one corresponds to the word on your answer sheet.

Here is a sample item in Italian:

Tape: A. Eccoli!   1. Eccoli!   A   B   C   (D)
        B. Eccola!
        C. Eccole!
        (D. Eccolo!)

Correct response: A

Short phrases or sentences may also be used in this type of item.

7.2.4 Handwriting

If the handwritten script of the target language differs markedly from the printed form, and if students are expected to read handwritten script, the teacher might wish to test the students' ability to decipher handwriting. Even if the target language and the native use the same alphabet, as is the case with American students learning one of the European languages, the handwritten forms of the two languages sometimes differ.

SAMPLE ITEM TYPE *8*   DECIPHERING SCRIPT—MULTIPLE-CHOICE FORMAT

Match the handwritten sentence with the appropriate printed version and mark the corresponding letter on your answer sheet.

Here is an example in Russian:

Кто-то смотрит в окно

A. КТО-ТО СТУЧИТ В ДВЕРЬ
B. КТО-ТО СМОТРИТ В ОКНО

Correct response: B

SAMPLE ITEM TYPE *9*   DECIPHERING SCRIPT—REWRITING

Rewrite the handwritten sentence in your own script.
(This is a more difficult item than simply identifying the appropriate printed version of the sentence.)

7.3   TESTING VOCABULARY VIA READING

Most standardized tests and many teacher-made tests contain items that measure the students' knowledge of vocabulary. While the student must "read" the target language in order to answer the items, it is the student's recognition of specific words and phrases that is being tested rather than his or her reading comprehension. This section will suggest ways of testing vocabulary in contexts where a student must know what a word or phrase means in order to respond correctly. (Section 7.5 will describe techniques for testing reading comprehension and will include aspects of reading such as inferring meaning from context and assigning appropriate meanings to unfamiliar words.)

In preparing discrete tests based on vocabulary, the teacher should take care to see that the comprehension problem lies in only one place, either in the stem or in the options. If the difficult vocabulary item is in the stem, all students should understand the meaning of the options. It is generally better to present the key word in a sentence with just enough context to limit the meaning of the word, but not too much to give away the right answer. If the problem lies in the choice of options, the meaning of the stem should be evident to all.

7.3.1   Picture tests

In reading tests as with listening tests, picture items can be used to test vocabulary knowledge, particularly with beginning students. Most of the items suggested for listening tests (Section 5.3.3) can be adapted to reading tests.

SAMPLE ITEM TYPE *10*   SINGLE ITEM PICTURES—MULTIPLE-CHOICE FORMAT

Select the sentence that best describes the picture.

A. La niña está comiendo.   *The girl is eating.*
B. La niña está corriendo.   *The girl is running.*
C. La niña está durmiendo.   *The girl is sleeping.*

Correct response: B

SAMPLE ITEM TYPE *11*   SINGLE ITEM PICTURES—MATCHING FORMAT

Match the words below with the corresponding pictures. Write the letter of the picture in the blanks provided.

_____ 1. der Zug
_____ 2. das Flugzeug
_____ 3. das Schiff
_____ 4. der Autobus

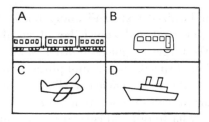

Correct responses: 1A, 2C, 3D, 4B

These items are more difficult if there are fewer pictures than words (or vice versa, although it is usually easier to add words than to add pictures). Instead of drawing pictures for this type of test, the teacher can use an available overhead transparency and prepare an overlay that contains the appropriate letters identifying the drawings.

SAMPLE ITEM TYPE *12*   MULTIPLE ITEM PICTURES—TRUE-FALSE
FORMAT

In items of this type, a composite picture is used for a series of items.

Look at the picture. Mike would like to take all the items you see on his trip to Europe, but his suitcase is too heavy. This means that he will only be able to take the items marked with an "X." Read the following statements and indicate whether they are true or false, according to the picture.

true   false   1. Mike is taking his tennis raquet.
true   false   2. Mike is taking his swimming trunks.

Correct responses: 1. false; 2. true

SAMPLE ITEM TYPE *13*   MULTIPLE ITEM PICTURES—MATCHING
FORMAT

Can you label the parts of the body in French? Write the number of the appropriate word in the corresponding box.

1. le bras
2. le cou
3. la jambe (etc.)

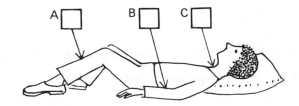

Correct responses: A:3; B:1; C:2

SAMPLE ITEM TYPE *14*   MULTIPLE ITEM PICTURES—
                                   MULTIPLE-CHOICE FORMAT

Look at the picture and complete the sentences to the right so that they correspond to the situations that are shown. Mark the corresponding letters on your answer sheet.

1. The cat is _____ the table.
   A. on   B. under   C. next to
2. The dog is _____ the chair.
   A. on   B. next to   C. over
3. The flowers are _____ the vase.
   A. in   B. next to   C. under

Correct responses: A, B, C

7.3.2   Vocabulary out of context

Standardized vocabulary tests, especially English vocabulary tests for American students, often measure the students' knowledge of meanings of words in isolation. Although most foreign language teachers prefer teaching and testing vocabulary in sentence context, some of the following item types may occasionally be appropriate.

SAMPLE ITEM TYPE *15*   SYNONYMS

Select the correct synonym or the word with the closest meaning.

Here is a French example:

vite   *quickly*

   A. rapidement   *rapidly*
   B. surtout   *especially*
   C. bientôt   *soon*
   D. constamment   *constantly*

Correct response: A

SAMPLE ITEM TYPE *16*   CLASSIFICATION: EXPLICIT

Select the appropriate category.

scarlet   A. a color
                B. a day of the week

C. an item of clothing

D. a songbird

SAMPLE ITEM TYPE *17*   CLASSIFICATION: IMPLICIT

In category items of the following type, the students must know which categories the words fall into and select the one word from a different category.

In each set of five words, one word does not belong. Circle it.

1. scarlet   green   violet   (robin)   lavender
2. (Monday)   March   April   August   January

Secondary students often enjoy items of this type. For homework and vocabulary review, they could be asked to prepare three items each. With some adaptation, these could be used for the next vocabulary test.

SAMPLE ITEM TYPE *18*   DEPTH OF MEANING

The depth-of-meaning item goes beyond the simple synonym or category, and asks the students for a more precise definition. This type of item is appropriate for more advanced students.

Here are some examples in French:

simple classification item:

Le phoque est	*The seal is*
A. un animal	*an animal*
B. une plante	*a plant*
C. un drapeau	*a flag*
D. un bateau	*a boat*

depth of meaning item:

Le phoque est un animal qui habite	*The seal is an animal that lives in*
A. la mer	*the sea*
B. le désert	*the desert*
C. les prairies	*the prairie*
D. la montagne	*the mountains*

simple synonym item:

apposer	to affix
A. mettre	*to put*
B. inspirer	*to inspire*
C. contredire	*to contradict*
D. fortifier	*to fortify*

depth of meaning item:

Apposer veut dire *mettre* dans le sens de	To affix *means* to put *in the sense of*
A. mettre une affiche au mur	*to put up a sign on the wall*
B. mettre une assiette sur une table	*to put a plate on the table*
C. mettre un jeton dans un téléphone	*to put a token in a pay phone*
D. mettre un obstacle devant quelqu'un	*to put an obstacle in front of someone*

SAMPLE ITEM TYPE *19*   DEFINITIONS

The students are asked to select the word that corresponds to a target language definition.

The stem of this Spanish item best defines which of the following words:

el habitante de una colonia	*the inhabitant of a colony*
A. Colón	*Columbus*
B. el colono	*the colonist*
C. el colon	*the colon*
D. el coloniaje	*the colonial period*

Correct response: B

SAMPLE ITEM TYPE *20*   NATIVE LANGUAGE EQUIVALENTS

Translation into the native language is typically not encouraged as a means of evaluating vocabulary knowledge. In American schools, teachers of the commonly taught European languages usually do not give vocabulary tests of this sort. (Translation items are regularly used in teaching Asian languages. For example, in a Chinese class the teacher may prepare a list of characters and ask the students to write out the meanings of these characters in English.) One area, however, where native language equivalents are often used is in the recognition of cognates.

Here are samples in Spanish and French:

Write the English equivalents of the following words:

(easy items: Spanish)

1. un secreto	*secret*
2. un prisionero	*prisoner*

(harder items: French)

3. un mât	*mast*
4. l'étable	*stable*
5. chérir	*to cherish*

SAMPLE ITEM TYPE *21*   ASSOCIATIONS

In items of this type, the students are asked to associate pairs of words. As a vocabulary review exercise, students may be asked to prepare their own lists of associations, and the teacher may use these lists as a point of departure in preparing the test.

Match the words that go together.

1. pilot   A. courtroom
2. doctor   B. airplane
3. judge   C. hospital

Correct responses: B, C, A

Here is an example in French:

1. avoir sommeil   A. dormir   *1. to be sleepy*   *A. to sleep*
2. avoir soif   B. manger   *2. to be thirsty*   *B. to eat*
3. avoir faim   C. boire   *3. to be hungry*   *C. to drink*

Correct responses: A, C, B

SAMPLE ITEM TYPE *22*   SEMANTIC CONGRUITY

In semantic congruity items, the students determine the acceptability of verb-adverb combinations.

Evaluate each of the combinations suggested. Mark your responses as follows:

A. The adverb strengthens the meaning of the verb: acceptable combination.
B. The adverb could be used with the verb: permissible combination.
C. The adverb contradicts the meaning of the verb: unacceptable combination.

Here is an example in English:

1. to shout loudly
2. to shout happily
3. to shout quietly

Correct responses: A, B, C

SAMPLE ITEM TYPE *23*   SEMANTIC INTENSITY

The following pairs of words have approximately the same meaning. Circle the word that is more intense.

1. hot—boiling
2. to nibble—to devour

Correct responses: boiling, to devour

NOTE: In preparing items of this sort, it is important to select pairs so that the more common word is not always the less intense. For instance, in considering pairs such as *thirsty—parched, cold—frigid,* the student may quickly decide simply to underline the less familiar word.

7.3.3   Vocabulary in context

The most common way of testing vocabulary in standardized foreign language tests is to present the items in sentence context. In this way the student can see how the item is used: Is it a verb? a noun? an adjective? However, the context is not strong enough to enable the student to infer the meaning of the word, for these are items of vocabulary knowledge and not of reading skill.

SAMPLE ITEM TYPE *24*   S Y N O N Y M S

Indicate which of the following words is closest in meaning to the underlined word (or words) in the sentence.

Here is a sample item in French:

Monique <u>assiste</u> au cours d'anglais.   *Monique <u>is attending</u> the English class.*

A. est présente   *is present at*
B. aide le professeur   *helps the teacher in*
C. est professeur   *is the teacher in*
D. regarde le professeur   *is looking at the teacher in*

Correct response: A

In this item, A is the correct choice. Option B is a form distractor: the French word *assiste* looks like the English *assist,* meaning to help or aid (hence *aide*). Option C is a content distractor: since the sentence mentions an English class, perhaps the student would think that *assiste* means *teaches.* Option D is a meaning distractor, similar in function to the correct response.[2]

---

[2] For more details on the selection of distractors in vocabulary items, see Robert Lado, *Language Testing* (New York: McGraw-Hill, 1964), pp. 191–97.

Here is a sample item in German:

Er will seinen Vater <u>umbringen</u>.   *He wants <u>to murder</u> his father.*

A. zum Flughafen fahren   *to drive to the airport*
B. holen   *to get*
C. töten   *to kill*
D. besuchen   *to visit*

Correct response: C

SAMPLE ITEM TYPE *25*   ANTONYMS

Indicate which of the following words is closest to meaning the *opposite* of the underlined word(s) in the sentence.

Here is a sample item in French:

Jean <u>se met</u> à son travail.   *Jean <u>begins</u> his work.*

A. n'organise pas   *doesn't organize*
B. veut quitter   *wants to stop*
C. termine   *finishes*
D. a faim pendant   *is hungry during*

Correct response: C

SAMPLE ITEM TYPE *26*   COMPLETION

The student is asked to complete a sentence by selecting the omitted word. Such items are effective in measuring his familiarity with certain idiomatic phrases. Occasionally it is possible to construct a series of items based on the same options.

Here are some sample items in French:

Complete the following sentences, using this key to indicate your choice: (A) a, (B) est, (C) fait, (D) va.

1. Comment _____ ta mère?   *How <u>is</u> your mother?*
    Est-elle encore malade?   *Is she still sick?*
2. Elle supporte mal la chaleur   *She is sensitive to heat*
    et il _____ très chaud.   *and it <u>is</u> very hot.*
3. Bien sûr, elle _____ toujours   *Of course, she always <u>has</u> a*
    mal à la tête.   *headache.*

Correct responses: D, C, A

More often, separate choices may be prepared for each item.

Here are two sample items in German:

1. Wir _____ ihm für seinen Brief.   *We _____ him for his letter.*

    A. denken   *think*
    B. danken   *thank*
    C. glauben   *believe*

2. Am Sonntag ist das   *On Sundays, the classroom*
    Klassenzimmer _____.   *is _____.*

    A. leer   *empty*
    B. heiß   *hot*
    C. spät   *late*

Correct responses: B, A

SAMPLE ITEM TYPE 27   LOGICAL INFERENCE

After reading the key sentence, select which of the subsequent sentences—A, B, or C—offers a logical explanation of or conclusion for the first sentence.

Here is a sample item in English:

He goes to sleep.   A. He likes candy.
    B. It's his favorite store.
    C. He is tired.

Correct response: C—He goes to sleep *because* he is tired.

In order to select the correct response, the student must be familiar with various items of vocabulary.

Here are two sample items in German:

1. Die Berge sind weiß.   *The mountains are white.*

    A. Sie sind mit Schnee bedeckt.   *They are covered with snow.*
    B. Das weiß ich nicht.   *I don't know that.*
    C. Sie sind weit von hier.   *They are far from here.*

Correct response: A

Here the student must know the meaning of *weiß* as used in the first sentence and know the meanings of *Schnee* and *bedeckt*.

2. Man kann sich auf diese Uhr   *You cannot depend on this clock.*
    nicht verlassen.

    A. Wir finden diese Uhr sehr   *We find this clock very pretty.*
      schön.

B. Es ist vier Uhr.   *It is four o'clock.*
C. Die Uhr geht nicht richtig.   *This clock doesn't work right.*

Correct response: C

In addition to understanding the use of the word *Uhr* in the first sentence, the student must know the meaning of *sich verlassen* in order to select the correct response.

SAMPLE ITEM TYPE *28*   CONTINUATION OF THOUGHT

This type of item is similar to Item Type 27, but the connection between the two statements is logically less rigorous. The student is asked to select the statement that best continues the thought of the first statement. Comprehension of such items generally depends on the recognition of familiar vocabulary in a new context.

Here are two sample items in French:

1. Quel temps affreux!   *What awful weather!*

   A. Regardez comme il pleut.   *Look how it's raining.*
   B. J'y vais de temps à autre.   *I go there from time to time.*
   C. Il est déjà trois heures.   *It is already three o'clock.*

2. L'ascenseur est occupé.   *The elevator is occupied.*

   A. Mais voici un fauteuil occupé.   *Here is a seat that is taken.*
   B. Il faut monter par l'escalier.   *We will have to walk up the stairs.*
   C. L'armoire est très commode.   *The wardrobe is roomy.*

Correct responses: A, B

SAMPLE ITEM TYPE *29*   QUESTION AND ANSWER

For a class with experience in dialogs and directed conversations, question-answer items appear natural.

Here is a sample item in French:

Avez-vous fait une bonne pêche   *Did you catch a lot of fish today?*
   aujourd'hui?

A. Non merci. Je préfère les poires.   *No thanks, I prefer pears.*
B. Mais oui. J'ai bien fait de   *Why yes. It was good I took*
   prendre ce papier.   *that paper.*
C. C'était mieux que la semaine   *It was better than last week.*
   dernière.

Correct response: C

This reading item is based primarily on vocabulary: the meaning of the phrase *faire une bonne pêche.*

SAMPLE ITEM TYPE *30*   STATEMENT AND REJOINDER

In statement-rejoinder conversations, the rejoinders range in length from one word to several sentences. If the terms "statement" and "rejoinder" are not within the grasp of younger students, the teacher may word the directions as follows: select the statement another person would most likely make in continuing the conversation without changing the topic.

Here are two sample items in German:

1. Es zieht.   *There's a draft.*

   A. Ja, dieser Platz ist belegt.   *Yes, this seat is taken.*
   B. Gestern ist sie abgefahren.   *She left yesterday.*
   C. Ich werde das Fenster   *I'll close the window.*
      zumachen.

Correct response: C

To answer this item correctly, the student must know the expression *es zieht.*

2. Er bekommt immer schlechte   *He always gets bad grades.*
   Noten.

   A. Ich habe auch eine reiche   *I also have a rich aunt.*
      Tante.
   B. Ja, aber er studiert wenig.   *Yes, but he doesn't study much.*
   C. Ich habe immer schrecklich   *I always have terribly much to do.*
      viel zu tun.

Correct response: B

7.4   TESTING GRAMMAR VIA READING

Multiple-choice items that evaluate passive knowledge of grammar may be considered "reading" items in that the student is reading the target language in order to select the correct answers. Such items are widely used on standardized tests for they allow the examiner to sample many aspects of grammar in a relatively short time. Moreover, the scoring of such items is rapid and objective.

The distractors in grammar items are correctly spelled words in the target language, but words which are inappropriate to the context. Misspelled or fictitious distractors are avoided, so that the testing time is also a learning time during which correct forms are reinforced.

Indirectly, grammar items test whether the student can use the target language correctly. The student of German who knows the construction "Ich gebe dem Mann das Buch" (I am giving the man the book) should be able to handle items like:

Ich gebe _____ das Buch.   A. der Mann
                              B. des Mannes
                              C. dem Mann
                              D. den Mann

The item could also be worded:

Ich gebe _____ Mann das Buch.   A. der
                                   B. des
                                   C. dem
                                   D. den
                                   E. die

While it is true that the multiple-choice item may suggest a response that the student would not otherwise have thought of, this happens only rarely. Generally, even the slow students are aware of the forms of articles and pronouns and the existence of systems of inflection. Hesitation occurs when they realize that an article is required but they are unsure of the correct choice.

Discrete reading items of the types suggested in this section have generally produced very reliable results. The teacher, however, must look at the objectives of his or her particular course to see which of the following types of questions would be valid for his or her class.

7.4.1 Elements of grammar

At the elementary and intermediate levels, the teacher frequently focuses on specific elements of grammar and wishes to test whether these elements have been mastered. This section contains a representative sampling of items that test the students' control of specific parts of the sentence.

7.4.1a DETERMINERS AND NOUNS

Since English has only one definite article orthographically, American students experience difficulty in learning the variety of definite articles in languages such as French, German, Spanish, and Italian. In highly inflected languages, students must learn the forms of nouns.

SAMPLE ITEM TYPE *31*   ARTICLES—SERIES ITEMS

On your answer sheet indicate the proper articles to be used in each sentence. Use the following key: (A) le, (B) la, (C) l', (D) les.

1. Paul achète _____ livre.   *Paul is buying the book.*
2. Marie lit _____ histoire.   *Marie is reading the story.*

Correct responses: A, C

A more informal item would have the student cross out the incorrect form:

Paul achète $\begin{smallmatrix}le\\la\end{smallmatrix}$ livre et Marie lit $\begin{smallmatrix}l'\\la\end{smallmatrix}$ histoire.

Such items test knowledge of gender rather than usage.

Here is an example testing the use of the partitive in French:

Complete the following sentences, using this key to indicate your answers: (A) le, (B) du, (C) de, (D) no word necessary.

1. Voulez-vous _____ pain?   *Do you want some bread?*
2. Je n'aime pas manger   *I don't like to eat too much*
     trop _____ pain.   *bread.*
3. _____ pain (Pain) fait grossir.   *Bread makes you gain weight.*

Correct responses: B, C, A

Since all choices are of the same gender, the vocabulary element is minimized.

Here is a German example involving case endings:

Complete the following sentences, using this key to indicate your answers: (A) ein, (B) eines, (C) einem, (D) einen.

1. Da steht _____ Stuhl.   *There is a chair.*
2. Ich kaufe meiner Mutter _____   *I'm buying my mother a chair.*
     Stuhl.
3. Legen Sie Ihren Hut auf _____   *Put your hat on the chair.*
     Stuhl!

Correct responses: A, D, D

SAMPLE ITEM TYPE *32*   NOUNS—DISCRETE ITEMS

Complete the following German sentence:

Der Wagen _____ fährt gut.   *Father's car drives well.*

A. der Vater
B. des Vaters
C. dem Vater
D. den Vater

Correct response: B

7.4.1b   PRONOUNS

In the use of pronouns, a foreign language often makes distinctions that do not exist in English; students consequently tend to confuse the pronouns used in such expressions. The teacher may test the student's knowledge of pronoun usage with an item like the one below, using four options to make the item more reliable. (Note: The student must have both pronouns correct in order to receive credit for the item.)

SAMPLE ITEM TYPE *33*   PRONOUNS—DOUBLE-CHOICE ITEMS

Complete the following sentences:

Connaissez-vous Marcel Dupont?   *Do you know Marcel Dupont?*
_____ professeur maintenant.   *He is a teacher now.*
_____ un très bon professeur,   *They say he is a very good*
dit-on.   *teacher.*

A. C'est, C'est
B. C'est, Il est
C. Il est, C'est
D. Il est, Il est

Correct response: C

SAMPLE ITEM TYPE *34*   PRONOUNS—SERIES ITEMS

Here is an example in Spanish:

Complete the following sentences, using this key to indicate your responses: (A) que, (B) quien, (C) quienes, (D) no word necessary.

1. Es el libro de _____ hablábamos   *That is the book we were talking*
   ayer.   *about yesterday.*
2. Ese es el amo del perro _____   *This is the dog's master who*
   llamó.   *called.*
3. Son los amigos con _____   *These are the friends with whom*
   hablaba.   *I was speaking.*

Correct responses: A, B, C

SAMPLE ITEM TYPE *35*   PRONOUNS—DISCRETE ITEMS

Here is a discrete item that tests the personal pronouns in German.

Complete the following sentence:

Geben Sie _____ zwei Paar   *Give me two pairs of socks.*
  Strümpfe!

A. ich
B. mir
C. mich
D. zu mir

Correct response: B

SAMPLE ITEM TYPE *36*   PRONOUNS—SENTENCE COMPLETION

In items of this sort, the student selects the appropriate completion to a sentence. The following item evaluates the students' familiarity with relative pronouns in French and with the constructions *se souvenir de* and *connaître*. (Although all the options in the English equivalent are acceptable, only one option is grammatically appropriate in French.)

Voilà une femme que   *There is a woman that*

A. je me souviens.   *I remember.*
B. nous connaît.   *knows us.*
C. je connais.   *I know.*
D. se souvient de moi.   *remembers me.*

Correct response: C

7.4.1c   PREPOSITIONS

Frequently the target language and the native language do not use prepositions the same way. For American students, if the target language uses prepositions in constructions where English does not, or if the choice of prepositions is not the same in both languages, conflict develops. Familiarity with prepositions and their use may be easily tested with multiple-choice items.

SAMPLE ITEM TYPE *37*   PREPOSITIONS—SERIES ITEMS

Here are some sample items in French:

Complete the following sentences, using this key to indicate your responses: (A) à, (B) de (d'), (C) pour, (D) no word necessary.

1. Il nous remercie _____ avoir téléphoné.
2. J'apprends à mon frère _____ nager.
3. Je n'ose pas _____ l'inviter.

Correct responses: B, A, D

7.4.1d CONJUNCTIONS

Series items, such as those in Sample Item Type 31, can also be used to test student familiarity with conjunctions. In many European languages, specific conjunctions are followed by a definite word order or verb form. Student sensitivity to the grammatical context in which conjunctions are used can be measured with discrete items.

SAMPLE ITEM TYPE *38*   CONJUNCTIONS—SELECTING THE WRONG
FORM

Indicate which of the following conjunctions may *not* be substituted for the underlined conjunction unless other changes in the sentence are made.

Il me donne un cadeau <u>quand</u> je suis sage.	*He gives me a present <u>when</u> I am good.*

A. puisque	*since*
B. parce que	*because*
C. pour que	*so that*
D. lorsque	*when*

Correct response: C

7.4.1e WORD ORDER

The target language and the native language often use different word order patterns. Knowledge of word order can be tested by asking students to indicate where in a sentence a given word or phrase should be inserted.

SAMPLE ITEM TYPE *39*   WORD ORDER—INSERTION ITEM

The word at the left belongs somewhere in the sentence that follows it. Indicate which letter in parentheses corresponds to the place where the word should be inserted and blacken the corresponding space on your answer sheet.

Here are two sample items in German:

1. nicht	Ich (A) werde (B) es (C) lesen (D).	*not*	*I will read it.*
2. mir	Er (A) wollte (B) ihn (C) geben (D).	*to me*	*He wanted to give it.*

Correct responses: C, C

7.4.1f VERBS

The items suggested in the previous sections can also be adapted to testing the students' command of verbs and verb forms. Here are several examples in French.

When certain indicative and subjunctive forms are identical, as is the case in French, items can be constructed to check the student's active knowledge of grammatical usage.

SAMPLE ITEM TYPE *40* IDENTIFICATION OF FORMS

Determine whether the underlined verb is in the subjunctive or in the indicative. Indicate your answer as follows: A = subjunctive, B = indicative.

1. Il faut qu'ils <u>viennent</u> demain.	*They have to come tomorrow.*

2. Je ne veux pas qu'elle <u>donne</u>
  le livre à sa mère.
	I don't want her to give the book
	  to her mother.

3. Nous pensons qu'elle <u>étudie</u> trop.	*We think that she studies too much.*

Correct responses: A, A, B

SAMPLE ITEM TYPE *41* SEQUENCE OF TENSES—DISCRETE ITEM

Complete the following sentence:

Quand vous _____ fini, passez
  chez moi.
	When you have finished, come by
	  my house.

A. êtes
B. serez
C. avez
D. aurez

Correct response: D

SAMPLE ITEM TYPE *42*   SEQUENCE OF TENSES—SENTENCE
COMPLETION

J'achèterai un manteau quand	*I will buy a coat when I go to town.*

A. je vais en ville.
B. j'allais en ville.
C. je suis allé en ville.
D. j'irai en ville.

Correct response: D

SAMPLE ITEM TYPE *43*   QUESTION-ANSWER FORMAT

A variety of grammatical material may be tested through discrete question-and-answer items. The French sample item below evaluates knowledge of verb forms and reflexive pronouns and general comprehension.

Est-ce que je vous dérange?	*Am I bothering you?*
A. Oui, je me dérange.	*Yes, I'm bothering myself.*
B. Oui, je vous dérange.	*Yes I'm bothering you.*
C. Oui, vous me dérangez.	*Yes, you are bothering me.*
D. Oui, vous vous dérangez.	*Yes, you are bothering yourself.*

Correct response: C

7.4.2   Intellectualization of grammar

In the mid-60s, Simon Belasco was already stressing the importance of "intellectualizing grammar."[3] By this he meant that students should be able to identify the systematic relationships between sentences and those sentences that underly them. As an evaluation technique, he suggested "transformation testing drills" for intermediate and advanced students.

SAMPLE TEST ITEM *44*   TRANSFORMATION TEST—MULTIPLE-CHOICE
FORMAT

For each sentence you will see two transformations. Mark your answer sheet as follows: A = both transformations are acceptable and correct; B = only transformation number 1 is acceptable; C = only transformation number 2 is acceptable.

[3] See "The Plateau, or the Case for Comprehension: the 'Concept' Approach," *Modern Language Journal* 51, no. 2 (February 1967), pp. 82–88. For examples in English, see his "Surface Structure and Deep Structure in English," *Midway* 8, no. 2 (Autumn 1967), pp. 111–23.

We urged John to sing.

1. We urged John, who sang.
2. We urged that John sing.

We persuaded John to dance.

1. We persuaded John, who danced.
2. We persuaded that John dance.

We required the audience to pay admission.

1. We required the audience, who paid admission.
2. We required that the audience pay admission.

Correct responses: A, B, C

NOTE: Instead of using an ABCD answer sheet, the teacher may prefer having the students place an asterisk (*) in front of any unacceptable sentence.

7.5   READING COMPREHENSION: WORD RECOGNITION

Word recognition is an important component of reading, be it reading in the native language or reading in the target language. In this section the focus is on recognizing familiar words in new contexts, and on discovering the meanings of unfamiliar words encountered in reading selections. These tests differ in intent and frequently in form from vocabulary tests as described in Section 7.3, for the emphasis here is on reading comprehension.

Students differ in their word recognition skills in reading their own native language. It is unrealistic to expect an American student, for example, to become more adept at word recognition in the target language than he or she is in English. Therefore, the teacher who is seriously focusing on the development of reading skills should be encouraged to check with the school guidance office to assess the students' reading level in English. (While these scores are never totally reliable, they do provide a general picture of the abilities of the class.)

The easiest way for the classroom teacher to test word recognition is to use available readings as a point of departure. If the class is developing newspaper reading skills, then an unfamiliar newspaper article could furnish sample sentences. If the students are reading a short story, the test material could be drawn from a chapter not yet read in class, or from a paragraph of similar difficulty in another of the author's works. The following sample items suggest some of the word recognition techniques that can be tested rather readily.

Word recognition tests may use either the target language or the native language for the student response. If the native language is used, the emphasis is not on translation but on recognition of meaning as conveyed by a native language equivalent. It is up to the teacher to determine which evaluation techniques best reflect the course objectives.

7.5.1 Recognizing cognates and false cognates

In order to read for meaning, it is not enough that students be able to identify cognate patterns (as in Sample Item Type 20). They must be able to identify these cognates when they occur in a reading passage. More important, they must be able to distinguish between true cognates and false cognates. Of course, cognates only exist in large numbers between related languages, such as French and Spanish, or English and Italian.

SAMPLE ITEM TYPE *45* COGNATE RECOGNITION

Read the following excerpt from a French newspaper. The cognates have been underlined. Circle any cognates that are false cognates.

"Le 3 décembre. Un hold-up avec prise d'otages: 21, cette fois. Aucun d'eux n'est blessé."

December 3. A hold-up with taking of hostages: 21, this time. No one is wounded.

Correct response: (blessé), false cognate, does not mean "blessed."

In an alternate form of this item, students may be asked to underline the cognates and to mark the false ones.

SAMPLE ITEM TYPE *46* COGNATE IDENTIFICATION

Read the following excerpt and write out the English equivalents of the underlined cognates.

"No desespere, hermano, no desespere."

Don't despair, brother, don't despair.

Die Übung ist gut für Ihre Armmuskeln.

The exercise is good for your arm muscles.

Correct responses: despair (*not* disappear); arm muscles

Typically, cognates in two languages do not possess the same frequency of usage. For example, in the Romance languages there are many cognates whose more usual English equivalent is a word of Germanic origin. Some students have difficulty with these cognates because their native English vocabulary is limited. To test whether students really understand a cognate, they may be asked to provide a native language synonym.

SAMPLE ITEM TYPE 47   INTERPRETATION OF COGNATES

Give the cognate and a more common English equivalent for the underlined words.

La acción comienza en Rota.   The action _____ in Rota.

Correct response: commences / begins

Françoise Giroud travaille pour   Françoise Giroud is working
améliorer la condition des   _____ the condition of
femmes.   women.

Correct response: to ameliorate / to improve

Many cognates across two languages are partial cognates. These words occasionally have the meanings of their counterparts, but have additional meanings that are not direct cognates.

SAMPLE ITEM TYPE 48   INTERPRETING PARTIAL COGNATES

For each underlined word, indicate whether A or B is the more appropriate English equivalent.

1. Recherche pour importante   Wanted for large Algerian
   société algérienne: company: budget director
   responsable de budget

   A. important
   B. large

2. Dans son journal, Arthur Bremer   In his journal, Arthur Bremer
   parle de son attentat sur   speaks of his assassination
   George Wallace.   attempt on George Wallace.

   A. journal
   B. newspaper

Correct responses: B, A

7.5.2   Recognizing word families

An important aspect of word recognition is the ability to identify members of word families and to guess intelligently the meaning of the unfamiliar word.

SAMPLE ITEM TYPE *49*   RECOGNIZING RELATED WORDS

Here is a list of words you already know:

1. haut   2. bas   *1. high   2. low*

Read the following selection and underline the new words that are related to them.

| Malgré la hausse du pétrole, les prix doivent baisser cet été. | *In spite of the increase in the cost of oil, prices should drop this summer.* |

Correct responses: haut—hausse; bas—baisser

SAMPLE ITEM TYPE *50*   GUESSING THE MEANINGS OF RELATED WORDS

As a follow-up to Sample Item Type 49, ask the students to fill in the missing words in the English equivalent.

In spite of the _____ in the cost of oil, prices should _____ this summer.

SAMPLE ITEM TYPE *51*   IDENTIFYING ROOT WORDS

The underlined words are related to words you already know. For each word, give the root word and guess the meaning of the unfamiliar word.

| Les écrivains ont fondé un syndicat. | *The writers founded a union.* |

Correct response: écrire (to write); écrivain = writer

7.5.3   Identifying forms of words

In reading a target language, students must be able to recognize inflected forms of nouns, adjectives, and verbs. The student of English, for instance, must realize that *went* is the past tense of *to go* and that *wives* is the plural of *wife*. Some languages have verb forms that are heavily used in narrative prose but not in conversation or informal letters. Students of French, for instance, should be able to recognize the *passé simple* although most of them will not have to know how to use that tense in writing.

SAMPLE ITEM TYPE *52*   IDENTIFYING INFLECTED FORMS:
                         WRITTEN FORMAT

Give the infinitives that correspond to the underlined verbs.

1. Qui a découvert le crime?   *Who discovered the crime?*
2. Un garçon qui a aperçu   *A boy who noticed the open*
   la fenêtre ouverte.   *window.*

Correct responses: découvrir, apercevoir

SAMPLE ITEM TYPE *53*   IDENTIFYING INFLECTED FORMS: MULTIPLE
                         CHOICE FORMAT

Read each sentence carefully and then indicate which of the infinitives
suggested corresponds to the underlined verb. Mark the appropriate letter
on your answer sheet.

1. Je vois une fille qui quitte   *I see a girl leaving the apartment*
   l'appartement et je la suis.   *and I follow her.*

   A. suivre
   B. être

2. Tout d'un coup je vis la maison   *All of a sudden I saw the house*
   qui brûlait.   *that was burning.*

   A. vivre
   B. voir

Correct responses: A, B

In addition to recognizing inflected forms of words, students should also
be able to identify prefixes and suffixes.

SAMPLE ITEM TYPE *54*   IDENTIFYING SUFFIXES—TRUE-FALSE
                         FORMAT

Read the following sentences. Are the underlined words all adverbs? If the
word ending in -ment is an adverb, mark A = true. If not, mark B =
false.

1. Il a répondu correctement.   *He answered correctly.*
2. Il parle couramment l'anglais.   *He speaks English fluently.*
3. C'est un bon raisonnement.   *That's a good line of reasoning.*

Correct responses: A, A, B

SAMPLE ITEM TYPE *55* IDENTIFYING PREFIXES—WRITTEN
FORMAT

Read the following sentences. Do the underlined words contain prefixes?
If so, separate the prefix from the root word.

1. Je ne peux pas le ranimer.   *I cannot revive him.*
2. Elle ne va pas le rançonner.   *She is not going to ransom him.*

Correct responses: re + animer; no

If desired, the students can also be asked to give either target language
synonyms or native language equivalents of the underlined words.

7.5.4 Understanding figures of speech and idiomatic expressions

In reading for meaning, the student who encounters a figure of speech should
understand the intent of the author even though he or she cannot translate
that figure into idiomatic English. Thus the student of French who encounters
the expression " bon comme le pain " (as good as bread) and who understands
it to mean " very good " can continue reading without having to come up
with an equivalent English comparison: " as good as gold."⁴

SAMPLE ITEM TYPE *56* PARAPHRASING

Complete the second sentence of each pair with a paraphrase of the
underlined expression.

English:

1. Benny is going bananas.
2. Benny is _____.

French:

1. "Pas maintenant, dit-elle, j'ai   *" Not now," she said, " I have*
   d'autres chats à fouetter."   *other fish to fry."*
2. "Pas maintenant, dit-elle,
   _____."

Correct responses: becoming or going crazy;
                    j'ai d'autres choses à faire (I have other things to do)

⁴ For a discussion of the differences between reading and translating, see Louise C. Seibert
and Lester G. Crocker, *Skills and Techniques for Reading French* (Baltimore: The Johns
Hopkins Press, 1958; subsequently published by Harper & Row). Hereafter this book is
cited as *Skills for Reading French.*

7.5.5 Knowing the meanings of key words

Every language has certain key words—frequently conjunctions, adverbs, and/or prepositions—with multiple meanings. In order to read a text properly, the student must recognize how these key words are used.

SAMPLE ITEM TYPE 57   RECOGNIZING KEY WORDS—
MULTIPLE-CHOICE FORMAT

Select the basic English equivalent for each of the underlined words. Mark the corresponding letter on your answer sheet. A = than   B = that C = only

1. Paul est plus riche que moi.   *Paul is richer than I am.*
2. Je sais qu'il a reçu 100 francs.   *I know that he got a hundred*
                                          francs.
3. Quant à moi, je n'ai que   *As for me, I only have*
   10 francs en ce moment.   *ten francs right now.*

Correct responses: A, B, C

7.5.6 Guessing word meanings from context

An important word recognition technique in reading both native language and target language texts is the ability to infer meanings from context.[5] The examples that follow are in English.

SAMPLE ITEM TYPE 58   INFERENCE QUESTIONS—MULTIPLE-CHOICE
FORMAT

Mark the option that best defines the underlined words.

1. From up there we had an aerial view of the unkempt lawns, the fruit trees, the wisteria climbing the weathered brick towards our window.[6]

Wisteria is   A. a kind of plant
               B. a kind of bird
               C. a kind of stone

[5] For a discussion of various inference techniques, plus dozens of sample exercises that can form the basis of test items, see Seibert and Crocker, Chapter IV in *Skills for Reading French*, (pp. 44–87).
[6] Quotations in this section are adapted from James Herriot, *All Things Bright and Beautiful* (New York: St. Martin's Press, 1974).

2. Tristam and I were in the dispensary one afternoon busy at the tasks which have passed into history—<u>making up fever drinks, stomach powders, boric acid pessaries</u>.

Tristam and James were   A. fixing dinner
                              B. preparing medicines
                              C. writing recipes

Correct responses: A, B

SAMPLE ITEM TYPE *59*   INFERENCE QUESTIONS—WRITTEN
                      RESPONSE

Give a synonym or equivalent for the underlined word.

1. I've never seen <u>owt</u> like that afore.
2. Is the water all gone? Aye, <u>nowt</u> left.

Correct responses: anything; nothing

SAMPLE ITEM TYPE *60*   INFERENCE QUESTIONS—FINDING
                      TEXTUAL CLUES

Read the following passage. Then circle those words which explain the meaning of the underlined word.

[The vet is examining a sick dog.] "Do you see how he's half closing his eyes as though he's frightened of the light?..." I looked down at the little dog. Occasionally he shivered, he had a definite <u>photophobia</u> and there was that creamy blob of pus in the corner of each eye.

Correct response: "he's frightened of the light"

7.5.7   Using the dictionary

When students encounter a difficult word whose meaning they cannot infer, and when they feel that the comprehension of this word is essential for an understanding of the text, they must turn to the dictionary. Whether they use a dictionary in the target language or a bilingual dictionary, they frequently find that the word they are looking up has several meanings. In testing word recognition skills, the teacher may wish to evaluate whether the students can pick out the appropriate definition among those given in the dictionary.

SAMPLE ITEM TYPE *61*   SELECTING DEFINITIONS—
MULTIPLE-CHOICE FORMAT

Read the following passage. Then select the appropriate dictionary definition from those suggested and mark the corresponding letter on your answer sheet.

Le <u>col</u> de sa chemise était fort sale.   *The <u>collar</u> of his shirt was very dirty.*

French definitions might read:
A. cou   *neck*
B. partie de vêtement qui   *collar*
   entoure le cou
C. passage entre deux montagnes   *pass*

Correct response: B

SAMPLE ITEM TYPE *62*   SELECTING DEFINITIONS—MATCHING
FORMAT

Each set of sentences contains an identical word. Match the sentences with the appropriate definitions.

1. Madame Duclos portait un <u>col</u>   *Madame Duclos was wearing a*
   de dentelle.   *lace <u>collar</u>.*
2. Après avoir passé le <u>col</u>, nous   *After crossing the <u>pass</u>, we will*
   pourrons voir l'océan.   *be able to see the ocean.*

(French definitions as in preceding item)

Correct responses: B, C

7.6 READING COMPREHENSION: UNDERSTANDING SYNTAX

In order to understand a text, the students must not only recognize the meanings of the individual words and expressions, they must also understand the interrelationships among these words. Students reading their native language usually handle the common syntactical patterns automatically. However, in the target language students tend to impose the syntax of their native language on what they are reading. Difficulties occur when the two languages use different syntactical patterns, such as word order, to express equivalent ideas. Tests to evaluate how readily students handle syntax are relatively easy to prepare.[7]

[7] For a detailed presentation of syntactic problems, plus dozens of exercises that can readily be adapted to reading test items, see Simon Belasco, *Reading College French* (New York: Harper & Row, 1975).

7.6.1   Recognizing the key elements

The first step in understanding a sentence is to locate the subject and the predicate. Then the student must be able to identify the roles of modifiers, objects, and phrases.

SAMPLE ITEM TYPE *63*   FINDING KEY ELEMENTS

Read the following passage carefully and underline the subjects. Then circle the finite verbs.

(Spanish) De esta manera (lamentaba) su adversa fortuna mi amo...	*In this way, my master was lamenting his bad fortune...*
(German) Durch die Tür (kam) plötzlich der Polizist.	*The policeman suddenly came through the door.*
(French) Les jeunes de ma connaissance (adorent) les sports.	*The young people that I know love sports.*

NOTE: Although only single sentences are given as illustrations, on a classroom test the teacher would probably use one or two paragraphs. As a variation, students can be asked to find the subjects of specific underlined verbs or the verbs corresponding to subjects that have been underlined.

SAMPLE ITEM TYPE *64*   RECOGNIZING STRUCTURAL SIGNALS

In items of this type, the students are asked to identify the tense of the verb, or indicate whether a noun is singular or plural.

For each sentence write the tense of the underlined verb.

1. Él tendrá un libro.	*He'll have one book.*
2. Él tuvo dos libros.	*He had two books.*

Correct responses: future; preterit

7.6.2   Identifying antecedents

When reading an unfamiliar text students must be able to find the antecedents of pronouns and possessive determiners. A wrongly identified antecedent will lead to a misreading of the passage.

SAMPLE ITEM TYPE *65*   IDENTIFYING ANTECEDENTS

Write the antecedents of the underlined pronouns.

"1975, année banale? Peut-être pas. Elle (1) pourrait marquer l'Histoire d'une date discrète: celle (2) de la fin des mythes." *1975, an ordinary year like the others? Perhaps not. It could mark History with an unobtrusive date: that of the end of myths.*

Correct responses: (1) 1975 (année); (2) date

7.6.3 Understanding deep structure

In reading a text, the students must not only understand the relationships among the words in the surface structure, but they must understand the deep structure—that is, they must determine the relationships between the underlying sentences. Let us look at Chomsky's oft-quoted example:

John is easy to please.
John is eager to please.[8]

The sentences look similar, but the underlying structure of the first is "It is easy to please John," whereas the underlying structure of the second is "John is eager to please someone." (One cannot say: "It is eager to please John" or "John is easy to please someone.") The students' awareness of underlying structures can be tested through multiple-choice items in the target language.

SAMPLE ITEM TYPE *66* UNDERSTANDING DEEP STRUCTURE

Indicate which of the interpretations of the underlined words is most appropriate.

1. As a teacher of French, one of my chief goals is stimulating conversation.

   A. to stimulate conversation
   B. conversation I find stimulating

2. I am looking forward to this evening at the O'Malley's: there is always good food and stimulating conversation.

Correct responses: A, B

[8] Noam Chomsky, "Current Issues in Linguistic Theory" in Jerry A. Fodor and Jerrold J. Katz, eds., *The Structure of Language: Readings in the Philosophy of Language* (Englewood Cliffs, N.J.: Prentice-Hall, 1964), p. 66.

SAMPLE ITEM TYPE *67*   SIMPLIFYING COMPLEX SENTENCES

Each sentence in this sample item is followed by two pairs of sentences. Which pair expresses the same meaning as the original?

1. Wie heisst der Mann, den   *What is the name of the man that*
   Monika gern hat?   *Monika likes?*

   A. Wie heisst der Mann?
      Monika hat ihn gern.   *...Monika likes him.*
   B. Wie heisst der Mann?
      Er hat Monika gern.   *...He likes Monika.*

2. Wie heisst der Mann, der Inge   *What is the name of the man that*
   gern hat?   *likes Inge?*

   A. Wie heisst der Mann?
      Inge hat ihn gern.   *...Inge likes him.*
   B. Wie heisst der Mann?
      Er hat Inge gern.   *...He likes Inge.*

Correct responses: A, B

7.7   READING COMPREHENSION: COMMUNICATION

When most people read a sign, a newspaper or a letter, they are reading for communication: they want to understand the message that the writer intended to convey. They will tolerate typographical errors, misspellings, and clumsy constructions as long as these are not so frequent as to interfere with communication. In testing reading ability at this level, the teacher strives to ascertain whether communication has taken place.

7.7.1   Reading aloud

Tests of reading aloud have proven to be very valid tests of reading ability in the native language. Their main drawback is that they are time-consuming to administer. The American child, for example, shows that he or she can read English well by reading a text aloud to the examiner.

Tests of reading aloud are valid measures of second-language reading ability only if the students speak the language with some ease. Often a student with a good pronunciation and a solid sense of the sound-symbol correspondences of the target language can read aloud texts that he or she does not really understand.

7.7.2   Getting the gist of the reading

At the beginning level, students should be able to determine the subject matter of an article or letter and get a feeling for the gist of the contents. When beginning students look at a target language newspaper, for instance, they realize they cannot read it the way they would read a similar newspaper in their native language. But gradually, as their familiarity with the target language increases, they should be able to determine what specific articles are about. In order to test performance at this level, the teacher should use authentic materials: newspapers, magazines, ads, letters.

SAMPLE ITEM TYPE *68*   UNDERSTANDING QUESTIONS

Read the following questions in German. You may answer in English, but be sure that your response shows that you understood the question.

Cue: Was halten Sie von der modernen Muzik?   *What do you think of modern music?*

Response: I hate modern music!

Cue: Von wem wurde Penizillin entdeckt?   *Who discovered penicillin?*

Response: I don't know who discovered penicillin.

SAMPLE ITEM TYPE *69*   DETERMINING THE GENERAL TOPIC

Look at each of the following clippings from a local Spanish newspaper. Can you tell the general topic of each clipping? Mark your answer sheet as follows:

A = news item, B = weather, C = sports item, D = entertainment.

NOTE: The articles the teacher chooses can be duplicated with a copy machine and, if desired, can be transformed into ditto masters. The articles can also be shown sequentially on an opaque projector.[9]

SAMPLE ITEM TYPE *70*   SCANNING

Look at this front page (inside page) of a German newspaper and find the following articles or features:

[9] Duplicating masters of selected newspaper articles are available commercially. Cf. H. Ned Seelye and J. Laurence Day, *The Newspaper: Spanish Mini-Culture Unit* and John A. Rallo, *The Newspaper: Italian Mini-Culture Unit*, both available from National Textbook Company, Skokie, Ill. 60076.

a. the weather report; b. the results of the soccer games; c. the report of a train accident; d. the visit of Queen Elizabeth.

In items of this type, the articles to be identified must be prepared for each newspaper page. If the test is given informally, each student can be given a different page to scan. The articles to be found should be of equivalent difficulty. (If desired, the pages and the instructions can be kept and redistributed for a second version of the same test.) As an informal test, students can also be allowed to work in pairs, especially if the pairs are changed in the course of the marking period.

SAMPLE ITEM TYPE *71* SKIMMING

Marylou is holding tryouts for a play. She has asked those interested to drop her a line indicating whether they can come on Monday, April 5 or Wednesday, April 7. You will now read the postcards she received in today's mail. Scan them quickly and sort them into four groups: A = people who can come April 5; B = people who can come April 7; C = people who cannot make those two dates; D = mail that has nothing to do with the tryouts.

1. Marylou, I'd love to try out for the part of Julie. I'll be there on Monday. See you then.
2. Dear Marylou, Sorry I can't make either date...but I do want to participate. Could you suggest another date?
3. Dear Marylou, Wednesday, April 7 is just fine. I'll come around four, if that's all right.
4. Dear Marylou, I am having a surprise party for Paul on Wednesday, April 7. Do you think you and Marty could come over? Be here at nine.

Correct responses: A, C, B, D

7.7.3 Obtaining information

In a natural, rather than a classroom, situation, people read material in the target language to obtain specific information. In other words, they have a question in mind (such as: What will the weather be tomorrow? What is showing at the movies tonight? Did the Bruins win their hockey game? When does Tour A leave and what places will we visit?) and are looking for an answer. In testing the students' ability to read for specific information, the questions are asked before the students begin reading. The material to be read can be taken from newspapers, magazines, advertisements, train and movie schedules, and letters. For more advanced students who are learning to read the target language for professional reasons, the reading material may consist of scientific articles, book reviews, or other appropriate selections.

SAMPLE ITEM TYPE 72 OBTAINING INFORMATION—SHORT ANSWER FORMAT

Look at the following descriptions from a brochure on the museums of Boston. Then answer the questions:

The Franklin Park Zoo

"A Bird's World"
Birds from around the world inhabit a series of natural environments in a spectacular exhibit that depicts a swamp, a rain forest, a desert, a river bank and a mountainside. Real plants, trees, rocks and water combine to transport the visitor into "A Bird's World". There are innovative educational exhibits that explain how the birds of the world survive. Outside, the huge flight cage and waterfowl pond add a "free-flight" dimension to the experience.
HOURS: Daily from 10-4.
ADMISSION: Free

Isabella Stewart Gardner Museum

Fenway Court, incorporated as a museum in 1900, houses the collection of paintings, tapestries, stained glass, furniture and other objects of art assembled by Isabella Stewart Gardner. The building is of Italian style and the central court has a display of flowers. Music programs are offered three times a week from September through June. Admission to the museum and to the concerts is free. Acoustiguide tour units are available during open hours. Photography for personal use is permitted. Children must be conducted by responsible adults. For information on hours and music programs call 734-1359. Other business: 566-1401.
HOURS:
September through June: Tuesday 1-9:30; Wednesday through Sunday 1-5:30. Closed Monday, national holidays, Sunday before Labor Day. Music Tuesday at 8, Thursday and Sunday at 4. July and August: Tuesday through Saturday 1-5:30. Closed Sunday, Monday and the 4th of July. No music.
ADMISSION:
Free

Museum of Transportation

The Museum has collections of antique carriages, bicycles, motorcycles, autos and all the bits and pieces of America's transportation history. Silent comedies, slide shows, old signs and gas pumps, games of discovery, rides in antique vehicles and a train board all invite children and adults to explore and discover what it was like to move around the countryside in years past. The Museum is housed in an 1880 carriage house in an 85 acre park.
HOURS:
Tuesday through Sunday 10-5.
ADMISSION:
Adults $2.00, Children 6-15 $1.00, 3-5 years 25¢. Senior citizens $1.00

Museum of Fine Arts

The Boston Museum of Fine Arts houses man's visual world from remote antiquity to the present day. It ranks as the second most comprehensive museum in the Western hemisphere with collections which are often unsurpassed. Resources include a school, library, research laboratory and a varied educational program of lectures, films, and musical performances.
HOURS:
Open every day of the week 10-6 and Tuesday and Thursday til 9 PM. Closed July Fourth, Labor Day, Thanksgiving, Christmas Eve, Christmas, and New Year's Day.
ADMISSION:
$1.50; Sundays 10-1 PM free. Free at all times to members, children under 16, holders of student or artist admission cards and servicemen in uniform. Free access to Museum Shop, Restaurant, and Lecture Hall. On MBTA Arborway Green Line.

New England Aquarium

On Boston's historic waterfront more than 2,000 fishes exhibited in life-like environments. The focal point is the 200,000 gallon giant ocean tank, the largest glass enclosed salt water tank in the world.
Opened in September, 1974, the "Discovery," home to bottle-nosed dolphins and sea lions. The ship, "Discovery" is berthed adjacent to the Aquarium where visitors find fascinating marine mammals "playing" daily.
HOURS:
Mon. thru. Thurs., 9-5; Fri., til 9, Saturday, Sunday, Holidays, 10-6. Closed Thanksgiving, Christmas, New Year's Day.
ADMISSION TO AQUARIUM OR DISCOVERY:
Adults $2.50; 6-15 $1.25; Senior Citizens, military, and college students with I.D. $1.25. Combination tickets to both Discovery and main Aquarium available at discount. Ask for membership and group rate information. Central Wharf, Boston, Massachusetts 02110 (742-8870)

The Prudential Skywalk

The shortest walk around Boston is a walk on the Skywalk. Located on the 50th floor of the Prudential Tower building, the Skywalk provides a 360° panoramic view of historical Boston. On a clear day you can see as far away as New Hampshire, Vermont, Gloucester and Cape Cod.
HOURS:
Open from 9 a.m. to 11 p.m., Monday through Thursday; 9 a.m. to midnight on Friday and Saturday; 1 p.m. to 11 p.m. on Sundays.
ADMISSION:
$1.00 for adults, 35¢ for children aged 6–12, Senior Citizens—50¢. Group rates—75¢ for adults in groups of ten or more; 20¢ for children.

1. Your family has no money. It is Wednesday afternoon. Which two places could you visit? (Note: You are not a member of a museum.)
2. You want an aerial view of Boston. Where would you go?
3. It is nine o'clock Monday morning. Which places are open?
4. You would like to go to a museum and also hear a concert. Which two choices do you have?
5. You are interested in old cars. Where would you go?
6. You are an adult. Which place is the most expensive?
7. You are fifteen years old. Where can you get in free? Where do you pay $1? Where do you pay $1.25?

Correct responses: 1. Zoo and Gardner Museum; 2. Skywalk; 3. Skywalk and Aquarium; 4. Gardner Museum and Museum of Fine Arts; 5. Museum of Transportation; 6. Aquarium; 7. Zoo, Gardner Museum, Museum of Fine arts: free; Museum of Transportation and Skywalk: $1; Aquarium: $1.25.

7.7.4 Passage comprehension

Passage items are the best-known reading tests. The selection may be unedited or edited material in the target language. In standardized tests, the items are in a multiple-choice format, whereas in informal reading tests, written or oral answers may be called for. The teacher must take care to make sure that the questions accompanying the passage are genuine reading-comprehension items, for there is the possibility that students could answer some poorly constructed items without having read the text. Reading-comprehension items are best pretested on individuals who have not read the accompanying passage.

7.7.4a PRINTED OPTIONS IN THE TARGET LANGUAGE

In the pure reading test, the student reads both questions and answers and selects the correct responses from the options given.

For elementary—and often intermediate—students, short passages with true-false sentences may be used as informal classroom tests. Care must be taken that the statements do not turn into exercises in logical thinking and problem solving.

SAMPLE ITEM TYPE 73 PASSAGE WITH TRUE-FALSE ITEMS

Here is a sample passage in French:

| Les enfants ne sont pas encore levés parce qu'ils se sont couchés tard hier soir. Mais nous sommes au mois de juillet et il n'y a pas d'école. Alors les enfants n'ont pas besoin de se lever de très bonne heure. | *The children are not up yet because they went to bed late last night. But it is July and there is no school. So the children don't need to get up very early.* |

After you have read the passage, decide whether the following statements are true or false. Indicate your answer as follows: A = true, B = false.

1. Les enfants sont encore couchés.	*The children are still in bed.*
2. Ils ont classe demain.	*They have school tomorrow.*
3. L'école commence en juillet.	*School begins in July.*

Correct responses: A, B, B

SAMPLE ITEM TYPE *74*   PASSAGE WITH VARIED MULTIPLE-CHOICE QUESTIONS

The following passage in French could be administered as a reading test to more advanced students:

| Je suis venue à Livry achever (1) les beaux jours, et dire adieu aux feuilles; elles sont encore toutes aux arbres; elles (2) n'ont fait que changer (3) de couleur: au lieu d'être vertes, elles sont aurores (4) ... | *I came to Livry to end the beautiful season and to bid adieu to the leaves; they are all still on the trees; they have just changed color: instead of green they are the color of dawn...* |

After you have read the passage, answer the following questions:

1. Qui est l'auteur?	*Who is the author?*
A. une femme	*a woman*
B. un homme	*a man*
C. ou un homme ou une femme	*either a man or a woman*

Correct response: A

To answer this item correctly, the students must understand the importance of the final *e* of *venue*.

2. (1) veut dire	*(1) means*
A. admirer	*to admire*
B. réussir	*to succeed*
C. finir	*to finish*

Correct response: C

This is a vocabulary item; B is a form distractor because *achever* looks like the English *achieve*, i.e., *réussir*.

3. (2) se rapporte aux   (2) *refers to*

    A. jours   *the days*
    B. feuilles   *the leaves*
    C. arbres   *the trees*

Correct response: B

This item tests whether the student has correctly identified the antecedent of the pronoun *elles*.

4. (3) est l'équivalent de   (3) *is the equivalent of*

    A. ont seulement changé   *only changed*
    B. doivent changer   *must change*
    C. n'ont pas encore changé   *have not yet changed*

Correct response: A

To select the proper response for this comprehension item, the student must be familiar with *ne...que* and this particular use of *faire*.

5. Dans le texte, (4) représente   *In the text, (4) represents*

    A. un phénomène lumineux   *a light phenomenon*
    B. le lever du soleil   *the rising of the sun*
    C. une couleur   *a color*

Correct response: C

In this item the student demonstrates his or her ability to select the proper definition of a word according to the context in which it is used. The item could be made a little more difficult if option C were to read *un teint* (a hue).

It is rather time-consuming to prepare passages followed by a variety of multiple-choice items. Often, however, it is possible to procure old copies or samples of New York Regents or College Board examinations. The items could be modified to meet the needs of the students. However, copyrights and permissions must first be checked.

7.7.4b WRITTEN ANSWERS IN THE TARGET LANGUAGE

For classroom use, reading tests with questions to be answered in writing are often more efficient than multiple-choice tests because they can be prepared in less time. However, the teacher must realize that two skills, reading and writing, are involved in such a test. The student may understand the passage, but produce an unacceptable written answer. Two grades could be assigned: one for comprehension (correct content) and one for written expression (correct form).

The range of questions will be limited by the teacher's objectives and by the level of the class. Elementary students will write only short summaries or answer questions that require more or less a restatement of the passage. The types of questions asked of more advanced students will be determined by their vocabulary and their background. If the writing sample contains too many mistakes (other than spelling), the teacher should review the difficult structures and vocabulary in class. On the next test the questions should be modified so that the students are encouraged to use expressions they know and can handle accurately.

7.7.4c   ORAL ANSWERS IN THE TARGET LANGUAGE

For informal classroom use, it is possible to combine comprehension passages with oral responses. The passage may be given to the students for a stated length of time; they are asked to prepare an oral résumé or to prepare oral answers for specific questions.

If such a passage is used as a laboratory test, all students will record their responses simultaneously on their tapes. If the teacher must see students individually, they should be allowed equal preparation time. Thus, while Student A answers the questions, Student B may read the text; as Student B recites, Student C is given the text, and so on. Those not being tested could be given a written assignment. In scoring such a test, the teacher must determine from his or her course objective what percentage of the grade is allotted to reading comprehension and what percentage to speaking ability (fluency, pronunciation, correctness, etc.).

7.7.4d   ANSWERS IN THE NATIVE LANGUAGE

In courses where the emphasis is on comprehension rather than self-expression, the teacher may wish to ask questions in the native language about the material in the passage. These reading tests may include résumés, specific questions on content, and explanations of lexical items or structures.

7.7.5   Translation

Many teachers find translation to be an excellent way of testing reading comprehension. Other teachers shy away from translation, for fear that this testing technique will lead to heavy classroom use of translation exercises and thus encourage the students to speak their native language more than the foreign language. Translation exercises are more appropriate in reading courses and less valid in courses stressing the audio-lingual skills.

To be effective, the translation test of reading comprehension must be carefully planned. The following guidelines may prove useful:

1. Select a passage unfamiliar to the students that is written by the same author whose work they have been reading (or that has appeared in another issue of a magazine they have been studying). Stylistically and lexically the passage should be similar to passages treated in class.
2. Determine whether students will use a dictionary or not. If not, gloss any unfamiliar words or expressions whose meanings cannot be inferred from the context.
3. Plan a scoring system. Determine how many points will be allotted for the entire translation, and then assign points to each sentence as a function of length and complexity. Determine whether extra points will be given for fluency.

Two types of translation tests are commonly used in the foreign language classroom.

SAMPLE ITEM TYPE 75 COMPLETE TRANSLATION

In a complete translation the student gives a native language equivalent of the entire passage.

SAMPLE ITEM TYPE 76 PARTIAL TRANSLATION

In a partial translation test, one part of the page contains the target language text. The other part of the page contains segments of the native language equivalent, with portions omitted. The student writes in the missing words, phrases and/or sentences. This type of translation test is longer to prepare, but it is generally shorter to grade since the attention of the teacher is focused only on the problem areas and not on the entire text.

7.8 READING COMPREHENSION: SPECIAL ASPECTS

With intermediate and advanced students for whom the linguistic content of the reading passages selected is familiar, the teacher may wish to employ evaluation techniques that are also used in testing reading ability in the native language. Some of the special aspects of reading that may be measured are: ease of reading, reading speed, retention ability, reconstitution of the text, and critical reading.

7.8.1 Ease of reading

Studies in native language reading skills indicate that the student who is able to break a sentence into meaningful chunks reads more easily than the student who attacks a sentence word for word. The following types of tests may be tried with low intermediate students of a second language, using texts written at their level.

SAMPLE ITEM TYPE 77 PHRASING

Read the following paragraph. Divide the sentences into phrases, using slash lines (/).

Here is an example in English:

An irate taxpayer / took direct action / when a street sweeping machine / woke him at 2 a.m. / He telephoned Town Manager Harry Tee, / routing him out of bed, / and dangled the phone out the window / so Tee could hear the racket.

NOTE: In scoring this type of test, the teacher deducts points for slash-marks that are incorrectly placed, e.g., "An irate / taxpayer took direct action..." Some students will break the sentence into smaller phrases than others, and phrase length is not a consideration.

SAMPLE ITEM TYPE 78 MARKING STRESSED SYLLABLES

Read the text at your normal reading speed. Underline the accented syllables.

Here is an example in English:

...Tee said he investigated the complaint and was able to halt the sweeper's post-midnight rounds. To insure the taxpayer's satisfaction, he called to ask if the noise had stopped—at 1 a.m. the next morning. "I would rather not comment on what his reaction was," Tee told the Town Council.

NOTE: This item is scored like Sample Item Type 77. The teacher deducts points for syllables that are wrongly underlined. Some students may mark secondary stress, while others may mark only primary stress. The emphasis is on reading fluency, not on phonetic analysis.

In native language reading tests in English, performance on such items correlates well with general reading ability. Experimentation will have to show how applicable this technique is to second-language reading.

7.8.2 Reading speed

Speed is one of the features that clearly distinguish the reading skill from the other three skills. Rapidity of writing or speaking is limited by the muscular functioning of the hand or the speech organs; rapidity of listening comprehension is determined by the speed at which others speak. Only in reading can the mind assimilate information in much less time than that required for writing it down.

As students learn to read the target language, they gradually develop speed in reading; advanced students should be able to read the target language as quickly as their native language. Even intermediate students should be able to read appropriate texts with maximum direct association. Fluency in reading is a sign that the students are not mentally transposing the text, partially or entirely, into their native language.

Students do not have a single reading speed, even in their native language. Simple texts are read more quickly than complex ones. However, relative reading speed remains rather constant: that is, the student who is ranked in the top 10 percent of the class for reading speed on an easy text will probably also rank in the top 10 percent on more difficult texts.

In order to measure reading speed, the test must allow the students to read without interruption for at least five minutes.[10] Two general formats are possible:

a. The students are given a text that no one in the class can finish in the allotted time. After five minutes, the teacher calls time and the students mark the point where they stopped reading.

b. The students are given a text that everyone can finish in five to ten minutes. When a student finishes, he or she signals the teacher's attention and the reading time is marked.

In both instances, it is advisable to check whether the students have understood what they have read. Comprehension may be tested by simple comprehension questions in the target language, or by asking students to write a brief summary in the target or native language.

7.8.3 Retention

Most reading tests permit the students to refer to the reading passage while answering related questions. In order to measure retention, as in the case of

---

[10] Three minutes has been found to be the absolute minimum. For more data on reading speed, see Roger Farr, ed., *Measurement and Evaluation of Reading* (New York: Harcourt Brace Jovanovich, 1970), pp. 31–32, 223 (hereafter cited as *Measurement*).

speed tests in the previous section, the students answer comprehension questions without looking back at the text. The types of questions asked depend on the nature of the reading selection. They might include questions about the topic of the selection, the conclusions, the organization, or specific points of information.

Students have different levels of retention when reading in their native language. Therefore, it is inappropriate to expect students to do better in the target language than in their native language.

7.8.4   Cloze tests

The *cloze test procedure* was developed by Wilson Taylor in the early 1950s.[11] The students are presented with a reading selection in which certain words have been deleted in a mechanical and objective manner. For instance, in a paragraph, the student is given the entire first sentence (to set the scene) and then must supply every fifth word for the remainder of the text. It is possible to omit every sixth or even every tenth word, as long as a regular pattern is followed. Cloze tests presented by computer often omit words according to a random table of numbers. The important factor is objectivity in selecting the words to be omitted, with no consideration for the context or the importance of the omitted word. The student receives points for every blank that is properly filled.

A recent variation of the cloze test is the reading-input test, in which every fifth word presents the student with the choice between the right response and a distractor.[12] There are two ways of generating the distractors: a) the test writer selects a word at random from the passage; b) the test writer specifically chooses the distractor. In the first instance, the distractor and the key word might be different parts of speech. In the second case, the distractor and the key word are usually the same part of speech, although the distractor may not be a word that appears elsewhere in the passage. The reading-input format has the advantage that the student does not need to interrupt his or her reading to write in a needed word, but simply circles the preferred option.

[11] See his article, "Cloze Procedure: a New Tool for Measuring Readability," *Journalism Quarterly* 30 (1953), pp. 415–33. See also Earl F. Rankin, Jr., "The Cloze Procedure—its Validity and Utility" in Farr, *Measurement*, pp. 237–53.

[12] See Ronald P. Carver, *New Techniques for Measuring and Improving Reading Comprehension* (Washington: American Institute for Research, 1973) and Oscar Ozete, "Assessing Reading Comprehension in Spanish as a Foreign Language: An Information Process Approach" (Ph.D. diss., Indiana University, 1974). Hereafter this dissertation is cited as "Assessing Reading Comprehension."

SAMPLE ITEM TYPE *79*   CLOZE TEST—STANDARD FORMAT

Fill in the missing words.

The great murder wave of the 1970s appears to have ebbed at last in big-city America. _____ reports from police departments _____ twelve selected cities show _____ in nine of them, _____ number of homicides dropped _____—and in some cases _____—last year. The drop _____ have halted for the _____ being a steady upward _____ in killing that reached _____ peak in 1974, the _____ lethal year since uniform _____ statistics have been kept _____ the United States.

Correct responses: First; in; that; the; markedly; sharply; may; time; trend; a; most; crime; in.

Scoring: When cloze tests are scored in the traditional manner, only the exact deleted word is acceptable (exact-cloze scoring). It is felt that the cloze test thus measures the degree of communication between the writer and the reader, for the latter is able to reconstitute the exact message the former intended to disseminate. Some cloze tests are scored so that the student receives credit for close synonyms (acceptable-cloze scoring). In this type of scoring it is felt that the student should receive credit for understanding the sense of the message, even if the precise form of the message was not reconstituted. In a recent experiment, Irvine, Atai and Oller found a .97 correlation between scores obtained with acceptable-cloze and exact-cloze scoring and conclude that it is possible to substitute one for the other with little loss of information. They also found that exact-cloze correlated more highly with dictation scores than did acceptable-cloze scoring. Scorer reliability, especially with non-native scorers, is obviously higher with exact-cloze scoring.[13]

SAMPLE ITEM TYPE *80*   CLOZE TEST—READING-INPUT FORMAT

Circle the word that most appropriately completes the thought expressed in the passage. (Note: Distractors were randomly selected from the text.)

The great murder wave of the 1970s appears to have ebbed at last in big-city America. (First/Have) reports from police departments (last/in) twelve selected cities show (from/that) in nine of them, (the/at) number of homicides dropped (markedly/cities)—and in some cases (swiftly/nine —last year. The drop (police/may) have halted for the (reports/time) being a steady upward (them/trend) in killing that reached (a/of) peak in

[13] Patricia Irvine, Parvin Atai and John W. Oller, Jr., "Cloze, Dictation and the Test of English as a Foreign Language (TOEFL)," *Language Learning* 24, no. 2 (December 1974), pp. 245–52.

1974, the (most/selected) lethal year since uniform (crime/cases) statistics have been kept (year/in) the United States.

NOTE: The presentation and instructions may be varied. For instance, students may be asked to cross out the inappropriate option. If preferred, the options may be typed one above the other: ... $\frac{\text{First}}{\text{Have}}$ reports from police departments $\frac{\text{last}}{\text{in}}$ twelve...

SAMPLE ITEM TYPE *81*   CLOZE TEST—MULTIPLE-CHOICE FORMAT

The cloze test may also be presented in a multiple-choice format, where the student chooses the correct response among three or four options. In preparing the distractors, the teacher can utilize the wrong responses furnished in a standard administration of the passage as a cloze test.

Underline the word that most appropriately completes the thought expressed in the passage.

The great murder wave of the 1970s appears to have ebbed at last in big-city America. [First / When / Few / Since] reports from police departments [over / and / in / at] twelve selected cities show [why / up / that / us] in nine of them, [the / a / many / any] number of homicides dropped [off / often / markedly / gently]—and in some cases [better / nine / rose / descended]—last year. The drop [would / may / can / might] have halted for the [instant / present / time / year] being a steady upward [number / line / bound / trend] in killing that reached [a / high / his / her] peak in 1974, the [least / small / most / very] lethal year since uniform [policemen / crime / traffic / population] statistics have been kept $\begin{bmatrix} \text{at} \\ \text{up} \\ \text{among} \\ \text{in} \end{bmatrix}$ the United States.

Cloze tests have the advantage of being easy to prepare and quick to score. Furthermore, they are totally objective. In his research, Oscar Ozete[14] found that reading-input tests with randomly selected distractors discriminated effectively among students in different levels of Spanish instruction. The tests seem to require both analytic and synthetic processes. The possibility of using cloze tests as placement tests should be explored.

Cloze tests can also be used to check student comprehension of a longer passage, short story or other reading. The teacher prepares a résumé of the material, and then systematically deletes every fifth word. The students complete the cloze résumé. Again, such a test allows the teacher to verify easily and rapidly whether students have done the assigned outside reading.

7.8.5 Textual criticism

In more advanced classes, teachers may use reading passages as a point of departure for textual criticism. The types of questions asked depend on the nature of the selection:

Evaluation of aptness of certain words or expressions: Why did the author use this word in the text rather than...?

What is the attitude of the author toward his subject? How is that attitude expressed?

Does the passage reflect the point of view of one of the characters? Which one? How is the reader made aware of this? (for fiction passages)

Specific suggestions for testing the cloze reading of literary works are made in Chapter Ten: The Literature Test.

[14] Ozete, "Assessing Reading Comprehension."

outline

eight
The Writing
Test

Of the four language skills, writing may truly be considered the most sophisticated. In listening and in reading, the students receive a message formulated by another; their role is receptive even though they may be actively interpreting and analyzing what they are hearing or reading. In speaking, the students are engaged in communicating their own ideas and feelings, but with approximations and explanations; conversation involves give-and-take with an interlocutor. Communication through the written word, on the other hand, possesses a certain degree of finality and demands real proficiency from the writer if it is to be effective. Many American college students have not even mastered the art of writing English, their native language.

The student learning a foreign language follows a series of steps in developing the writing skill. The mechanics—vocabulary, spelling, grammar—must be mastered before the student can aspire to precision of expression, fluency, and style. At the early levels, communication consists of messages and short paragraphs. Later, the student writes longer papers. Tests must consequently be so structured that they measure the various aspects of student progress toward the acquisition of this fourth skill.

8.1 GENERAL CONSIDERATIONS

Historically, writing was not a transcription of the spoken language but an independent system of visual communication. Pictorial symbols or hieroglyphs, such as those used by the ancient Egyptians and the American Indians, were gradually replaced by more abstract forms of writing that eventually attempted to represent the spoken language. This transition, though still incomplete, has passed through three major stages:[1]

Characters are formal items, such as those used in classical Chinese (which possesses from five to six thousand commonly used characters); even English uses certain characters such as % and &.

Syllabaries, containing from fifty to five thousand symbols, note only consonant articulations, indicating vowels, when necessary, by a system of dots or other marks. This partly phonological type of writing is characteristic of the ancient Semitic languages, such as Hebrew and Arabic, several languages of India, and Javanese. Japanese combines characters (borrowed from the Chinese) with a syllabic script.

Alphabets, invented in ancient Greece, use well under fifty single symbols to represent all consonant and vowel sounds. They are the easiest script to learn and to use; even Chinese is changing very slowly to a phonological system based on the Roman alphabet.

The phonological scripts—syllabaries and, particularly, alphabets—are imperfect transcriptions of the spoken language; stress and intonation are shown in a sketchy manner if at all. While spelling and pronunciation are quite close in Italian, English has an extremely ambiguous spelling system, and French writing reveals many vestigial sounds that are no longer pronounced. Since the invention of printing, the written language has exercised a conservative influence over the speech community. The continual evolution of the spoken language is counteracted by the presence of the "correct" forms in newspapers, magazines, and books.

Written language possesses its own conventions, which in certain cases do not parallel the spoken language. Sometimes the written language is entirely different from the spoken language; note the use of Latin in the Middle Ages or the use of English, French, or Swahili by many African tribesmen who speak other dialects. In French, the *passé simple* may be considered uniquely a written form.

What are the problems encountered by English-speaking students learning to write the target language? What particular aspects of the writing skill should the teacher test and evaluate?

American students learning to write a foreign language are literate in English. They know the Roman alphabet, even though they have learned to equate letters and letter combinations with English sounds. They realize, from their experience in spelling, that a written language can be a very imperfect transcription of the spoken language. One letter or cluster of letters can represent a variety of sounds (for example, *tough, bough, though, thought*); consequently, Americans do not think it strange when they find a

[1] See R. H. Robbins, *General Linguistics* (Bloomington: Indiana University Press, 1965), pp. 121–25.

similar phenomenon in French (bie*n*, renne, e*n*, parle*nt*). Moreover, they realize that one sound may be transcribed in a number of ways (English: *soul, sole;* French: *fin, faim*). They adapt even more happily to a language with a more phonological writing system, such as Spanish or Russian (in spite of the new accent marks of the former and the modified alphabet of the latter).

Furthermore, American students are familiar with certain morphemes in both their oral and written forms. On the printed page they recognize 's as a sign of possession, even though in spoken English they listen for /s/ (as in *Pat's*), /z/ (as in *Sal's*), and /ɪz/ (as in *Gus's*). A morphological consistency in spelling coupled with an inconsistency in the spoken language is nothing new.

The commonly taught foreign languages possess, as does English, a rapid spoken form that is not transcribed phonetically in writing. Many Americans say "Ya gonna come?" but write "Are you going to come?" Similarly, whereas many Germans say something that sounds like "Chaps nicht," they write "Ich habe es nicht."

English uses punctuation marks to separate elements of the sentence. Other languages have slightly different systems of punctuation that must be learned. The rules of punctuation in German are strict but the marks are fairly similar to English marks; punctuation rules in Spanish are freer but there are new symbols to be learned. In all writing exercises, the proper use of punctuation should be stressed.

Each language possesses certain typographical conventions that are quite evident—in business letters, for example; certain types of spacing, punctuation, and margins are used in each country. Written conventions also exist: salutations and closings. These elements, totally independent of the spoken language, must be learned. Written conventions exist in other specialized areas, too—in law, medicine, science, and so on.

The conservative nature of the written language explains the stricter conventions and the narrow margin of tolerance that educated natives have in regard to inaccuracies in writing. A heavy "foreign" accent, if it does not greatly interfere with comprehension, is permitted and is sometimes appreciated (note the success of Maurice Chevalier), but a letter poorly worded or containing misspellings elicits a negative reaction. The student and the teacher must strive for perfection in the writing skill.

The mastery of the elements of writing and the acquisition of new vocabulary and grammatical structures via writing comprise the skill-getting aspect of the writing skill. Traditionally these aspects of writing were evaluated through translation tests, which took the form of paragraphs and sentences to be translated or incomplete sentences in the target language containing words to be translated. Such tests were relatively easy to prepare and lent themselves to efficient and fairly reliable scoring. More recently, however, both teachers and language specialists have begun to question the *validity* of such translation tests.

Basically, the translation test hinges on a knowledge of vocabulary: if the student cannot recall the foreign-language equivalent of the English word, he or she obviously cannot demonstrate his or her ability to handle the structures of the language. Thus, in testing the language proficiency of beginners or intermediate students, the teacher obtains more valid results in testing vocabulary and structure separately.

The dictation is another traditional test eliciting a written response. During the 1960s, its role in second-language evaluation was played down, for testing specialists felt that it measured more than one skill. Now the dictation is finding new favor among those engaged in testing research, for it seems to provide a global measure of language proficiency.

With the strong current interest in communicative competence and the focus on self-expression, teachers are beginning to make heavier use of written tests of communication. In tests of this sort, the mastery of the elements of language, and specifically spelling, is of secondary importance. (Even native speakers make spelling mistakes.) Attention is focused on the content: Is the message clear and unambiguous? Is the paragraph well organized? Is the choice of words appropriate to the context? Could a native speaker understand the text without difficulty? Obviously communication tests are not as objective in their scoring as the short-answer tests of the elements of language. However, a carefully planned scoring system will increase the scorer reliability. The key consideration is validity, and written communication tests definitely test the ability to write.

8.2   THE WRITING SYSTEM

In order to write a foreign language, the student must first be familiar with the alphabet or characters in which that language is transcribed. Since the most commonly taught languages, such as Spanish, French, and German, employ the Roman alphabet, the student must learn only certain accent marks or an occasional new letter or digraph. If the target language is Russian, a greatly modified alphabet must be learned; in the case of Chinese, a new and voluminous set of characters is to be mastered. The assimilation of these mechanical aspects of writing entails practice and drill.

If the second language uses the same alphabet as the native language, the student must learn to master a new spelling system. Letters and groups of letters in the target language may represent sounds entirely different from those they represent in the native language.

8.2.1   Copying

The student is graded on his or her accuracy in copying characters or sentences. The teacher must be extremely strict in demanding a legible copy. Both spelling and punctuation should be checked.

SAMPLE ITEM TYPE *1*   SCRIPT WRITING—ACCURACY

The student is given a printed sentence that he or she is to copy in script.

SAMPLE ITEM TYPE *2*   SCRIPT WRITING—SPEED

The students are given a limited period (perhaps three minutes) in which to copy a printed paragraph or paragraphs in script. A student who finishes before time is called should begin copying the paragraph again. The work is graded on the basis of the length of the material copied and accuracy.

8.2.2 Spelling tests

In the spelling test, the teacher reads the words or phrases that the student is to write. At the elementary level, it is essential that the student be familiar with the text so that no problem of comprehension exists. In languages like English, where each word has a single spelling independent of its grammatical function, spelling tests usually take the form of lists of words in isolation. In languages like French, where a word may have several spellings, depending on its use in a sentence, spelling tests generally consist of dictations.

To provide the desirable reinforcement, these spelling tests should be corrected immediately; good results are often obtained by having the students exchange papers with one another. To save class time, the teacher could distribute mimeographed copies of the test or raise a wall chart to uncover the correct words or phrases, written before class on the blackboard.

SAMPLE ITEM TYPE *3*   WORD LISTS—WITHOUT CONTEXT

The teacher reads a list of words that the students are to write down. Often each word is read twice, followed by a pause for writing. At the end of the list, the entire set of words is read rapidly one final time. It is important that the teacher state in advance how often each word is to be read, and then not deviate from this method.

You will hear each word twice. Write it out the second time you hear it.

1. animal # animal #
2. bear # bear #

SAMPLE ITEM TYPE *4*   WORD LISTS—WITH CONTEXT

The teacher reads each word alone, and then places it in a sentence context.

1. animal # The lion is a large animal. # animal #
2. bear # The bear is also an animal. # bear #

NOTE: The sentence context helps clarify homonyms. For instance, bare #
His feet were bare. # bare. #

SAMPLE ITEM TYPE 5   SPOT DICTATION

The spot dictation tests the spelling of words in context. It also permits
the testing of grammatical forms and homonyms.

1. The lion is an _____ that lives in the jungle.
2. The tiger lives in the jungle _____.

You will hear each sentence read twice. Then fill in the missing words.

1. The lion is an animal that lives in the jungle. (repeat) #
2. The tiger lives in the jungle too. (repeat) #

SAMPLE ITEM TYPE 6   FULL DICTATION

The teacher reads a familiar paragraph or set of dialog lines. Usually the
entire text is read once, and then reread slowly with pauses for the students
to write out what they hear. At the end of the dictation, the entire text is
read once more. When dictations are used as spelling tests, the text to be
used is announced in advance so that students can study it.[2]

8.2.3   Punctuation tests

Sometimes the target language has unfamiliar punctuation marks, or uses
punctuation differently from the native language. In punctuation tests, the
student is asked to supply missing punctuation and capital letters.

SAMPLE ITEM TYPE 7   WRITTEN PUNCTUATION TEST

Rewrite the following sentence, adding punctuation and capital letters
where needed.

(English) my uncle writes that henry has just finished a good book called
gone with the wind
(German) meine mutter sagt dass   *My mother says that you know*
   du weisst wo die bücher sind   *where the books are.*

Correct responses: My uncle writes that Henry has just finished a good book
                   called *Gone with the Wind.*
                   Meine Mutter sagt, dass du weisst, wo die Bücher sind.

_____

[2] For suggestions on the scoring of dictations, see Section 8.5.3.

SAMPLE ITEM TYPE *8*   DICTATED PUNCTUATION TESTS

You will hear each sentence read twice. Complete the sentence on your answer sheet by adding the appropriate punctuation marks.

(Spanish) Sí ... Caramba ... Por qué no se lo aceptaste Tonto

Really? Blast it! Why didn't you accept it, stupid?

Correct response: ¿Sí? ... ¡Caramba! ... ¿Por qué no se lo aceptaste? ¡Tonto!

8.3 TESTING VOCABULARY VIA WRITING

The ability to write a foreign language presupposes a knowledge of the lexical units of the language. In this sense, a lexical unit is a word or group of words possessing a specific meaning. Just as one word can have different meanings in different contexts, so may that word represent several lexical units. Consider the following example in English:

Joe belongs to the human *race*.
Joe went to the dog *race*.
Joe and Sam *race* each other.
Joe and Sam *race* across the room and out the door.
Joe and Sam *race* their turtles.

The effective vocabulary test should be constructed around lexical units rather than words.

Written vocabulary tests evaluate the student's ability to recall and to produce lexical units in the new language. Vocabulary items may be developed for use in conjunction with visual, printed, or oral cues.

8.3.1 Picture tests

Visual cues, while particularly effective in the elementary school, may be profitably used at all levels of instruction. If stick figures or simplified line drawings have been used in class, they may also be used in vocabulary tests. Pictures may be cut from magazines and mounted on cards. Care must be taken to avoid the possibility of an ambiguous interpretation of a picture; if necessary, scoring can be modified to allow a certain range of correct responses. The visual cue may also be accompanied by a written cue to focus student attention on the specific lexical unit to be furnished.

SAMPLE ITEM TYPE *9* PICTURE TEST—LABELS

Look at the following picture and write out the names of the parts of the car.

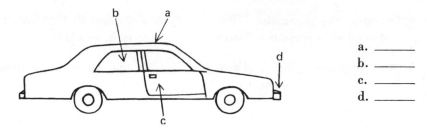

a. _____
b. _____
c. _____
d. _____

Correct responses: roof; window; door; bumper

SAMPLE ITEM TYPE *10* PICTURE TEST—SHORT QUESTIONS

Answer the questions according to the pictures.

(French)

Cue:

Qu'est-ce que c'est?   *What is it?*
Response: une maison (la maison   *a house; the house; It's a house.*
   or C'est une maison.)

(Spanish)

Cue:

¿Qué hace?   *What is he doing?*
Response: Duerme.   *He's sleeping.*

The cue question can also be worded so that students must furnish the infinitive. For example:

Qu'est-ce qu'il aime faire?   *What does he like to do?*
Response: Dormir.   *Sleep.*

SAMPLE ITEM TYPE *11* PICTURE TEST—COMPLETION ITEMS

Pictures or diagrams may be used to define prepositions directly and unambiguously. If only the meaning of prepositions is to be tested, then a written cue should be included.

Here is a sample item in French:

Cue:

Le chapeau est _____ la chaise.   *The hat is on the chair.*
Response: sur

In an inflected language such as German, the same item could require the use of the appropriate article; in this case the gender of the word *chair* should be given unless everyone is totally familiar with the word. For example:

Cue: Da ist der Stuhl.   *There is the chair. My hat is*
    Mein Hut ist _____   *on the chair.*
    Stuhl.
Response: auf dem

SAMPLE ITEM TYPE *12*   PICTURE WRITING

With picture writing, test items can be developed in which the students' performance will be measured independently of their listening and reading skills. In addition, the students will not have recourse to their native language. The system of ideograms has been briefly described in Section 6.5. Once the students know the symbols, they will be able to understand the ideogram easily; the test will then evaluate only their proficiency in writing.

Here are two sample items in English:

The school is far from here.

The hospital is three kilometers from here. (The symbol × means here; ←· · ·→ means far.)

The school is near the church.

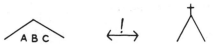

The school is very near the church; (↔ is near; ! means very).[3]

[3] See *TAVOR Aids Bulletin*, No. 5 (May 1966), p. 2.

8.3.2   Vocabulary out of context

Although vocabulary is generally taught in context and should consequently also be tested in context, it is sometimes expedient to test vocabulary knowledge out of context.

SAMPLE ITEM TYPE *13*   SERIES COMPLETION

Write in the word that completes the series.

(French) lundi, mardi, _____, jeudi	*Monday, Tuesday . . . Thursday*
(Spanish) febrero, _____, abril	*February . . . April*
(German) achtzehn, neunzehn, _____	*eighteen, nineteen . . .*

Correct responses: mercredi; marzo; zwanzig

SAMPLE ITEM TYPE *14*   SYNONYMS AND ANTONYMS

Write a word or expression similar in meaning to the word given.

(German)	Cue: Gewiß!	*certainly*
	Response: Sicher!	*sure*

Write a word or expression whose meaning is the opposite of the word given.

(Spanish)	Cue: oscuro	*dark*
	Response: claro	*bright*
(German)	Cue: schwer	*heavy; difficult*
	Response: leicht	*light; easy*

SAMPLE ITEM TYPE *15*   WORD FAMILIES

As the students continue their language instruction, they learn to recognize related words. Vocabulary items can assess their ability to produce related forms.

(German) Give the related nouns.

Cue: dumm	*stupid*
Response: die Dummheit	*stupidity*
Cue: pünktlich	*punctual*
Response: die Pünktlichkeit	*punctualness*

(Spanish) Give the related verbs.

Cue: narración	*narration*
Response: narrar	*to tell a story, to narrate*
Cue: sonriente	*smiling*
Response: sonreír	*to smile*

(French) Give the related adjectives.

Cue: salir	*to make dirty*
Response: sale	*dirty*
Cue: fausser	*to falsify*
Response: faux	*false*

SAMPLE ITEM TYPE *16*   TARGET-LANGUAGE DEFINITIONS

Items of this sort should only be used with students who read the target language easily: the difficulty should lie in the production of the desired word and not in the comprehension of the definition.

Write the words that correspond to the following definitions:

(English)   Cue: an instrument used to remove the cork from a bottle of wine
          Response: corkscrew

(French)   Cue: Qu'emploie-t-on   *What do you use to cut meat?*
          pour couper la
          viande?
          Response: un couteau   *a knife*

SAMPLE ITEM TYPE *17*   NATIVE-LANGUAGE EQUIVALENTS

Many teachers avoid items of this sort because of their lack of context and their tendency to make students feel that a one-to-one correspondence exists between words in the target language and their native language.

Give the French equivalent of the following words:

     Cue: can opener
Response: un ouvre-boîte

Such items can be improved by providing a situational context.

Imagine you are in Paris. An American friend has arrived and she wants to purchase a few items at the neighborhood hardware store. Tell her the names of the following objects in French:

1. a broom
2. a frying-pan
3. sponges

Correct responses: un balai; une poêle; des éponges

SAMPLE ITEM TYPE *18*   COGNATES

At the initial stages in foreign language instruction, emphasis is on recognizing cognate patterns. Gradually, however, students learn, under guidance, how to generate cognates in the target language. In preparing items of this type, the teacher must be sure that the students are indeed able to produce the desired cognates and that no unexpected spelling changes will be encountered.

Write out the equivalent French verbs.

1. animate
2. agitate
3. navigate

Correct responses: animer, agiter, naviguer

NOTE: In the above example, students may have difficulty producing "naviguer" unless they realize that the "gu" spelling is needed to maintain the "hard" sound /g/.

8.3.3   Vocabulary in context

Pedagogically it is more effective to test vocabulary knowledge by providing or requesting an appropriate sentence context for the item under consideration.

SAMPLE ITEM TYPE *19*   SYNONYMS IN SENTENCE CONTEXT

Rewrite the following sentences, replacing the underlined words with appropriate synonyms.

(French)   Cue: Marie est   *Marie is happy.*
                     contente.
             Response: Marie est
                     heureuse.

Variation: Complete the second sentence with the synonym of the underlined word.

Marie est <u>contente</u>. Marie est _____.

Items of the type shown, could be scored 1 point for choice of word and 1 point for accuracy in spelling and adjective agreement.

SAMPLE ITEM TYPE *20*   SYNONYMS IN SITUATIONAL CONTEXT

Harry hates repeating words. Complete each of his statements by providing a synonym for the underlined expression.

"We have to leave <u>immediately</u>. Hurry up! If we don't go _____ we will miss the beginning of the film."

Correct response: right away

SAMPLE ITEM TYPE *21*   ANTONYMS IN SENTENCE CONTEXT

Rewrite the sentences below, giving the antonyms of the underlined words.

(French)   Cue: Sa tasse est   *His cup is empty.*
                  <u>vide</u>.
            Response: Sa tasse est   *His cup is full.*
                  pleine.

SAMPLE ITEM TYPE *22*   ANTONYMS IN SITUATIONAL CONTEXT

The following sets of fraternal twins have little in common. Fill in the description of the second twin with the antonym of the underlined word.

1. Paul is <u>tall</u>, but Paula is _____.
2. Robert is <u>fat</u>, but Roberta is _____.

Correct responses: short; thin

SAMPLE ITEM TYPE *23*   CONTEXTUAL DEFINITIONS

Complete the following sentences:

(French)   Cue: J'emploie mon   *I use my knife to _____ the*
                  couteau pour   *meat.*
                  _____ la
                  viande.
            Response: couper   *cut*

SAMPLE ITEM TYPE *24* SENTENCE CONSTRUCTION

Use each of the following words in a sentence that shows that you understand its meaning.

(German)   Cue: klopfen   *to knock*
        Response: Der Mann   *The man is knocking at the door.*
        klopft an die
        Tür.

NOTE: Items of this type are more appropriate for intermediate and advanced students. Each item should be assigned 2 points: 1 for comprehension and 1 for accuracy of expression. If desired, the student might receive two separate grades on the test.

Variation: Construct as many sentences as you can using the suggested words as different lexical units.

(French)   Cue: compte
        Responses: Jean compte   *Jean is counting his money.*
        son argent.
        Marie compte   *Marie plans to come tonight.*
        venir ce soir.
        Il a écrit son   *He wrote his paper.*
        compte rendu.
        Tout compte   *All in all, he had a good time.*
        fait, il s'est
        bien amusé.

SAMPLE ITEM TYPE *25* PARAPHRASING

Reword the following sentences according to the instructions:

1. (increase the intensity) The noise was too loud.
2. (lessen the intensity) That was a stupid response.

Correct responses: 1. It was a deafening noise. The noise broke my eardrums. Etc.
               2. That was not a very good response. That was a poor response. Etc.

SAMPLE ITEM TYPE *26* NATIVE LANGUAGE EQUIVALENTS

Vocabulary translation tests are most effective when both the native language and the target language expressions are given in context. Such items are particularly effective for testing knowledge of adverbs, conjunctions, and idiomatic expressions. They may also be used for testing false cognates and other difficult lexical problems.

Complete the second sentence of each pair with the appropriate expression.

1. (French)
   Jean is coming as soon as possible.
   Jean vient _____ possible.

Correct response: aussitôt que

2. (Spanish)
   He's not tall, but short.
   No es alto _____ bajo.

Correct response: sino

3. (German: false cognate)
   He wants to become a soldier.
   Er will Soldat _____.

Correct response: werden

4. (French: two equivalents of the English word "rather")
   Jeanne was rather sad, but tried to hide her feelings.
   Jeanne était _____ triste, mais elle essayait de cacher ses sentiments.

Correct response: assez

   I'd rather go to the movies than to the theater.
   J'aimerais _____ aller au cinéma qu'au théâtre.

Correct response: mieux (or plutôt)

NOTE: It is sounder linguistically to present the native-language sentence first and then the incomplete equivalent in the foreign language rather than mix a native-language word in parentheses with the target-language sentence. The students are able to grasp the entire idea in their own language before formulating the equivalent idea in the target language. Moreover, such items serve to reinforce the correct native-to-target-language correspondence between the other elements in the sentence.

8.4   TESTING GRAMMAR VIA WRITING

Written grammar items are the staple of most elementary and intermediate classroom tests. Items of this sort, however, should be used in moderation. First, the teacher should realize that written grammar tests do not evaluate the students' ability to use the written language as a medium of personal communication (see Sections 8.7 and 8.8). Second, the teacher whose course stresses the development of all four language skills will want to make adequate allowance for testing grammar via listening and speaking.

8.4.1   Completion items

Completion items ask the student to furnish the missing elements in a sentence. As much as possible, this writing activity should resemble a natural and normal use of language. The following guidelines will help the teacher improve his or her completion items:

a. Completion sentences are *not* sentences written in a mixture of the two languages. Nothing more effectively defeats the goals of contemporary language classes and the intentions of any language teacher eager to have the students develop fluency in the target language than hybrid sentences such as: Ich gehe _____ (home). Nous _____ (have just bought) une maison. Haga el favor de _____ (study) la lección.
If the native language must be used to cue the correct completion, then entire sentences should be used: (I am going home.) Ich gehe _____. (We have just bought a house.) Nous _____ une maison. (Please study the lesson.) Haga el favor de _____ la lección. (See Section 8.4.3.)

b. Especially at the elementary levels, it is better to avoid completion items in which the verb to be employed is presented in the infinitive, such as: Pierre _____ (venir) chez moi. Student dependence on the infinitive is unnatural and should not be encouraged.

c. The sentences should be presented in a meaningful situational context. If possible, the sequence of completion items should read as a paragraph or conversation.

The following sample item types are frequently presented in isolation. On a classroom test, several such items would be grouped with one set of instructions.

SAMPLE ITEM TYPE *27*   PICTURE CUES

Certain grammatical elements, such as descriptive adjectives, can be tested in completion items using picture cues.

Complete the following sentences according to the pictures:

(German)

Cue:

Hier ist ein _____ Hut und da liegt ein weißer Hut.

Response: schwarzer

Here is a black hat and there is a white hat.

(French)

Cue:

Jean est grand, mais sa mère est _____ que lui.

Response: plus grande

Jean is tall, but his mother is taller than he is.

SAMPLE ITEM TYPE *28*   PREFIXES AND ENDINGS

This type of writing test tends to be artificial and should be used, if at all, only with advanced students.

Here are some sample items:

Fill in the blanks in the following sentences:

1. Nous sommes all_____ en ville.   *We went downtown.*
2. Die Kinder geh_____ zur Schule.   *The children are going to school.*
3. Los automóviles blanc_____ son de los Estados Unidos.   *The white cars are from the United States.*

Correct responses: allé(e)s, gehen, blancos

SAMPLE ITEM TYPE *29*   FUNCTION WORDS

Entire words may be left out of sentences if the student can easily deduce which elements must be added. However, this type of item should not be reduced to a guessing game or an exercise in puzzle-solving. The sentences could be composed to form an entire paragraph.

Here are some isolated sample items:

1. Chantal veut aller _____ Etats-Unis.   *Chantal wants to go to the United States.*
2. Die Frau hat eine schlimme Wunde _____ Kopf.   *The lady has a bad cut on her head.*
3. Son _____ diez menos cuarto.   *It is quarter to ten.*
4. Sandro ha fatto _____ viaggio molto bello.   *Sandro made a magnificent trip.*

Correct responses: aux, am, las, uno

SAMPLE ITEM TYPE *30*   VERBS

Complete the following conversation with the appropriate forms of *prendre*.

Garçon: Qu'est-ce que vous _____?   *Waiter: What are you having?*
Paul: Moi, je _____ un café.   *Paul: I'm having a cup of coffee.*
  Chantal _____ un café aussi,   *Chantal is having coffee too,*
  et Claire va _____ une bière.   *and Claire is going to have a*
                                            glass of beer.

Robert: Marc et moi, nous _____   *Robert: Marc and I are having*
  un Coca-cola. Quant à Eric et   *Coke. As for Eric and Anne,*
  Anne, ils _____ toujours du thé.   *they always have tea.*

Correct responses: prenez; prends; prend; prendre; prenons; prennent

SAMPLE ITEM TYPE *31*   PHRASES OR CLAUSES

In items of this type, a phrase or clause is omitted and the student is given the words to be used in finishing the sentence. The missing part of the sentence is sometimes referred to as a "dehydrated clause" or a "frozen clause." Such items are very effective for testing word order and sequence of tenses.

Here are some sample items:

1. J'ai peur que _____   *I am afraid that Marie is*
   (Marie / venir / maintenant)   *coming now.*
2. Ich weiß, daß _____   *I know that Father is sick.*
   (Vater / sein / krank)
3. En realidad José era un   *In reality José was a man who*
   hombre _____ (preferir /   *preferred doing nothing.*
   hacer / nada)

Possible responses: Marie ne vienne maintenant; Vater krank ist; que prefirió no hacer nada

8.4.2   Directed sentences

An important step in the acquisition of the writing skill is learning to write sentences. At first this practice is carefully structured so that the students will produce accurate and natural sentences. Most oral classroom drills may be adapted to written testing. As students progress in language ability, they are asked to construct more difficult sentences within predetermined limits. The following sample items show how exercises may be used in written classroom tests.

SAMPLE ITEM TYPE *32*   SIMPLE SUBSTITUTION

Replace the underlined words with the expression in parentheses.

(French) Je vais <u>en ville</u>.   *I am going <u>downtown</u>.*
    (à la campagne)   (*to the country*)

Correct response: Je vais à la campagne.

In written format, these items are primarily copying exercises for elementary students. This type of item may be made more difficult by administering the cues orally. Since comprehension should pose no problem, the student is free to concentrate on spelling.

SAMPLE ITEM TYPE *33*   CORRELATION

In items of this type, the student replaces one element in the sentence and subsequently must effect other changes.

Replace the underlined words with the expression in parentheses. Make any other necessary changes.

(French: changes in the verb)
<u>Il</u> mange du pain. (nous)   *<u>He</u> is eating bread. (we)*

Correct response: Nous mangeons du pain.

(German: changes in the determiner)

Wo ist der <u>Hund</u>? (Katze)   *Where is the <u>dog</u>? (cat)*
Seine <u>Mutter</u> kam schnell. (Vater) *His <u>mother</u> came quickly. (father)*

Correct responses: Wo ist die Katze? Sein Vater kam schnell.

(Spanish: changes in adjective position)

Este es un <u>buen</u> libro. (español)   *This is a <u>good</u> book. (Spanish)*

Correct response: Este es un libro español.

(German: changes in case)

Fritz kommt <u>mit</u> seiner Schwester.   *Fritz is coming <u>with</u> his sister.*
    (ohne)   (*without*)

Correct response: Fritz kommt ohne seine Schwester.

SAMPLE ITEM TYPE *34* MODIFIED SUBSTITUTION

Here the students must modify the new element before substituting it in the sentence. Sometimes the change also necessitates a different word order.

(English) Joan <u>read</u> the book. (put away)

Correct response: Joan put the book away.

(German) Er <u>brachte</u> die Butter.   *He brought the butter.*
  (wegnehmen)   *(take away)*

Correct response: Er nahm die Butter weg.

SAMPLE ITEM TYPE *35* PRONOUNS

Replace the underlined nouns or noun phrases with the appropriate pronouns.

(French) Il donne <u>le livre à Pierre.</u>   *He is giving <u>the book to Pierre.</u>*

Correct response: Il le lui donne.

SAMPLE ITEM TYPE *36* TRANSFORMATION

In items of this type, students are asked to transform sentences according to a specific pattern. Although the suggested items are single sentences, the teacher may want to arrange items of this type into a situational context. Situational directions are given in parentheses for each example.

(French: number) Change the following sentences from the singular to the plural. (Copycats: Paul and Yves are doing what their big brother Simon does. Read Simon's activities and then write out Paul and Yves' activities.)

Simon regarde la télévision.   *Simon is watching television.*
Il mange un sandwich.   *He is eating a sandwich.*

Correct response: Paul et Yves regardent la télévision. Ils mangent un sandwich.

(German: word order) Rewrite the following sentences, beginning with the underlined word. (Kid sister: To tease her brother, Monika likes to repeat his sentences and turn them around. Write out her responses beginning with the underlined word.)

Ich weiß nicht, <u>wie</u> sie es macht.   *I don't know <u>how</u> she does it.*

Correct response: Wie sie es macht, weiß ich nicht.

(English: tense) Rewrite the following sentences in the past tense. (When Mary visited London, she did all the things her sister Linda had done last year. Read Mary's activities, and then write out what Linda did, using the past tense.)

Mary arrives at Heathrow Airport. She goes through customs.

Correct response: Linda arrived at Heathrow Airport. She went through customs.

(English: negative) Rewrite the following sentences in the negative. (Out of luck: Betty has none of the advantages that Nancy does. Describe Betty's position.)

Nancy has a rich uncle. She is going to Bermuda for spring vacation.

Correct responses: Betty doesn't have a rich uncle. She's not going to Bermuda for spring vacation.

(Spanish: interrogative) Rewrite the following sentences in the interrogative. (Curiosity: You will hear what Pablo is doing. Ask whether José is doing the same things.)

Pablo irá al concierto.   *Pablo is going to the concert.*

Correct response: ¿Irá José al concierto?

SAMPLE ITEM TYPE *37*   OBEYING COMMANDS

Items of this type test primarily word order and verb forms. Complex commands can necessitate changes in pronouns.

Here are two sample items in French:

1. Dites à Madame Lasalle de   *Tell Madame Lasalle not to get*
   ne pas se lever.   *up.*
   Ne vous levez pas, Madame.   *Don't get up, Ma'am.*
2. Dites à Pierre qu'il vous rendra *Tell Pierre that he will give you*
   le journal ce soir.   *back the paper this evening.*
   Tu me rendras le journal ce soir. *You will give me back the paper*
                                     this evening.

SAMPLE ITEM TYPE *38*   JOINING SENTENCES

The students' ability to use conjunctions and relative pronouns, as well as their understanding of verb tenses, modes, and word order, can be evaluated with the following type of written test. The students are given two independent statements and are asked to join them into one complex or compound sentence.

Here are some sample items in French using the indicative and the subjunctive:

Rewrite each pair of sentences as a single sentence. Where appropriate, use the expression in parentheses.

1. Je suis certain. Paul viendra à deux heures.

   Je suis certain que Paul viendra à deux heures.

   I am sure. Paul will come at two.

   I am sure that Paul will come at two.

2. Je suis content. Pierre va à l'école.

   Je suis content que Pierre aille à l'école.

   I am happy. Pierre is going to school.

   I am happy that Pierre is going to school.

3. J'aide ma sœur. Elle peut finir son travail.   (pour que)

   J'aide ma sœur pour qu'elle puisse finir son travail.

   I help my sister. She can finish her work.   (so that)

   I help my sister so that she can finish her work.

4. Nous n'y allons pas. Il fait trop froid.   (parce que)

   Nous n'y allons pas parce qu'il fait trop froid.

   We are not going. It is too cold. (because)

   We are not going because it's too cold.

Items of this type are also effective for testing the use of relative pronouns:

Mr. Harris is a teacher. His exams are very difficult.

Mr. Harris is a teacher whose exams are very difficult.

SAMPLE ITEM TYPE *39*   DIRECTED ANSWERS

Question-answer items, in which the proper response is suggested to the student, offer still another variation of the brief writing-test item that can be easily and objectively scored.

Question-answer items lend themselves equally well to oral and to written presentation. If only one element is to be tested, each item must be carefully checked to remove any words that would require an additional transformation. In other instances, it might prove valuable to examine several aspects of the language in the same item.

The following questions in French show how different elements can enter into the answers.

1. (negative: word order)

   Votre mère arrive-t-elle ce matin?   (non)

   Non, elle n'arrive pas ce matin.

   Does your mother arrive this morning?

   No, she doesn't arrive this morning.

2. (negative: partitive)

Désirez-vous de l'eau? (non, merci)	*Would you like water?*
Non, merci, je ne désire pas d'eau.	*No thanks, I don't want any water.*

3. (verb forms)

Lisez-vous ce roman? (oui)	*Are you reading this novel?*
Oui, je lis ce roman. (*or* Oui, nous lisons ce roman.)	*Yes, I'm reading this novel. or Yes, we're reading this novel.*

4. (pronouns)

A-t-il écrit cette lettre à son frère? (non)	*Did he write that letter to his brother?*
Non, il ne la lui a pas écrite.	*No, he didn't write it to him.*

NOTE: The item shown tests pronoun forms, word order, and the agreement of the past participle.

The English equivalents above sound somewhat stilted, for French does not have the short answer forms: No, she doesn't. No, I don't. Yes, I am. No, he didn't.

5. (prepositions)

Où allez-vous cet été? (Canada)	*Where are you going this summer?*
Je vais au Canada. (*or* Nous allons au Canada.)	*I'm going to Canada. or We are going to Canada.*

SAMPLE ITEM TYPE *40* DIRECTED QUESTIONS

Items of this type are similar to the previous ones, except that the student is given the response and is asked to write out the related question.

Write out the questions that would give you the following answer. The underlined word represents the information you are looking for.

1. J'aime le livre <u>bleu</u>.	*I like the <u>blue</u> book.*
Quel livre aimez-vous?	*Which book do you like?*
2. Marie a <u>cinq</u> ans.	*Marie is <u>five</u> years old.*
Quel âge a Marie?	*How old is Marie?*
3. J'écris avec <u>mon stylo</u>.	*I am writing with <u>my pen</u>.*
Avec quoi écrivez-vous?	*What are you writing with?*

NOTE: This type of item can be integrated into a "hard-of-hearing" situation. Grandmother is eighty-five and never hears the end of your statements. Write out the questions she would ask.

SAMPLE ITEM TYPE *41*   SENTENCE CONSTRUCTION

An effective writing test may be created with "dehydrated" or "frozen" sentences. The students are to construct a sentence from a selected group of nouns, pronouns, adjectives, verbs, and adverbs. Nouns and pronouns would be given in the nominative; verbs would appear in the infinitive form. Thus, a sample item in French would look like this:

Cue: hier / tante / aller / église

Response: Hier ma tante est allée   *Yesterday my aunt went to*
à l'église.   *church.*

In a more highly inflected language, such as German, this type of test permits effective examination of the students' grasp of a large variety of morphological forms.

Cue: gestern / groß / Mann / gehen / Stadt

Response: Gestern ist der große   *Yesterday the tall man went into*
Mann in die Stadt   *town.*
gegangen.

It is also possible to furnish a model sentence and then provide a set of elements to be incorporated into a similar sentence. Here is a sample item in Spanish:

Model: Ha venido para que yo   *He came so that I could help him.*
lo ayude.
Cue: llegar / sin que / tú / la / llamer
Response: Ha llegado sin que tú   *She came without your calling her.*
la llames.

Sentence-construction items constitute an excellent test for students of junior-high age or over. Most students enjoy the challenge such a test provides. Moreover, it reproduces the problems the student faces writing in the target language with the aid of a dictionary.

From the examiner's point of view, such a test may be scored objectively, and the scores are reliable because it removes the stumbling block that traditional translation tests create for the students with poor vocabulary recall. If there is only one acceptable way of writing out the "dehydrated" sentence, a scoring system may be devised where each element of the sentence is assigned a specific number of points. For example:

hier / tante / aller / église

Hier ma tante (1) est (2) allée (3) à l'église (4).

1. 1 point for appropriate determiner: feminine singular
2. 1 point for correct auxiliary: est
3. 2 points for correct past participle: 1 point for allé; 1 point for ending
4. 1 point for appropriate preposition and article

Total points for sentence: 5

However, if there are several acceptable sentences, it is easier to assign a global score to each item. For example:

tante / aller / église / prier

Ma tante va à l'église pour prier.	*My aunt goes to church to pray.*
Quand ma tante va à l'église, elle prie.	*When my aunt goes to church, she prays.*
Si ma tante pouvait aller à l'église, elle pricrait.	*If my aunt were able to go to church, she would pray.*
Il faut que ma tante aille à l'église pour prier.	*My aunt has to go to church to pray.*

Here, the teacher might assign 4 points globally to each sentence.

8.4.3   Sentence translation

Many teachers find that translation items do not fit in with their course objectives. However, translation items may be used effectively to test grammatical problems where the native-language structures seem to interfere with proper use of the target language.

Another drawback of translation sentences is that some students may not perform well because they cannot recall the needed vocabulary. The recall problem can be minimized by providing students with needed words and expressions in a separate "test glossary."

SAMPLE ITEM TYPE *42*   PARTIAL SENTENCE TRANSLATION

Complete the sentences below so that they correspond to the English (French) equivalents.

(German) The lady you met is my mother.
        Die Dame, _____, ist meine Mutter.

Correct response: die Sie getroffen haben

(Spanish) I wonder what time it is?
        ¿Qué hora _____ ?

Correct response: será

(English) Quand tu viendras, apporte-moi un verre d'eau.
     When you _____, bring me a glass of water.

Correct response: come

NOTE: The equivalent sentences in the native language and the target language help reinforce proper correspondences between the two languages. Moreover, they allow the teacher to focus student attention on the trouble spots without introducing other elements such as vocabulary.

SAMPLE ITEM TYPE 43   FULL SENTENCE TRANSLATION

Translate the following sentences into French. (Situational context: You are in Paris with a friend. He asks you how to say certain things in French. Write out your replies.)

Your friend:	You tell him:
How do you say...	
You're right!	_____
I need a guide.	_____

Correct responses: Vous avez raison! J'ai besoin d'un guide.

8.4.4   Intellectualization of grammar

Items of this type correspond to those described in Section 7.4.2. While the student in the reading test was instructed to recognize ungrammatical sentences, in the writing test the student is to produce only grammatical utterances.

SAMPLE ITEM TYPE 44   TRANSFORMATION TEST

Transform the sentences below so that the subject of the infinitive appears a. as an antecedent of a relative clause, and/or b. as the subject of a dependent clause. Write only grammatically correct sentences.

1. J'entends chanter l'enfant.   *I hear the child sing.*
   Responses: a. J'entends l'enfant   *I hear the child who is singing.*
              qui chante.
           b. J'entends que l'enfant   *I hear that the child is singing.*
              chante.

2. Elle regarde jouer l'enfant.   *She watches the child play.*
   Response: a. Elle regarde l'enfant   *She watches the child who is*
             qui joue.   *playing.*

8.5 DICTATION

Dictation, in which the student transcribes a passage he hears read (live or on tape), is used to some extent by almost all language teachers. In beginning classes, exercises in dictation give the student practice in associating the sounds of the new language with their written form. They are employed, as we have seen, in effecting the transition from the listening and speaking skills to the reading and writing skills and can be considered spelling tests.

With intermediate and advanced students, the dictation provides a measure of overall language proficiency.[4] Its ease of administration and scoring makes it an excellent instrument to evaluate year-end performance or to group incoming students according to ability levels. Oller also found that the student errors on a dictation lend themselves to a diagnosis of areas where further work is needed.

8.5.1 Kinds of dictations

Two types of dictations are used in the foreign language classroom.

SAMPLE ITEM TYPE *45*   SPOT DICTATION

In a spot dictation, or partial dictation, the student receives a printed copy of a passage in which certain words and phrases have been omitted. As the passage is read, the student fills in the blanks. Such dictations, while necessitating a certain amount of advance preparation, have two distinct advantages. First, they can be administered more rapidly and scored more objectively than conventional dictations. Second, they permit the teacher to test only the problem areas; students do not waste time writing words and phrases that they already handle relatively accurately.

SAMPLE ITEM TYPE *46*   FULL DICTATION

On a full dictation, the student writes out the entire passage. This type of dictation is somewhat longer to administer and score than the spot dictation, but it provides a more valid measure of overall language ability.

[4] Valette found that unless students receive a great deal of dictation work in class, the score on a final dictation correlates highly with the score on a full-length examination testing the skills of listening, reading and writing. See R. Valette, "The Use of the *Dictée* in the French Language Classroom," *Modern Language Journal* 48 (November 1964), pp. 431–34. More recently Oller has found dictation in English to be a good test of overall language ability for incoming foreign students at the college level. See J. W. Oller, "Discrete-Point Tests versus Tests of Integrative Skills" in John W. Oller, Jr. and Jack C. Richards, eds., *Focus on the Learner: Pragmatic Perspectives for the Language Teacher* (Rowley, Mass.: Newbury House, 1973), pp. 194–97.

NOTE: Dictations given primarily to test mastery of the writing skill are usually based on prepared selections, such as a textbook dialog or reading; dictations used to evaluate general proficiency are taken from texts that are unfamiliar to the students.

8.5.2   Giving the dictation

When a test dictation is given, certain precautions must be taken to make sure that the test is always administered in the same manner. Only in this way can the teacher make valid comparisons between the performances of different classes or of the same student on different occasions.

Here is one effective technique of administering a test dictation. First, the whole passage is read at normal speed. The students are told not to write, just to listen carefully. Then the passage is read a phrase at a time, with pauses during which the students write down what they have heard. At this time the teacher may read each phrase either once or twice, as long as he or she is consistent. (At the teacher's discretion, punctuation marks may be given in the target language.) Finally, the entire passage is read again at normal speed, and the students are given a few minutes for final revision. It is imperative that the teacher *never* repeat a particular phrase at a student's request.

The dictation may also be administered in the language laboratory. If the tape is to be played from a master console, the dictation script should be prerecorded in the described manner.

8.5.3   Scoring the dictation

In scoring dictations the teacher should realize that the major consideration is not so much the manner in which points are assigned, but rather the consistent use of a given scoring system.

8.5.3a   SCORING BY WORDS

The basic unit of scoring can be the individual printed word. Only one error per word should be counted, for the student who omits a word should not be penalized less than the one who tries to write the word and makes several mistakes. Various word-unit scoring systems exist. The most common include:

1. 1 point off for each incorrect or omitted word;
2. $\frac{1}{2}$ point off for each recognizable word with a spelling error, 1 point off for each omitted or unrecognizable word;

3. $\frac{1}{4}$ point off for a wrong or omitted accent, $\frac{1}{2}$ point off for a misspelled but recognizable word, 1 point off for each omitted or unrecognizable word;

4. like 3, but with 1 point off for a word containing a morphological error, such as an incorrect verb or adjective ending.

Generally a recurring word consistently misspelled counts as only one error.

System 1 places the emphasis on perfection: the student who has a word *almost* right receives no more credit than the student who omitted the word. Systems 3 and 4 are more detailed, and scoring according to these systems takes more time. It is recommended that the teacher select one system and employ it for all dictations so that by comparing performances he or she may reliably assess the progress of the class and the improvement of the individual student during the semester or year.

8.5.3b SCORING BY PHRASES

On the scorer's copy, the dictation may be divided into words or phrases. Within this framework, scoring variations may be devised similar to systems 1 through 4 above.

Here is a sample in French:

Hier* / nous avons vu / nos grands-parents / qui demeurent / à la campagne. / J'ai joué / avec mon cousin, / Henri,* / qui aime jouer / au football.

* Score $\frac{1}{2}$ point for this word and other similarly marked words or groups. Score 1 point for each of the other groups.[5]

8.5.4 The transcription test

The transcription test is similar to a dictation in that students write down a passage they hear. In fact, the transcription also uses the two dictation formats: the spot transcription, in which students provide the missing words, and the full transcription.

The transcription differs from the dictation in that the test is based on authentic recorded material: a newscast, a speech, a piece of dialog from a movie soundtrack, a song, and so on. The student is given the recording and can play and replay it as often as necessary for complete transcription. The teacher may decide that the students are also allowed to use dictionaries while working on the transcriptions.

[5] Taken from Harry L. Bratnober, *Teachers' Guide, Recorded Text and Key for Test Tapes to Accompany New First-Year French, New Junior French by O'Brien and Lafrance* (Boston: Ginn, 1964), p. 28.

The transcription is scored like the dictation. Scores from transcription tests (which are power tests) may be compared with each other, but not with scores from dictations (which are partial speed tests).

8.6   CONTROLLED COMPOSITION

In a controlled composition, the students are writing full dialogs or paragraphs under definite guidelines. These are not yet true communication activities, for the students are told what to write. However, they provide a transition from sentence exercises and partial sentences to free self-expression. In the controlled composition, the teacher is expecting everyone to produce more or less the same paragraph: therefore, scoring is quite objective and reliable.

8.6.1   Passage transposition: focus on vocabulary

In passage transposition tests, the students are told how to transform a text according to specific guidelines.

SAMPLE ITEM TYPE 47   SYNONYMS AND ANTONYMS

Rewrite the following paragraph, replacing the underlined words first with synonyms and then with antonyms.

"Oh," said Amy, "this test is going to be very hard! Mr. Craigie dislikes giving a lot of A's."

Response: "Oh," said Amy, "this test is going to be extremely difficult! Mr. Craigie hates giving a lot of A's."
"Oh," said Amy, this test is going to be quite easy! Mr. Craigie enjoys giving a lot of A's."

NOTE: The choice of words to be underlined will generally vary, depending on whether students are to provide synonyms or antonyms.

SAMPLE ITEM TYPE 48   EXPANSION

Rewrite the following paragraph, adding a word or phrase at each asterisk (*). Be sure that the new paragraph makes logical sense.

When the (*) man (*) opened the (*) door, he saw a (*) sight.

Response: When the old man cautiously opened the cellar door, he saw a strange sight.

Variation: The students may be asked to insert only words chosen from a list given at the bottom of the test page. In this way, the teacher can limit the breadth of selection and can focus attention on specific expressions.

8.6.2 Passage transposition: focus on structure

Passage transposition tests require the students to demonstrate their control of the structures of the target language.

SAMPLE ITEM TYPE *49* CHANGE OF TENSE

Rewrite the following passage in the past, using the appropriate tenses. (Situational context: Read the description of Paul's activities, then rewrite the paragraph as if these activities had taken place yesterday.)

(French) Ce matin Paul est en retard. Quand il arrive en classe, le professeur fait déjà l'appel....

This morning Paul is late. When he arrives in class, the teacher is already taking the roll. . . .

Response: Hier matin, Paul était en retard. Quand il est arrivé en classe, le professeur faisait déjà l'appel....

SAMPLE ITEM TYPE *50* CHANGE OF SUBJECT

Rewrite the following dialog. Replace "Robert" with "Alice," and make the necessary changes. (Situational context: In the following dialog, Anne and Christine are planning to invite Robert to a party. Rewrite the dialog so that they are planning to invite Alice.)

Anne: Shall we invite Robert to the party?
Christine: Who is he?
Anne: He's a new boy in my biology class. His father teaches at the high school....

Response: Shall we invite Alice to the party? Who is she? She's a new girl in my biology class. Her father teaches at the high school....

SAMPLE ITEM TYPE *51* CHANGE OF MODE

Rewrite the following passage, placing the underlined verbs in the negative and making any other necessary changes. (Situational context: Jean-Luc is rather sure of his statements, but Nicole is not. Rewrite the passage giving Nicole's view.)

Jean-Luc: Je <u>crois</u> que nous irons
au musée demain. Et je <u>pense</u>
que nous ferons du tennis ce
week-end....

*I <u>think</u> that we will go to the
museum tomorrow. And I <u>think</u>
that we will play tennis this
week-end. . . .*

Response: Je ne crois pas que nous allions au musée demain. Et je ne crois
pas que nous fassions du tennis ce week-end....

SAMPLE ITEM TYPE 52   COMBINING SENTENCES

Rewrite the following paragraph so that it consists of only three sentences.

Tomorrow we are going to New York. In New York we will visit the
Planetarium. My brother is a doctor. He lives in New York. His place is
near Central Park. He is in Paris this week. Therefore, we will stay at his
apartment.

Response: When we go to New York tomorrow, we will visit the Planetarium.
My brother, who is a doctor, lives in New York near Central
Park. Since he is in Paris this week, we will stay at his
apartment.

SAMPLE ITEM TYPE 53   DIRECT AND REPORTED SPEECH

Rewrite the following paragraph in the third person, giving the content
of the letter. (Situational context: You have just received this letter from
Sylvia. Tell your mother what Sylvia said.)

I am really excited today since we are going to Disney World this week.
We are going to fly to Orlando and visit cousins of my father's....

Response: Sylvia writes that she is really excited today since they are going
to Disney World this week. They are going to fly to Orlando
and visit cousins of her father's....

NOTE: This type of test item can also require the student to transpose a
passage into the first person. For example: Write a letter saying that you
are really excited today since you all are going to Disney World....

Students frequently find this type of transposition rather difficult; it is
advisable to go through several examples in their native language so that
they understand what sort of transformation is expected.

8.7   WRITING FOR COMMUNICATION: DIRECTED COMPOSITION

In asking the students to write for communication, the teacher's main
concern is the intelligibility of the written work. Could a native speaker of
the language easily understand the text? If so, the student has been success-

ful in communicating. If the native speaker would have difficulty under-standing the text, the student's effort at communication has been only partially successful.

The scoring of directed compositions reflects this concern for effective communication. Spelling mistakes and missing accent marks, for instance, usually do not hinder the native speaker who is reading the text. Errors in choice of vocabulary and word order, however, may make comprehension difficult. The teacher will have to determine the relative seriousness of mistakes for the specific foreign language under instruction and develop an appropriate scoring system.

The directed composition differs from the free composition in that the student is provided with a rather detailed framework. The directed composi-tion tests primarily the students' ability to express themselves in writing on a carefully prescribed topic. The free composition places heavy emphasis on the elements of organization, imagination, and style.

8.7.1   Visual cues

The framework for the directed composition may be introduced with visual cues. Before giving this type of test, the teacher is advised to give the students experience in writing such compositions as part of their classwork. In this way the entire class will understand what is expected of them.

SAMPLE ITEM TYPE *54*   FILMSTRIP

The teacher shows the class a filmstrip—preferably one with an easily identifiable series of actions. Then the teacher shows the filmstrip a second time, stopping after every frame so that the students can write a descriptive sentence. Finally, the filmstrip is shown once more so that the students can check their work. Note that it may be advisable to darken the room for the first showing of the filmstrip and then use only a semi-darkened room while the students are writing.

Variation: The teacher shows the filmstrip and narrates the story or asks students to narrate the action. In this way the entire class understands the pictures. The narration may be in the target language (and provide a linguistic warm-up for the composition) or in the native language (so as not to provide any lexical or structural cues).

Suggested scoring: For each frame of the filmstrip score:

> 2 points, if the sentence is appropriate to the frame
> plus 3 points, if the sentence is grammatically and lexically accurate (with no attention paid to minor spelling errors);

or plus 2 points, if the sentence is understandable but contains some grammatical or lexical errors;

or plus 1 point, if the sentence would be very difficult for a native speaker
to understand.

SAMPLE ITEM TYPE 55   SILENT MOVIE OR CARTOON

The teacher shows the class one of the 4-minute silent movies or cartoons
commercially available for super-8 projectors. The film is then rewound and
projected a second time, with the action stopped at intervals so that students
can write down a description of what has happened. Then the film is shown
once more in its entirety, and the students check their work. If desired, the
teacher can tell the class how many sentences to write each time the film is
stopped. (For variations and scoring suggestions, see Sample Item Type 54.)

SAMPLE ITEM TYPE 56   SERIES OF PICTURES

The teacher prepares a series of pictures that tell a story. These may be
magazine pictures, comic strips, or hand-drawn cartoons. The pictures may
be taped on the chalkboard, prepared on ditto masters, or projected via
overhead transparency. (For scoring suggestions, see Sample Item Type 54.)

8.7.2 Oral cues

The directed composition may also be based on oral cues. Since this format
introduces the variable of listening comprehension, an interpretation of the
scores must take into account the fact that two aspects of communicative
competence are being tested simultaneously. If primary emphasis is on the
writing skill, the oral cues should be relatively easy for the students to
understand.

SAMPLE ITEM TYPE 57   INTERVIEW

You will hear Mr. Jacobson interviewing a candidate for the position of
salesperson. Take notes on the candidate's responses. At the end of the
interview write up as complete a description as you can of this candidate.

Tape: Mr. Jacobson: Please come in. Are you Mr. Smith?
      Mr. Smith: Yes, my name is Jack Smith and I am applying for the
        position you advertised.
      Mr. Jacobson: Where do you live, Mr. Smith? (etc.)

Suggested scoring: Count the number of bits of information contained in the
interview. For each bit of information score:

2 points for accuracy of the information
plus 3 points, if the corresponding sentence is grammatically and lexically
accurate (with no attention paid to minor spelling errors);
or plus 2 points, if the corresponding sentence is understandable, but contains some grammatical or lexical errors;
or plus 1 point, if the sentence would be very difficult for a native speaker
to understand.

Variation: To facilitate the students' notetaking, the teacher may wish to
provide an annotated sheet with appropriate categories:

Name:
Address:
Age: (etc.)

SAMPLE ITEM TYPE 58   MESSAGE TAKING

You are working as a receptionist in an insurance company. A young lady
comes in to see Mrs. Golden, one of the agents, but Mrs. Golden is out.
You ask the young lady if you can take a message. Listen to what she tells
you and take notes. Then write up the message for Mrs. Golden.

Tape: Young lady: My name is Bessie Sterling. I went to college with
Mrs. Golden. She perhaps does not know my married name and
remembers me as Bessie Marx. (Etc.)

(For variations and scoring suggestions, see Sample Item Type 57.)

SAMPLE ITEM TYPE 59   LETTER WRITING

Imagine you are working as a secretary. Your boss dictates the following
letter. Type (write) it up appropriately.

Tape: Please write a letter to Mr. George Johnson, 29 Fifth Avenue,
New York, New York 10011. Tell him that the book he ordered,
LANGUAGES MADE EASY, is temporarily out of stock and
that we will send him a copy on February 15.

Suggested scoring:

10 points = correct business letter format
10 points = message conveyed accurately, including correct address
 5 points = grammatically and lexically correct sentences
 5 points = stylistically appropriate sentences

NOTE: This is a rather special type of guided composition, and its use is
probably limited to courses teaching business correspondence.

SAMPLE ITEM TYPE *60* SUMMARY OR "NACHERZÄHLUNG"

The teacher reads a paragraph or short narrative that the students are to retell in their own words. To minimize the element of recall, a poster or series of pictures could be used to illustrate the story. If desired, students may be allowed to take notes.

Suggested scoring: accuracy of summary:

5 points = all major elements included
3 points = most major elements included
1 point = less than half the major elements included

intelligibility of summary:

5 points = a native speaker could easily understand the summary
3 points = a native speaker could understand the summary only with effort
1 point = a native speaker would have serious difficulty understanding the summary

use of tenses:

5 points = all verbs were in the appropriate tense
3 points = there were 1–3 errors in verb tense
1 point = there were four or more errors in verb tense

NOTE: The scoring category on verb tenses is more appropriate for the summary of a narrative than for the summary of a factual description.

8.7.3 Written cues

Guided compositions are usually based on written cues, either in the students' native language or in the target language. Many teachers prefer using only the target language for pedagogical reasons. Other teachers feel that since students will occasionally be asked to provide a foreign language equivalent for a friend who speaks only the native language, such compositions can validly be based on native language cues. This decision rests with the teacher.

SAMPLE ITEM TYPE *61* SKELETON DIALOG

Write out a conversation built around the suggested cues. Use all the key words in your dialog.

Joe: nice day!
Janet: walk?
Joe: where?
Janet: forest / flowers
Joe: fine

Suggested scoring: For each person's cue in the dialog, count:

> 2 points if the cue words are appropriately used
> plus 2 points if the utterance is understandable to a native speaker
> plus 1 point if the utterance would sound natural to a native speaker

NOTE: Since this type of guided composition is an indirect measure of conversational skill, the students will be producing a written version of spoken exchanges. Therefore the emphasis in the scoring is primarily on how the dialog would sound to a native speaker if it were read aloud.

SAMPLE ITEM TYPE *62*   WRITING NOTES OR PERSONAL LETTERS

Imagine you are spending a month in Spain. An American friend of yours who speaks very little Spanish wants you to help her write a note.

"I want to tell my landlady that I am going to go to Barcelona for three days. Write that I am going by car with some English students, and that we will be staying at the ... Hotel. A friend may phone me from Paris and she should tell him where to reach me. I will be back on Monday evening around 9:30 p.m."

(Suggested scoring: see Sample Item Type 57.)

SAMPLE ITEM TYPE *63*   WRITING BUSINESS LETTERS

Imagine you are working as a bilingual secretary. Your boss has directed you in English to write the following letter.

"Please write Mr. Georges Blanchette, 85, rue de la Boëtie, Paris 75008, and tell him that we have received his letter of November 30. We are delighted that he will be visiting our company when he comes to Boston. We will meet him at Logan Airport on December 11."

(Suggested scoring: see Sample Item Type 59.)

SAMPLE ITEM TYPE *64*   ANSWERING AN AD

Look through a local newspaper and find a help-wanted ad for a job that might interest you. Write a short letter responding to the ad and furnishing the desired information.

Variation: The teacher may select an ad to which all students in the class must respond.

Suggested scoring: 50 percent for the amount of information conveyed, 50 percent for accuracy of form. Form plays a definite role here, for prospective employers are often looking for candidates who handle the second language accurately.

SAMPLE ITEM TYPE *65*   FILLING OUT AN APPLICATION

Here is a copy of an application for a learner's driving permit (or other appropriate application form in the second language). Fill in all the information required.

Suggested scoring: 1 point for each item correctly filled in.

NOTE: Writing tests of this sort do not require long sentences. In fact, they are a combination of reading comprehension and short-answer writing. They are valid writing tests, however, for they duplicate the type of writing a second-language student might frequently be expected to carry out.

8.8   WRITING FOR COMMUNICATION: FREE COMPOSITION

While controlled and directed compositions measure certain writing skills in a fairly objective manner, the free composition allows the students to demonstrate their ability to organize their thoughts, to choose appropriate vocabulary, to formulate paragraphs—in short, to express themselves in writing.

Yet free composition tests, like English essay tests, have two drawbacks: scoring is time-consuming, and grades tend to lack objectivity. Not only will different teachers assign different grades to the same paper, but a teacher reading a set of papers for a second time will rarely give them the same grades as he or she gave after the first reading. However, since composition is an art in which students—especially advanced language students —are expected to gain proficiency, composition tests cannot be ignored. This section will suggest ways of improving composition tests through careful preparation, pre-planned scoring, and appropriate selection of composition topics.

8.8.1   Methods of evaluation

Free composition may be evaluated formally or informally. On a formal test, the student produces a composition on a specific topic under specific conditions. Such tests have the advantage of increased objectivity, and the results on such tests can be compared from student to student. The informal evaluation of composition skills usually takes the form of a daily diary in which the students can write about whatever interests them. This informal evaluation is not as objective as the formal test, but it does provide the teacher with a longer and more valid measure of the student's writing skill.

Formal composition tests may be administered in or out of class. If the composition is written in class, the students are all composing under the same conditions. However, such a timed test may favor students who can organize their thoughts quickly and provide less valid results for students who need a long period of time to settle down to the writing task. The out-of-class test permits the students to determine how much time they need to produce a composition of a specific length, but the lack of teacher control might encourage some students to seek unwarranted help.

If the teacher determines to administer a formal test in class, the students must be told whether they may use their textbooks and/or dictionaries. By allowing the students to use reference materials, the teacher administers the test under conditions that closely parallel those under which students might at some later time be writing notes or letters to speakers of the target language. However, if students tend to make heavy use of the reference materials, this may significantly limit their writing time. The teacher is the best person to determine which are the most appropriate testing conditions for a specific class.

8.8.2 Methods of scoring

If the composition test is to be a learning experience for the students, the scoring system must provide diagnostic feedback. Rather than just receiving a global score, the students should be informed as to areas in which improvement is needed. A diagnostic scoring system has the further advantage that its results are more objective than those obtained by simply assigning a letter grade to a composition. The three sample scoring systems described below may serve as a point of departure for the teacher setting up his or her own scoring system.

8.8.2a RATING SPECIFIC ELEMENTS

The teacher announces in advance that specific elements will be evaluated. For instance, in a vocabulary-based composition the teacher may provide ten key words (see Sample Item Type 61). The student receives one point for each word that is used correctly. In addition to this score, the composition may be rated outstanding, satisfactory, or unsatisfactory. Writing errors may be indicated, with the expectation that the student is to correct them.

8.8.2b   TEACHER-PREPARED RATING SCALE

The teacher determines which aspects of the composition are to be scored and prepares a rating scale. Here is an example of elements that such a scale might contain:

Organization:	excellent 6 5 4 3 2 1	nonexistent
Clarity of expression:	easily understood 6 5 4 3 2 1 by native speaker	incomprehensible to native speaker
Breadth of vocabulary:	imaginative use 6 5 4 3 2 1 of vocabulary	repetitive use of high-frequency vocabulary

It is advisable that the teacher share the scoring system with the class *before* giving the composition test so that the students will know which aspects of the composition merit their special attention.

8.8.2c   STUDENT-PREPARED RATING SCALE

The establishment of a student-prepared rating scale is a two-day class project. On the first day the class is divided into groups of four or five, and each group prepares a composition on an announced topic. The teacher circulates among the groups, answering questions and making corrections if needed. Once a group has finished a composition and the work has been checked to delete spelling mistakes and gross grammatical errors, a member with good handwriting copies the composition onto a ditto master.

On the second day the teacher distributes copies of the resulting group compositions. The students, either individually, in pairs, or in groups different from those of the first day, rank the papers in order of preference. Then the class ranking is placed on the board, and the students are asked to compare the top-ranked composition with the bottom-ranked paper and determine what elements make it superior. These elements are then listed on the board, and may include: imagination; organization; longer sentences; choice of words; etc. Each element is then followed by a set of numbers; for instance,

Imagination   5 3 1

Then the students, in pairs or groups, are asked to apply this rating scale to all the group compositions and to add up the total score for each one. The composition they consider the best should receive the highest number of points, and the poorest should receive the lowest number of points, with the others appropriately distributed in between. If this occurs, the rating scale has been "validated." If not, the rating scale is revised until the proper result is obtained. This revision might include the addition of additional categories, of the weighting of specific categories. For instance, if Imagination were found to be more important than the other elements, the scale might be modified to read:

Imagination   10 6 2

The teacher will subsequently use this student-prepared scale to score the next composition tests.

NOTE: Some teachers do not give students credit for a composition test until the students have rewritten their compositions, correcting all grammar, spelling, and vocabulary mistakes. In this way students are encouraged to go over their written work carefully, rather than simply file it in a notebook or toss it in a wastebasket.

8.8.3   Composition topics

The choice of a composition topic is an important factor. The ideal topic is one that students have no trouble handling, for the students' efforts during the test should be directed toward how to express themselves rather than what to write about.

SAMPLE ITEM TYPE 66   VOCABULARY-BASED COMPOSITION

In a vocabulary-oriented composition, the main objective is to evaluate the richness and appropriateness of the student's recall or active vocabulary. To score this type of composition, the teacher could assign one grade for richness and another for appropriateness (that is, accurate choice of words). To simplify the scoring, these grades could be limited to three categories: poor, satisfactory, and good.

Use of nouns: Students are asked to describe a room, a street scene, a farmyard, a menu, or the like. Objectivity is greatly increased if all students are asked to describe a particular picture, perhaps a textbook illustration or a large picture hung at the front of the classroom.

Use of adjectives and adverbs: Students are asked to compare and contrast two similar pictures. Illustrations can be chosen that elicit number and color words or that require the comparative and superlative forms of adjectives and adverbs.

Use of verbs: Students are asked to narrate an imaginary experience: a day at school, a typical Sunday, a trip. To increase the reliability of the test, students may be asked to use 10 out of 12 suggested words.

SAMPLE ITEM TYPE 67 GRAMMAR-ORIENTED COMPOSITION

In a grammar-oriented composition, the students are led to use specific structures. A direct system consists of telling the students to write a paragraph, for instance, containing ten verbs in the future tense.

Here is an example in French:[6]

Racontez l'un des événements suivants, en employant au moins 5 verbes à l'imparfait et 5 verbes au passé composé.	*Write about one of the following events, using at least 5 verbs in the imperfect and 5 verbs in the passé composé.*
Voici les événements:	*Here are the events:*
1. votre dernier dîner de Thanksgiving	*1. your last Thanksgiving dinner*
2. votre dernière fête de Noël	*2. your last Christmas*
3. un pique-nique ou une surprise-partie	*3. a picnic or a party*
4. votre anniversaire	*4. your birthday*
Et voici ce que vous pouvez décrire:	*And here is what you can describe:*
Les circonstances ...	*The circumstances...*
La date: le jour? l'heure?	*the date: the day? the time?*
L'endroit: la ville? chez vous? chez des amis?	*the place: in town? at your house? at the home of friends?*
Les invités: combien étaient-ils? qui étaient-ils?	*the guests: how many were there? who were they?*
Le repas: qu'est-ce qu'il y avait à manger? à boire?	*the meal: what was there to eat? to drink?*
Ce que vous avez fait ...	*What you did...*
A qui avez-vous parlé? De quoi avez-vous parlé?	*whom did you talk to? what did you talk about?*
Qu'est-ce que vous avez mangé? bu?	*what did you eat? drink?*
Y a-t-il eu une surprise? pour vous? pour vos amis?	*was there a surprise? for you? for your friends?*
Qu'est-ce que vous avez fait d'ordinaire? d'extraordinaire?	*what ordinary things did you do? what extraordinary things?*

NOTE: This sample topic provides a great deal of guidance for the students. For more advanced classes, the teacher may simply list the suggested events without the lead questions.

[6] Taken from Jean-Paul Valette and Rebecca M. Valette, *French for Mastery: Book Two* (Lexington, Mass.: D. C. Heath, 1975), pp. 154–55.

SAMPLE ITEM TYPE *68*   PARAGRAPH WRITING

In tests of this sort, the emphasis is on the ability to construct a unified paragraph. An English paragraph, for instance, in expository prose consists of three parts: an introduction or topic sentence, the body, and the conclusion. The scoring system would evaluate how well the student has handled these three factors.

Here is an example in English for foreign students: [7]

Go to the school cafeteria. Watch Americans eat, talk, move around the room, pick up or put down things. Make a note of these gestures. Write a descriptive paragraph about your observations of one or more people.

SAMPLE ITEM TYPE *69*   "POINT OF VIEW" COMPOSITION

The "point of view" composition challenges the students' imagination and tests their consistency of style. The target language becomes a vehicle of individual expression. The possibilities are endless and can be adapted to all levels.

Physical descriptions: Descriptions may concern units studied in class. When students have finished a unit based on the house, they may be asked to describe a house as seen by a midget, or by the family dog, or by an American Indian of the past century.

Emotional states: Students are asked to describe a scene or situation as seen through the eyes of someone who is elated (or sad or extremely tired).

Personality: Students are asked to describe a scene or narrate an event in the style either of a specific onlooker—a grandmother, for example—or of two different observers, an old miser and a poor orphan, a teen-age girl and a grandmother, and so on.

SAMPLE ITEM TYPE *70*   THOUGHT-PROVOKING ESSAYS

Composition topics should be precisely worded to make the grading as objective as possible. Subjects may be drawn from political events, school happenings, current controversies. Papers may be scored on logical reasoning, organization, sophistication, or effective communication. If language and expression are the primary points to be tested, the subject could be discussed in class orally and the written test given at the end of the period.

[7] Taken from Jewell A. Friend, *Writing English as a Second Language* (Glenview, Ill.: Scott, Foresman and Co., 1971), p. 23.

Here is an example in English: [8]

What do you think about the short poem that follows?

Patience is a virtue.
Possess it if you can.
It's seldom in a woman
But it's never in a man.

Are the statements in this folk poem true? Write a paragraph that explains the meaning of the folk poem and relates your opinion of its truth or lack of truth. Then provide an example to illustrate and defend your contention.

8.9 TRANSLATION

For advanced students, familiar with vocabulary and structure, the translation of a passage from English into the target language becomes a refined exercise in style. In this context, the translation test becomes both reliable and valid. Translations may be scored for accuracy (in a scientific article, for example) or for literary expression (in selections where tone and mood are of greater importance than a word-for-word rendering of the text).

[8] Taken from Friend, *Writing English*, p. 76.

outline

nine

The Culture Test

As the teaching of culture has become an accepted part of the second-language course, teachers are realizing how broad and how complex this subject matter really is.

Culture in the broad sense has two major components. One is anthropological or sociological culture: the attitudes, customs, and daily activities of a people, their ways of thinking, their values, their frames of reference. Since language is a direct manifestation of this phase of culture, a society cannot be totally understood or appreciated without a knowledge of its language. The other component of culture is the history of civilization. Traditionally representing the "culture" element in foreign-language teaching, it includes geography, history, and achievements in the sciences, the social sciences, and the arts. This second component forms the framework for the first: it represents the heritage of a people and as such must be appreciated by the students who wish to understand the new target culture.

As language teachers strive to introduce their students to a second culture so as to free these young people from the strait jacket of monoculturalism, some specialists are beginning to warn of the dangers of immersion into the great tradition of a second high culture. Margaret Mead writes:

When students saturate themselves deeply and meaningfully in one other culture and language, and that in a high culture with whose members they can engage in sophisticated discourse, they tend to become locked into a kind of we-they position, in which one language and culture tends to become better, higher, than the other. ... There is no doubt that learning a second language is a releasing activity and is much more difficult than learning subsequent languages. But we need to go further and consider how to rescue students from the various traps that lie in the intense immersion in a second high culture, whether it be the trap of romanticism, of finding a counter culture, of excessive guilt over past imperialism and western chauvinism, or the development of a kind of double personality, complete with kinesics.[1]

She suggests increased cooperation between teachers of the commonly-taught languages and the anthropologists who work with primitive cultures and unwritten languages. The study of a third language and culture could help avoid the dangerous polarization that bilingualism and biculturalism may produce.

9.1 GENERAL CONSIDERATIONS

Although most foreign language teachers do not deny the importance of culture in their course curriculum, few teachers actively test whether students are attaining their cultural goals. The problem seems to be that many teachers are uncertain as to what specifically their goals are and how they may be evaluated.

For many years, the New York State Regents Examinations in modern languages contained a "culture" section. This part of the text asked the student to respond to ten out of fifteen questions in a multiple-choice format. Here are some typical examples:[2]

1. Orly et Le Bourget sont deux aéroports situés dans la banlieue
   A. du Havre
   B. de Lille
   C. de Marseille
   D. de Paris

   Orly and Le Bourget are two airports located in the suburbs of
   Le Havre
   Lille
   Marseilles
   Paris

2. Aujourd'hui la population de la France est d'environ
   A. 20.000.000
   B. 50.000.000
   C. 80.000.000
   D. 100.000.000

   Today the population of France is about
   20,000,000
   50,000,000
   80,000,000
   100,000,000

[1] Margaret Mead, "How Anthropology Can Become a Component in a Liberal Arts Education," in Howard B. Altman and Victor E. Hanzeli, eds., *Essays on the Teaching of Culture: a Festschrift to Honor Howard Lee Nostrand* (Detroit: Advancement Press of America, 1974), pp. 14–15.
[2] Taken from the University of the State of New York Regents High School Examination: *Comprehensive Examination in French: form B* (June 24, 1975).

3. Louis XIV fit construire l'Hôtel   *Louis XIV had the Hôtel des*
   des Invalides pour y   *Invalides built in order to*
   A. enterrer Napoléon   *bury Napoléon*
   B. abriter des reliques   *shelter relics*
   C. présenter des spectacles   *give shows*
   D. soigner les militaires   *give medical aid to soldiers*

4. Au théâtre, les Français sifflent   *At the theater, the French*
   parfois pour exprimer leur   *sometimes whistle to express*
                                            their
   A. enthousiasme   *enthusiasm*
   B. impatience   *impatience*
   C. dissatisfaction   *dissatisfaction*
   D. reconnaissance   *appreciation*

Correct responses: D, B, D, C

These items test the knowledge of discrete cultural facts and are therefore relatively easy to prepare and score. The disadvantage of such items on broadly administered tests is that students are likely to cram lists of names, places, dates, and facts as a last-minute preparation for the examination. In explaining why the Regents Examinations were dropping the Culture Section as of June 1976, Paul Dammer of the New York State Education Department wrote:

> In essence, then, the type of questions most suitable, from the technical point of view, for inclusion in the Regents examinations has encouraged the pursuit of pedagogically unsound practices which, while retarding pupils' intellectual growth in understanding how discrete cultural items function and interact, in most cases assured pupils of a high grade in this part of the examinations— provided, of course, that they could readily recall the facts with which they were confronted. . . . Therefore, the Bureau decided to recommend removal of the culture section from the Regents examinations in modern foreign languages in order to stimulate a greater interest on the part of teachers in making cultural understanding a more meaningful learning experience for pupils.[3]

For the classroom teacher, cultural goals may be divided into four categories: developing a greater awareness of and a broader knowledge about the target culture; acquiring a command of the etiquette of the target culture; understanding differences between the target culture and the

---

[3] Paul E. Dammer, "A Rationale for the Elimination of the Culture Section from the Regents Examinations in Modern Foreign Languages," *Language Association Bulletin* [of the New York State Association of Foreign Language Teachers] 27, no. 2 (November 1975), pp. 6–7.

students' culture; and understanding the values of the target culture. Each of these goals will be treated in a separate section of this chapter.

However, before considering cultural goals, the teacher must define his or her view of the target culture. For example, in a French class, is the emphasis on the culture of Paris? of a village in Auvergne? of Guadeloupe? of Québec? of Dakar? or of the Franco-American community in Manchester, New Hampshire? In the Spanish class, is the course to focus on Spain? Argentina? Mexico? Cuba? the Puerto Ricans? the Chicanos? the Cuban-Americans? Probably the teacher will want to convey the complexity of the target culture in its many facets, or perhaps focus on one regional variation of the target culture (the one with which the teacher is most familiar through travel, residence, research, and/or study) while discouraging overgeneralization. The actual choice of testing techniques will depend on the goals of the course.

9.2   CULTURAL AWARENESS

As students progress through a foreign language program, it is expected that they will increase their awareness of the culture or cultures characteristic of the speakers of the language under study. This broadened awareness may touch on all aspects of culture: the people's way of life as well as the geographic, historical, economic, artistic, and scientific aspects of the target society.

Tests of cultural awareness are generally built around items measuring cultural knowledge. The student who is aware of American history can identify people like Washington and Lincoln. These bits of knowledge constitute the general background of members of the target culture, and the student who shares this knowledge demonstrates an increased awareness of the parameters of that target culture.

Cultural awareness tests are typically administered in pairs: pretests and posttests. The pretest establishes the baseline or point of departure: how great is the students' cultural awareness before entering a course of study? The posttest allows the teacher to determine the degree of progress that the students have made.

9.2.1   The geographical parameters of the target culture

One goal in the area of cultural awareness is bringing students to realize the breadth and variety of countries and areas where the target language is spoken.

SAMPLE ITEM TYPE *1*   GEOGRAPHIC LISTS

List the countries and places where Spanish is spoken.

Correct responses: Spain, Mexico, United States, Argentina, Cuba, etc.

NOTE: At the end of a course, the students probably have a much more accurate picture of where the target language is used.

SAMPLE ITEM TYPE *2*   MAP IDENTIFICATION

Identify the French-speaking countries and places on the map of the world (p. 268).

Correct responses: 1. l'Algérie, 2. la Belgique, 3. le Cambodge, 4. le Cameroun, 5. le Congo-Brazzaville, 6. la Corse, 7. la Côte d'Ivoire, 8. la France, 9. le Gabon, 10. la Guadeloupe, 11. la Guinée, 12. la Guyane, 13. Haïti, 14. le Laos, 15. le Liban, 16. le Luxembourg, 17. le Madagascar, 18. le Mali, 19. le Maroc, 20. la Martinique, 21. la Mauritanie, 22. le Niger, 23. Québec, 24. la République Centrafricaine, 25. la Réunion, 26. le Sénégal, 27. la Suisse, 28. la Syrie, 29. le Tchad, 30. le Togo, 31. la Tunisie, 32. le Vietnam, 33. le Zaïre (Congo-Kinshasa).

9.2.2   Contributions of the target culture

This category includes an awareness of the contributions of the target culture to world civilization in general and to the history of the students' home country, where appropriate.

SAMPLE ITEM TYPE *3*   ORIGINS OF PLACE NAMES—IDENTIFICATION

Explain the origins of the names of the following United States cities:

1. Germantown, Pennsylvania
2. Detroit, Michigan
3. Santa Barbara, California

Correct responses: 1. Germantown was the first settlement of Germans who arrived in America in 1683.
2. Détroit in French means strait: the city is situated on on a strait between Lake Saint Clair and Lake Erie.
3. Santa Barbara is the name of a Spanish mission founded in 1786.

PAYS ET TERRITOIRES OÙ L'ON TROUVE DES GROUPES FRANCOPHONES

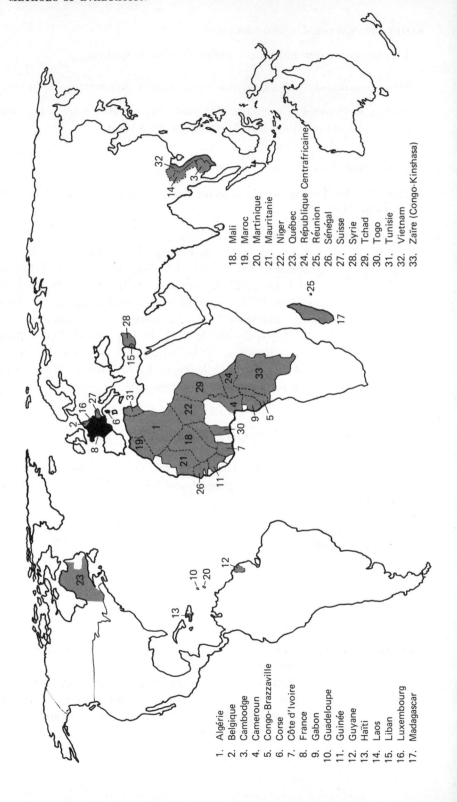

1. Algérie
2. Belgique
3. Cambodge
4. Cameroun
5. Congo-Brazzaville
6. Corse
7. Côte d'Ivoire
8. France
9. Gabon
10. Guadeloupe
11. Guinée
12. Guyane
13. Haïti
14. Laos
15. Liban
16. Luxembourg
17. Madagascar

18. Mali
19. Maroc
20. Martinique
21. Mauritanie
22. Niger
23. Québec
24. République Centrafricaine
25. Réunion
26. Sénégal
27. Suisse
28. Syrie
29. Tchad
30. Togo
31. Tunisie
32. Vietnam
33. Zaïre (Congo-Kinshasa)

SAMPLE ITEM TYPE *4* FAMOUS PEOPLE—MATCHING

Match the following persons with their contributions:

1. Rochambeau	a. poet and president of Sénégal
2. Senghor	b. feminist writer
3. De Beauvoir	c. pioneer aviator and novelist
4. Curie	d. discoverer of radium
	e. commander of French troops during the American Revolution

Correct responses: 1e, 2a, 3b, 4d

NOTE: In items of this sort it is better to ask the students to match two lists of unequal length. This reduces the opportunity for guessing.

9.2.3 Differences in way-of-life patterns

One goal of many foreign language classes is to sensitize the students to the existence of differences in daily life patterns between the target culture and the native culture. The first step is increasing student awareness of the existence of these differences.

SAMPLE ITEM TYPE *5* LISTING DIFFERENCES

Imagine you are living with a family in Germany. List outward cultural differences you would be likely to observe.

Correct responses: different ways of making beds, different ways of setting the table, tendency to keep all doors closed, etc.

9.2.4 Differences in values and attitudes

Students learning a new language learn that the target culture and the native culture do not always have identical values and attitudes. At first, students are made aware of the existence of these differences. Then, an effort is made to develop an understanding of these new values (see Section 9.5).

SAMPLE ITEM TYPE *6* IDENTIFYING PATTERNS—TRUE-FALSE
FORMAT

Indicate whether the following statements are true or false.

1. French young people may earn money by baby-sitting.
2. Most French parents encourage their teenage children to find part-time jobs.
3. Most French young people would like to earn their own money.

Correct responses: 1. true   2. false   3. true

9.3 COMMAND OF ETIQUETTE

Most foreign language programs introduce the students to the polite behavior expected of persons living in the country or countries where the target language is spoken. The command of etiquette may be tested either with written tests or through role-play activities.

9.3.1 Knowledge of etiquette

Each target culture has different etiquette patterns. French etiquette in Paris, for instance, differs from patterns in Sénégal or Québec or Tahiti. As the students learn about certain polite codes of behavior, they should also know when and under which conditions such behavior is appropriate.

SAMPLE ITEM TYPE 7 DESCRIBING ETIQUETTE

What is the traditional American pattern when a man and woman are walking down a city street?

Correct response: The man always walks on the curb side.

SAMPLE ITEM TYPE 8 INTERPRETING CODES OF BEHAVIOR—
MULTIPLE-CHOICE FORMAT

Imagine you are in France near a school. You observe a teenage girl meet a boy and watch them kiss each other on the cheeks. What should you conclude? Explain your answer.

a. They are going steady.
b. They are friends.
c. They are cousins.

Correct response: Either *b* or *c*. Members of a family (including distant family) tend to kiss each other upon meeting. Often teenagers also greet friends this way. Of course, *a* is also a possible explanation, but not the only one.

It should be noted that multiple-choice items of this sort are difficult to prepare. The options should all be equally plausible to a person who is not aware of the meaning of a specific behavior pattern. At the same time, the item should be validated by asking native speakers to take the test. Often the test writer will find that native speakers do not all agree to one correct response.[4]

[4] For an excellent discussion on the problems of preparing multiple-choice culture items, see H. Ned Seelye, "Preparing end-of-course objective tests," *Teaching Culture: Strategies for Foreign Language Educators* (Skokie, Ill.: National Textbook Company, 1974). Hereafter this book is cited as *Teaching Culture*.

9.3.2   Ability to adopt patterns of etiquette

The ability to react appropriately to situations in the target culture is frequently taught through role-play activities and "culture capsules." If desired, students can be evaluated informally on their participation in such activities. In a more formal test, each student would be expected to carry out specific instructions or demonstrate specific behaviors.

SAMPLE ITEM TYPE *9*   GREETINGS

Demonstrate how you would greet the parents of a French friend.

Correct response: The student should use the phrases "Bonjour, Monsieur" and "Bonjour, Madame" and should shake hands.

SAMPLE ITEM TYPE *10*   TABLE MANNERS

Imagine you are eating in the home of a French family. Show how you would behave.

Correct response: The student should keep his or her hands on the table rather than in the lap. When eating meat, the fork is kept in the left hand both while cutting and while putting the food in the mouth. Pieces of bread may be used for pushing food and for soaking up sauce.

SAMPLE ITEM TYPE *11*   LEVELS OF LANGUAGE

Imagine that you had written the following persons, indicating that you were unable to meet them as planned, but the letters were not received. How would you excuse yourself?

a. Monsieur Boutron, professor
b. Marc, a close friend

Correct responses: a. Je suis désolé, Monsieur, que vous n'ayez pas reçu ma lettre....
(use of formal language and the pronoun *vous*)
b. Ça m'embête que t'aies pas reçu le mot que j'ai laissé....
(use of informal language and the pronoun *tu*)

NOTE: Items of this type combine linguistic and cultural goals. The emphasis is on communication in a cultural context.

9.4 UNDERSTANDING OF OUTWARD CULTURAL DIFFERENCES

Many facets of daily life are organized differently in another culture. In the foreign language course, the students should learn how to interpret unfamiliar cultural conventions and realia. This understanding will help those students who travel to the foreign country to function more easily. Even students who are unable to travel will be better able to understand foreign films and magazines.

9.4.1 Unfamiliar conventions

Often the foreign culture has a different way of indicating dates and times. Meals may be served at different hours, and foods may be served in different combinations or at unexpected times of day. Driving codes and street signs may be different in the foreign culture.

SAMPLE ITEM TYPE *12*   READING TIMETABLES

Answer questions about the arrival and departure times of French airplanes according to the following timetable:

AÉROPORT
DE CLERMONT-FERRAND/Aulnat

PRINTEMPS - ÉTÉ 76
jusqu'au 31-10-1976

TÉL. 91.71.00 - 92.28.28 et Agents de voyages
Télex 390024

I.C.A.A.
MEMBER

Lignes Directes à destination de :	Heure Départ	Heure Arrivée
Service en Caravelle	07.55 (1)	08.50 (1)
⟶ PARIS	11.00 (2)	12.10 (2)
	18.30 (3)	19.40 (3)
Service en Caravelle	21.30 (1)	22.25 (1)
⟶ LYON	08.20 (6) *	09.00 (6)
	18.45 (1)	19.25 (1)
⟶ TOULOUSE	10.35 (1)	11.35 (1)
⟶ BORDEAUX	21.00 (3) **	22.15 (3)
⟶ TOURS	21.05 (1)	22.00 (1)
⟶ NANTES	10.30 (1)	11.50 (1)
⟶ MENDE a/c du 12/4	08.05 (1)	08.55 (1)
	21.35 (1)	22.25 (1)
⟶ MONTPELLIER a/c du 12/4 via MENDE	08.05 (1)	09.50 (1)
⟶ LA ROCHELLE du 1/8 au 4/9	21.05 (1)	22.25 (1)
⟶ GENEVE	08.10 (1) ***	08.00 (1) *
	18.35 (1) ***	18.25 (1) *
⟶ LONDRES a/c du 02/5	19.00 (4) du 19/5 au 15/9	20.10 (4) du 19/5 au 15/9
	19.00 (5) du 20/6 au 12/9	20.10 (5) du 20/6 au 12/9
	18.10 (5) **** du 2/5 au 13/6 et du 19/9 au 24/10	18.30 (5)
	16.10 (4) **** du 22/9 au 20/10	16.30 (4)

(1) Q. sf Sa et Di - (2) Sa - (3) Q sf Sa - (4) Me - (5) Di - (6) Q. sf Di
* Sa 08.30   * Compte tenu décalage heure légale
** Di 21.05
*** Arr. GENEVE 1 h plus tard a/c du 26/9
**** Dép. CLERMONT-FERRAND 1 h plus tôt a/c du 26/9

ATTENTION ! Les horaires ci-dessus indiqués peuvent être modifiés sans préavis. De même certaines lignes fonctionneront à des fréquences réduites ou seront supprimées de fin juillet à fin août.
Se renseigner auprès des agences de voyage.

If you leave Clermont-Ferrand a little after 9 p.m., when will you arrive in Tours?

Correct response: At 10 p.m.

Look at the following schedule of movies from an American newspaper.

Which one is appropriate for an eight-year-old child?
Which one is restricted to adults?

Regent, 7 Medford st. 643-1197.
  EARTHQUAKE (PG)★
  Through Tues. Shows at 7 and 9:15 p.m.
  Also Sun. at 4:45.
Burlington — Cinema, Rte. 128, exit 42.
272-4410.
  BLACKBEARD'S GHOST (G)
  Through Feb. 12. Shows at 1, 3, 5, 7 and 9.
  DOG DAY AFTERNOON (R)★★★★
  Through Tues. Shows at 1:45, 4:25, 7:20
  and 9:40 p.m.
Danvers — Sack Danvers, Liberty Tree Mall.
777-1818 or 599-3122.
  CUCKOO'S NEST (R)★★★★
  Due Wed. Call theater for times.
  STORY OF O (X)★
  Through Tues. Shows at 7:30 and 9:30
  p.m. Also Sat.-Sun. at 1:30, 3:30 and 5:30.

Correct responses: Blackbeard's Ghost; Story of O

9.4.2   Linguistic cultural referents

In order to understand a conversation among speakers of the target language or an article in a target language magazine it is frequently necessary to interpret cultural referents. The state of Florida, for instance, is not just one of the fifty states, nor is it simply a southern state: it is a place where elderly people retire and where college students go for spring vacation. Therefore, an American would interpret a reference to Florida differently than a reference to Alabama or South Carolina.

A French student mentions that she will be visiting her grandparents in "Bretagne" during the "Toussaint" holidays.

1. She will be traveling from Paris toward
   a. central France
   b. the Mediterranean
   c. the Atlantic
2. She plans to be with her grandparents on
   a. October 15
   b. November 1
   c. December 24

Correct responses: 1c, 2b (*Toussaint* is All Saints' Day, November 1)

SAMPLE ITEM TYPE *15* INTERPRETING REFERENTS—SHORT
ANSWER FORMAT

A German pen pal writes that his sister is attending a boarding school and is in "Unter Sekunda." About how old do you think she is?

Correct response: About 15 (*Unter Sekunda* is the tenth year of schooling)

9.4.3 Performing according to unfamiliar conventions

Items of this type are appropriate for courses that are preparing the students for residence in the target culture. As part of the course objectives, students might learn how to fill out hotel forms, how to write business letters, how to buy train tickets, and so on.

SAMPLE ITEM TYPE *16* WRITING CHECKS

Demonstrate your ability to write checks in France by completing the blank check below. Request that Jean-Michel Vergne be paid one thousand francs.

Correct response:

9.5   UNDERSTANDING OF CULTURAL VALUES

A major aim in the teaching of culture is to bring the students to the real-
ization that the target culture may have a system of values that differs from
their own. While we may expect students to imitate the social conventions
of this target culture, we do not normally expect them to adopt a new set of
values. However, students should understand the foreign system of values
and come to respect it.

9.5.1   Interpreting behavior of members of the target culture

In items of this sort, the student is presented with an example of behavior
in the target culture. For a French course, for example, the teacher might
describe a situation, or project a situation via video or film clips. The American students would interpret the situation in terms of the French system of
values. (It should be remembered that there is no single system of values in
the target culture, but rather a range of value systems that varies according
to social position, age, sex, region, etc.)

SAMPLE ITEM TYPE *17*   OPEN INTERPRETATION

> Mireille plans to invite an American student to her home. She tells her
> parents that this new friend is "très cultivé" and they react by saying
> they look forward to meeting him. What is meant by "cultivé" and how
> do you explain the parents' reaction?

Correct response: The French respect culture and admire people whom they consider "cultivés" or cultured, that is, people who can express themselves easily on a wide variety of subjects —especially art and literature. The French tend to stereotype the Americans as "uncultured." Mireille knows that her parents will react favorably to the idea of meeting a student who represents the exception: the cultured American.

It should be noted that the described situation reflects a predominantly urban and middle-class to upper-middle-class attitude. As a variation to such an item, the students might be asked to transfer the situation to their native culture. For example:

What would you tell your parents about a visiting French student so that they would wish you to invite him to your house? Or would you simply invite him without even asking your parents?

SAMPLE ITEM TYPE *18*   MULTIPLE-CHOICE INTERPRETATION

The film "Amarcord" has several scenes that take place in a classroom. How would a middle-aged Italian probably view these scenes?

a. As examples of very poor teaching, reminiscent of the Fascist period
b. As examples of very undisciplined students, whose parents failed to inculcate in them the proper sense of respect
c. As examples of classroom situations with which he or she easily identifies.

Correct response: c

Multiple-choice interpretation items are extremely difficult to prepare. Either the distractors are so wrong as not to attract the students, or the distractors contain an element of truth and become ambiguous. In his validation of test items about Guatemalan culture, Seelye discovered that test items that did work were multiple-choice questions referring to the understanding of outward cultural differences (how stores indicate whether fresh meat is available or whether tamales are being sold). Multiple-choice items requiring interpretation of behavior frequently gave ambiguous results.[5] John Clark in his description of culture tests also points out the problems involved in multiple-choice items of this type and suggests that teachers use free response techniques similar to Sample Item Type 17.[6]

[5] Seelye, *Teaching Culture*, pp. 147–52.
[6] John L. D. Clark, *Foreign Language Testing: Theory & Practice* (Philadelphia: Center for Curriculum Development, 1972), p. 140.

9.5.2 Interpreting behavior of members of the native culture

Here the students are expected to anticipate aspects of their own culture that would strike a foreign visitor as strange. In items of this type, the teacher would specify, for example, which segment of the target culture the foreign visitor represents: is the Spanish speaker a businessman from Madrid? a student from Peru? a farm worker from Mexico?

SAMPLE ITEM TYPE *19* ANTICIPATING REACTIONS

Robert Duroc is staying at the home of an American family in a Boston suburb. The family consists of Mr. Paul Brand, a business associate of Monsieur Duroc's; Mrs. Margaret Brand; and Mary, Mrs. Brand's daughter by a previous marriage. Which of the following behaviors would probably shock Monsieur Duroc? Explain.

1. Mary calls her stepfather Paul.
2. Mary phones home after school to tell her mother that she will not be coming home for supper.
3. Mary kisses her parents goodnight before going to bed.

Correct responses: 1. (because French children do not call parents or stepparents by their first names); 2. (because French children are expected home for supper, and if there were an invitation to eat elsewhere they would ask their mothers' permission, rather than simply inform them of a decision)

9.6   ANALYSIS OF THE TARGET CULTURE

The analysis of the target culture is as challenging as the investigation of one's native culture. As students begin to study various facets of the target culture in depth, they will begin to realize that their own culture incorporates a complexity of patterns they were never aware of. They will also discover that a culture is not a static but an ever-changing phenomenon. In the United States, for instance, the hair length that symbolized revolt and rebellion in the mid-1960s became the accepted style for most adults in the mid-1970s.

In testing the students' ability to analyze the target culture, teachers will probably adopt evaluation techniques that parallel those employed in their classroom approach to the topic. The following sections suggest some directions that have been explored in recent years.

9.6.1   Beaujour and Ehrmann: the semiotic approach [7]

In the semiotic approach to culture the objective is to interpret natural language signs, such as "mercredi" (Wednesday), in terms of their implicit cultural signs (a school holiday for French children).

Beaujour and Ehrmann stress the semiotic analysis of raw cultural data, such as interviews, pictures, television commercials, and magazine ads.

SAMPLE ITEM TYPE *20*   ANALYZING AN AD

The student is shown an unfamiliar ad that relates to a topic studied in class (e.g.: the French attitude toward vacations).

Look at this ad prepared by the Club Méditerranée. Discuss the following topics:

1. The visual impact of the ad and the choice of images.
2. The text of the ad: what impression does it create in the reader?
3. The role of vacations for the French: how are they organized? what possibilities are open to the individual? how does the individual view vacations? does the ad fit this general vacation picture?
4. The role of vacations in an industrial society: is there a conflict between advanced technology and the happiness of the individual? what solution does the ad offer? is the Club's main concern the happiness of the individual or the financial profit of the organization? Explain.
5. Would such an ad be appropriate for an American readership? If so, why? If not, what changes would you suggest and why?

Scoring: Detailed instructions of this type permit a more objective scoring system than a simple one-line statement, such as "Analyze the following ad." The teacher would assign a specific number of points to each part of the essay. Then the teacher would read the responses to question number 1, and place the essays into four piles: outstanding response, good response, average response, and poor response. These scores would be recorded on the backs of the test papers. Then the papers are shuffled, and the teacher would read the responses to question number 2, and so on.

9.6.2   Nostrand: the thematic approach [8]

Nostrand has found it possible to summarize the shared patterns of a culture into about a dozen major "themes," which are defined as the pervading

[7] Michel Beaujour and Jacques Ehrmann, "A semiotic approach to culture," *Foreign Language Annals* 1, no. 2 (December 1967), pp. 152–63.
[8] See Howard Lee Nostrand, ed., *Background Data for the Teaching of French* (Seattle: University of Washington, 1967), EDRS: ED 031 964, ED 031 989 and ED 031 990. See also

concerns that make up a culture's value system. For French culture, he has identified the following main themes:

l'individualisme, l'intellectualité, l'art de vivre, le réalisme, le bon sens, l'amitié, l'amour, la famille, la religion, la justice, la liberté, la patrie.

For Hispanic culture, he suggests:

individualism, dignidad, orientation toward persons, serenidad, beauty, leisure valued over work, human nature mistrusted, "cultura" despite "la realidad del medio," rising expectations.

Students who are aware of the underlying themes of the target culture are more likely to react appropriately or, at least, to appreciate the reactions of members of the culture, to stimuli such as jokes, cartoons, television programs, movies, songs and even literature.

SAMPLE ITEM TYPE *21*   IDENTIFYING CULTURAL THEMES

The student is shown an unfamiliar cartoon, or listens to a popular song that he or she may have heard before but never analyzed.

Read the lyrics of Georges Moustaki's well-known song "Le Métèque" as you hear it played. Then study the lyrics and identify the underlying themes of French culture. Explain how each theme is exemplified in the song, and give a second example of the same theme from a play, comic book, film, ad, song (etc.) studied in class.

Correct response: The students would probably identify individualism, love, and liberty.

9.6.3   Santoni: the contextual approach [9]

For Georges Santoni, the language used by an individual in society is not only an expression of that person's thought but also of his or her culture. The culture of a worker is not that of an intellectual or a high school student,

Nostrand, "Levels of Sociocultural Understanding for Language Classes" in H. Ned Seelye, ed., *A Handbook on Latin America for Teachers* (Springfield, Ill.: Superintendent of Public Instruction, 1968), pp. 19–24; and Nostrand, "Empathy for a second culture: motivations and techniques" in Gilbert A. Jarvis, ed., *Responding to New Realities*, ACTFL Review of Foreign Language Education 5 (Skokie, Ill.: National Textbook, 1974), pp. 263–327. See also, Howard L. Nostrand and Frances B. Nostrand, "Testing Understanding of the Foreign Culture" in H. Ned Seelye, ed., *Teaching Cultural Concepts in Spanish Classes* (Springfield, Ill.: Superintendent of Public Instruction, 1972).

[9] Georges V. Santoni, "Langue et culture en contexte et contraste," *French Review* 59, no. 3 (February 1976), pp. 255–65 (hereafter cited as Langue et Culture). See also Jean-Noël Rey and Georges V. Santoni, *Quand les Français parlent: langue en contexte, culture en contraste* (Rowley, Mass.: Newbury House, 1975).

and this difference in culture is also reflected in a difference in language. Santoni stresses the complexity of the target culture and insists on a careful study of relevant cultural data: facts, descriptions, interviews, and documents. Most questions do not have clear-cut answers, and the students should learn to analyze possible options in the light of the data they have been working with.

SAMPLE ITEM TYPE *22*   THE CULTURE GRID

Read the following statement and the suggested explanations. In the light of the data you have studied, indicate which option (or options) are most likely to be true. Then indicate which option (or options) are probably false. Substantiate your choices by referring to material studied in class or other cultural data.

L'absence de toute communication entre les parents et les élèves est assez rare...

It is rare to find that there is absolutely no communication between high school students and their parents...

PARCE QUE:

A. En France, la famille joue toujours un rôle important et l'heure du repas est un moment privilégié pour la discussion en famille.

B. La morale a beaucoup changé depuis quelques années et les jeunes se sentent plus libres de s'exprimer ouvertement.

C. Les jeunes sont tous d'accord avec la manière de vivre de leurs parents.

D. Les jeunes Français reçoivent une éducation très sévère et profondément catholique. Ils sont obligés de se confier à leurs parents.[10]

BECAUSE:

A. *In France, the family still plays an important role and mealtime is a special part of the day set aside for family discussion.*

B. *Morals have changed a great deal in recent years and young people feel freer to express themselves openly.*

C. *Young people are all in agreement with their parents' life style.*

D. *French young people are brought up in a strict and profoundly Catholic setting. They feel obliged to confide in their parents.*

Correct responses: A and B tend to be true, C and D tend to be false. However, the essential feature of the answer is the explanation.

[10] Quoted from Santoni, "Langue et culture," p. 364.

Scoring: This type of item is scored on how effectively the students justify their choices. In a more informal setting, small groups of students may be asked to pool their reactions and information and arrive at a consensus. In this case, scoring would reflect each individual's participation in the discussion.

9.6.4   Applying an unfamiliar model

After the class has spent a given amount of time, from one unit to an entire semester, studying the target culture, the teacher might suggest analyzing aspects of that culture through the framework of a model unfamiliar to the class. For instance, if the students in a French course had not worked with Nostrand's cultural themes, the teacher might describe the parameters of selected themes and ask the students to find illustrations for each from material studied in class. The following sample item type introduces the viewpoint of a psychologist.

SAMPLE ITEM TYPE *23*   ANALYSIS ACCORDING TO A NEW MODEL

In preparation for the test, the American teacher of a course on German culture explains Maslow's five Basic Needs to the students.[11]
Here are the five Basic Needs determined by Maslow:

1. comfort and survival
2. safety
3. belongingness and love
4. self-esteem and the esteem of others
5. self-actualization

Determine in what way the Germans meet these needs and to what extent the German pattern differs from the American pattern. Give examples.

Scoring: The students' replies are scored on appropriateness and on the ability to substantiate their interpretations. In an informal test, pairs or small groups of students can discuss their views and submit a joint oral or written response.

[11] See Abraham Maslow, *Motivation and Personality* (New York: Harper & Row, 1954 and 1970).

outline

10.1 GENERAL CONSIDERATIONS

10.2 TYPES OF LITERATURE TESTS

    10.2.1 Objective tests
    10.2.2 Essay tests
    10.2.3 Oral tests

10.3 PLANNING THE LITERATURE TEST

    10.3.1 Knowledge
    10.3.2 Comprehension
    10.3.3 Expression
    10.3.4 The teacher's schematic outline

10.4 MULTIPLE-CHOICE ITEMS

    10.4.1 Knowledge items
    10.4.2 Comprehension items

10.5 ESSAY QUESTIONS

    10.5.1 Essay-test reliability
        10.5.1a Language of test
        10.5.1b Length of test
        10.5.1c Vagueness of subject
        10.5.1d Non-comparative scoring
    10.5.2 Essay-test validity
        10.5.2a Knowledge questions: class discussion
        10.5.2b Knowledge questions: reading
        10.5.2c Thought questions

ten

The Literature Test

L iterature is the written transcription of man's thoughts, feelings, and aspirations. While cultures or societies that do not have developed literatures exist, literature cannot come into being without culture. Fortunately many good features of a literary work survive translation; otherwise, few Americans, for example, could enjoy the Bible, the *Arabian Nights*, *War and Peace*, and Dante. Even so, the student who possesses a near-native command of Spanish has a marked advantage when reading Calderón over persons who must either rely on a translation or work slowly through the text, dictionary in hand. This student has the advantage because he or she can appreciate the *untranslatable*: both the tangible elements, such as the rhythm and flow and the precision of the author's expression, and the intangible—the intellectual and emotional response created by the tangible elements. The study of literature as an art and of the stylistic techniques of this art can only be approached through the language in which the literature was written.

10.1   GENERAL CONSIDERATIONS

In this section we must draw a distinction between reading texts and literature. It is obvious that the student should be able to read the target language with a certain facility before undertaking a study of the literature. Facility is important; otherwise the study of a literary text is an exercise in decoding or deciphering. The student becomes engrossed in discovering what the author is saying without being able to analyze why or how it is said.

Often the reading skill is developed by having the student work with carefully selected short texts or excerpts.[1] At a more advanced level, longer literary works are read, and are read in their entirety. Yet at this point even novels will be treated primarily as vehicles for the development of vocabulary, ease of expression (both oral and written), and direct comprehension of plot.

In this chapter we shall consider tests for advanced literature courses where the accent is on an appreciation of the artistic work and its background. This category includes Advanced Placement classes, survey of literature courses, and specialized courses organized by genre, period, or author.

10.2 TYPES OF LITERATURE TESTS

There are three types of literature tests: objective tests, essay tests, and oral tests. Each has certain advantages and limitations.

10.2.1 Objective tests

An objective-test item (whether a multiple-choice item or a direct question) is designed to elicit a specific response. The student's response, therefore, will be either clearly right or clearly wrong. The teacher can keep a record of the common wrong answers to certain questions and use them as distractors in multiple-choice items.

An objective test in literature *can* measure the following:

knowledge of chronology, authors, works, even content (plots, ideas, characters);

vocabulary: key words, their importance, their specific interpretation and use by the author;

ability to analyze specific features of a poem or a prose passage, to draw comparisons between works, periods, etc.

However, the objective test *cannot* measure:

accuracy and sophistication of student expression in the foreign language;

ability to interpret a literary selection;

ability to organize an essay, develop an introduction, choose related and salient examples, and draw a valid conclusion.

---

[1] Consult the MLA Conference Newsletter: *Teaching Language Through Literature*. Published quarterly. Address correspondence to 501 Philosophy Hall, Columbia University, New York, NY 10027.

The question of literary interpretation is particularly delicate. Faced with several credible interpretations in a multiple-choice item, the students are prevented from searching for any other interpretation. In addition, the danger exists that the students will concentrate on discovering not the interpretation they find most valid, but the interpretation they think the teacher most likely to have selected. On a particular item, either one interpretation is obviously correct and the three others are total misreadings of the text (the item is consequently relatively simple), or the choices are ambiguous, each containing an opinion that might be supported. It seems that a more reliable type of interpretation item could be developed, one containing the "interpretation" in the stem and requiring the student to select the best supporting quotation(s); however, such an item would tend to evaluate analysis and logical thinking rather than valid personal interpretation.

Test items for advanced students pose another problem. Literature courses of the type we are discussing are usually offered to fifth-year language students in high school or third-year language students in college. At this stage in their language education, students have become sophisticated objective-test takers. Thus, the teacher must take great care in the composition and selection of distractors.

10.2.2   Essay tests

Essay tests require the students to organize their thoughts and to substantiate their interpretations. Since almost all literary criticism is in essay form, from brief book reports to lengthy critical works, the essay test in literature is a highly valid test form. The limitations of the essay-type test must also be taken into account. First, there is the inequity of scoring. Those students who express themselves well and easily in the target language often obtain a high score even though their ideas are mediocre, while students who can give a more valid interpretation but possess less facility in the target language receive a lower grade. Some teachers, taking this phenomenon into account, occasionally give an essay test in English. Other teachers tell students that they may answer in the target language *or* in English, but that the highest possible grade for an English essay will be B + .

Second, many essay tests sample only limited aspects of the material that has been covered. Fortunately, a structured test can be developed in which the student is asked to introduce a greater amount of specific material.

Finally, essay tests are extremely difficult to score reliably. There is the ever-present tendency to expect good papers from good students and to make an *a priori* negative judgment about the work of the poor students. Some teachers admit that they grade by the "hunch" system: they have a "feeling" about how good a paper is. While an experienced teacher would probably not categorize a particular set of papers as "very good," "average," and "poor" on the first reading and then drastically revise these grades on a second reading a week later, the difference between a C+ and a B— is very hazy indeed, as it often is even between a C and a B. Two teachers reading the same set of papers will find that their scores vary even more sharply than those given by one teacher on two different occasions. In preparing a testing program for a literature class, the teacher must not forget these considerations.

10.2.3 Oral tests

At the graduate school level, oral literature tests are part of the comprehensive examinations for the master's and doctor's degrees. In advanced literature courses, some teachers give short oral tests, in part as preparation for the degree examinations.

Oral literature tests favor the students who express themselves fluently in the target language. Like the essay tests, the oral tests are difficult to score with complete reliability. Not only are the results not always predictable, but the personalities of the teacher and student and the rapport they have with one another may tend to influence the test grade. Oral tests do have an advantage over essay tests in that they permit a broader sampling of the subject matter. In an essay test students may camouflage their ignorance by selectively including only those elements they are sure of; students in an oral test are confronted with more direct questions. In a typical oral test there is a mix of objective or short-answer questions and more complex thought questions.

10.3   PLANNING THE LITERATURE TEST

Usually very few tests are administered in a literature class. Therefore, many students study the types of tests and the content of the test items their teacher has given in the past in order to determine what material to learn. If the teacher planning a literature test has first reviewed the course objectives, such reviews can be helpful in orienting the students toward these objectives, which are generally divided into three areas; factual knowledge, textual comprehension, and individual expression.[2] Each teacher determines the relative importance of the areas for each particular class.

[2] For an alternate classification system based on the Valette-Disick taxonomy, see Chapter 15: "Literature," in Rebecca M. Valette and Renée S. Disick, *Modern Language Performance Objectives and Individualization* (New York: Harcourt Brace Jovanovich, 1972).

10.3.1   Knowledge

Most literature teachers expect their students to have learned a certain number of facts. Some courses are built around facts about authors, works, characters, historical situations, and so on. Often students have to be able to identify quotations. Most teachers consider such knowledge as basic to any further discussion of the texts. They use factual tests or quizzes primarily to encourage a careful reading of major works and background material; since the tests are conceived primarily as "incentives," the grades scored on these tests, frequent in number though they may be, have little weight when the final grade is determined. Other teachers may consider the acquisition of factual knowledge a major objective of the course, rather than a step toward a major objective; in this case scores made on "knowledge" tests are an important factor in determining the student's final grade.

10.3.2   Comprehension

A primary objective, particularly in undergraduate literature classes, is comprehension. The course is so constructed that students will learn to read, analyze, and understand different types of texts. Both classwork and tests are built around series of questions designed to lead the student to pick out specific points, identify styles, determine themes and character development. The emphasis is on analysis, on the dissection of a literary work. On a test for such a class, the student usually identifies works and authors and answers questions on works studied in class or prepared outside of class, or even on an unfamiliar text.

10.3.3   Expression

There are two aspects to expression, both of which may be objectives of the literature class. One aspect is command of the target language: the acquisition of a literary vocabulary and an impersonal style. The second aspect is ability to synthesize or organize. Once the students have demonstrated their ability to examine a literary work, they must prepare an outline of their findings, and draw the relevant conclusions. Only a written essay test will enable the students to demonstrate their organizational ability. At its best, this type of test presents the students with a new idea or thesis that they are to criticize and interpret in the light of the course material.

10.3.4   The teacher's schematic outline

In order to see how a written literature test may be scored, let us take as an example the first-semester midterm examination of a French literature survey course. Generally the teacher assigns the following percentages to the objectives:

knowledge: 20 percent
comprehension: 30 percent
expression: 50 percent

The expression part of the examination will be an essay question. Knowledge of the subject matter and comprehension will be tested by objective multiple-choice items.

The multiple-choice items will also be planned so that the course material is covered and so that the number of questions per subject will more or less correspond to the importance given that particular subject in the course. The teacher makes the following brief outline (subject to revision as he or she prepares the test):

The multiple-choice section will include 50 questions: 20 to determine the students' knowledge of authors, themes, works, plot, etc., and 30 to assess their comprehension, that is, their ability to analyze a poem, to analyze a prose passage, and to draw comparisons between works and passages. Five questions will treat the literary terms studied, and, since more study was given to the Middle Ages than to any other period, 27 questions will concern the Middle Ages; 18 will cover the Renaissance.

With this outline in mind, the teacher draws up the chart on page 289. As the multiple-choice items are prepared, he or she classifies each item according to the prior specifications. If necessary, the chart may be somewhat modified as the construction of the test progresses. The chart permits a certain degree of flexibility of choice as the items (indicated by tallies) are being written.

10.4   MULTIPLE-CHOICE ITEMS

The preparation of a multiple-choice section for a literature test is an especially challenging (and time-consuming) enterprise. The teacher who enjoys precise logical exercise and who does not become easily discouraged when the item analysis shows that certain items have furnished poor results (ambiguous? too difficult? too easy? more than one possible answer?) will appreciate the stimulation the preparation of such tests provides.

If possible, the teacher should prepare the outline chart for the examina-

Figure 22

	OBJECTIVES	authors and characters	works and times	content:ideas and plot	content:themes	analysis of a poem	analysis of prose	drawing comparisons between passages	
	CONTENT	KNOWLEDGE				COMPREHENSION			TOTALS
Middle Ages	literary terms					ҬHL			5
	background		//						2
	chansons de geste		/				/	//	4
	Tristan			///			///	///	9
	littérature courtoise	/			/				2
	littérature bourgeoise	/		/				/	3
	poésie	/	//	/	//		/	/	8
Renaissance	background	/							1
	Rabelais			/			/	//	4
	La Pléiade		/		/	ҬHL		/	8
	Montaigne	/					////		5
	TOTALS	5	5	5	5	10	10	10	50

tion well in advance, see Figure 22. Throughout the course, he or she will note the material that might be useful for future test items. Items from past examinations should be filed; often a good item can be modified and used on a later examination. The writing and editing of the test must be completed a week or so in advance of the examination date so that the items can be typed up and duplicated. During the pressure of examination time, a set of such papers can be scored and graded very quickly.

10.4.1 Knowledge items

Knowledge items, often of the identification type, are the easiest to write and tend to prove quite reliable statistically. The advantage of the multiple-choice item over the simple question with written answer is twofold. First, students can answer a greater number of them within a given period of time; thus, the grade for that particular exam is based on a broader sampling of the subject matter. Second, the multiple-choice examination, even though more time-consuming to prepare, can be scored very rapidly. Third, it exclusively examines knowledge; a student's command of writing in the foreign language plays no role in the test. Moreover, the teacher is freed from the necessity to correct the inevitable errors of vocabulary and grammar.

The sample items in this section are taken from a French literature test.

SAMPLE ITEM TYPE *1* AUTHORS

The student is asked to describe a writer or to identify the author of a quoted passage.

Lequel des écrivains suivants *n'est pas* un « chroniqueur » ?

Which of the following authors is not a "chroniqueur"?

A. Agrippa d'Aubigné
B. Philippe de Commynes
C. Geoffroy de Villehardouin
D. Jean de Joinville

Correct response: A

SAMPLE ITEM TYPE *2* WORKS

Le sonnet « Heureux qui, comme Ulysse... » a paru dans quel recueil ?

The sonnet "Heureux qui, comme Ulysse..." appeared in which collection?

A. *Antiquités de Rome*
B. *Hymnes*
C. *Regrets*
D. *Elégies*

Correct response: C

In other items concerning works, the student may be asked to identify the work in which a particular quoted passage is found.

SAMPLE ITEM TYPE *3*   PLOT AND CHARACTER

Le gant comme symbole apparaît
dans quel chapitre de *Tristan*?

*The glove as a symbol appears in
which chapter of* Tristan?

A. « L'Ermite Ogrin »
B. « Brangien livrée aux serfs »
C. « Le Jugement par le fer rouge »
D. « La Forêt de Morois »

Correct response: D

SAMPLE ITEM TYPE *4*   THEMES

La question *ubi sunt* paraît dans
un poème de du Bellay « Las! où
est maintenant ce mépris de
Fortune? » où le poète se plaint

The question ubi sunt *appears in
a poem of du Bellay "Las..."
in which the poet complains
about*

A. de la disparition de l'inspiration
poétique
B. du manque de richesses
C. de l'éloignement de ses amis
D. du mépris des gens de Rome

*the disappearance of poetic
inspiration*
the lack of wealth
the separation from his friends
the scorn of the Romans

Correct response: A

10.4.2   Comprehension items

Comprehension items are much more difficult to write and should be analyzed
statistically whenever possible. Often the test situation will reveal a second
valid response or some other kind of ambiguity; in this case the answer grid
should be modified to allow the student credit for having selected either of
the two possible responses. (Some teachers prefer to measure only knowledge
with multiple-choice tests and to measure comprehension with a series of
written questions and answers.)

SAMPLE ITEM TYPE *5*   LITERARY ANALYSIS

A short literary selection is followed by a series of multiple-choice items
that test the student's analytical ability. Here, for example, is a sample
selection from the poetry part of the French literature survey midterm
examination.

> France, mère des arts, des armes et des lois,
> Tu m'as nourri longtemps du lait de ta mamelle;
> Ores, comme un agneau qui sa nourrice appelle,
> Je remplis de ton nom les antres et les bois.

Si tu m'as pour enfant avoué quelquefois,
Que ne me réponds-tu maintenant, ô cruelle?
France, France, réponds à ma triste querelle!
Mais nul, sinon Echo, ne répond à ma voix.

Entre les loups cruels j'erre parmi la plaine,
Je sens venir l'hiver, de qui la froide haleine
D'une tremblante horreur fait hérisser ma peau.

Las! tes autres agneaux n'ont faute de pâture,
Ils ne craignent le loup, le vent, ni la froidure:
Si ne suis-je pourtant le pire du troupeau!

Joachim du Bellay, *Les Regrets*

1. Ce poème est un(e)	*This poem is a (an)*
A. sonnet	*sonnet*
B. rondeau	*rondeau*
C. ode	*ode*
D. élégie	*elegy*

Correct response: A

If such an item is too simple for the level of the class, it may be modified so that instead of a recognition question it becomes in part a recall question. In the two sample items below and in Item 2, the student must remember the word "sonnet" and the characteristics of a sonnet in order to select the correct responses. Two modifications are possible: options may be presented with the initial and terminal letters or with only the initial letters.

Ce poème a la forme d'un(e)		*This poem has the form of a (an)*	
A. s____t	A. é	s____t	e
B. r____u	B. o	r____u	o
C. o____e	C. r	o____e	r
D. é____e	D. s	e____y	s

In the second case, in this example, it is desirable to arrange the options in alphabetical order.

2. Les rimes des deux premières strophes sont des rimes	*The rhymes in the first two stanzas are*
A. croisées	*A. alternate rhymes: ABAB*
B. plates	*B. couplets: AABB*
C. embrassées	*C. ABBA*
D. redoublées	*D. AAAA*

Correct response: C

Below we see how this item, too, may be transformed into a partial-recall question by using first and last letters or first letters only:

Dans les deux premières strophes le poète emploie des rimes

In the first two stanzas, the poet uses

A. c_____ées	A. c	*A. a_____e rhymes:*	*ABAB*
B. e_____ées	B. e	*B.*	*: ABBA*
C. p_____es	C. p	*C. c_____ts*	*: AABB*
D. r_____ées	D. r	*D.*	*: AAAA*

3. Pour exprimer la détresse de l'exil, le poète s'identifie avec

In order to express the distress of his exile, the poet identifies himself with

A. la France, sa nourrice

France, his wetnurse

B. un agneau égaré

a lost lamb

C. le pire du troupeau

the worst of the flock

D. les loups cruels

the cruel wolves

Correct response: B

Such an item, which is relatively easy, tests whether the students have understood the major imagery of the poem.

4. Dans le vers quatorze, le poète met l'accent sur son

In the fourteenth line, the poet underlines

A. propre génie

his own genius

B. insuffisance

his inadequacy

C. besoin d'amitié

his need for friendship

D. amour pour la France

his love for France

Correct response: A

This item, built on the critical reading of one line, is much more difficult than Item 3, above.

5. Dans la dernière strophe le poète introduit l'idée de

In the last stanza, the poet introduces the idea of

A. solitude

solitude

B. l'injustice de son sort

the injustice of his fate

C. l'unité du troupeau

the unity of the flock

D. la tristesse de la séparation

the sadness of separation

Correct response: B

This question is similar to Item 4; it evaluates the student's critical reading of a part of the poem. While all four ideas expressed in the options are found in the poem, only B does not appear until the final verse.

6. Quel vers est particulièrement lent?   *Which line is particularly slow?*

A. 2
B. 6
C. 7
D. 13

Correct response: C

This item evaluates student appreciation of rhythm and movement.

Short prose passages may also be presented in a multiple-choice format. Reading questions based on prose passages are often difficult to prepare since paragraph analysis is open to diverse interpretations; reading items based on poetry are easier to compose since most languages have some formal rules of versification.

SAMPLE ITEM TYPE 6   DRAWING COMPARISONS

Good comparison items can constitute an effective test, for students are compelled to think about what they have read in order to arrive at valid conclusions.

Here is an example in French:

Si l'on juge l'amour de Tristan et Iseut selon les idées de l'« art de vivre » de Montaigne, on critiquera surtout

If one were to judge the love of Tristan and Iseut according to Montaigne's concept of the "art de vivre", one would most criticize

A. l'adultère.
B. leurs souffrances.
C. la volupté de leur amour.
D. les excès de la passion.

their adultery.
their suffering.
the voluptuousness of their love.
the intemperance of their passion.

Correct response: D

Comparison items may be presented in conjunction with literary-analysis items. In this case, the passage or poem may lead to such questions as:

The main theme of the passage is similar to that of...

or:

Rabelais' ideas on education are

A. identical with those expressed in the passage.
B. in total contrast to those expressed in the passage.
C. etc.

10.5   ESSAY QUESTIONS

In many literature classes, especially the more advanced ones, examinations are usually written tests often consisting of one or several essay questions. Since these classes are usually relatively small, the time saved scoring a multiple-choice test is often a consideration of minor importance. Unfortunately the written tests given in many literature classes are hastily prepared and of dubious validity and reliability.

10.5.1   Essay-test reliability

The reliability of an essay test tends to be limited by several factors: the language used (target or native), the length of the test, the vagueness of the subject, and non-comparative scoring.

10.5.1a   LANGUAGE OF TEST

Literature tests given in the target language unfortunately have the effect of favoring those students who possess the most fluency in the language. (While it is admitted that literature classes should best be offered only to students whose command of the language presents no barrier either to understanding or to expression, it is true that this is frequently not the case. In graduate school libraries, English translations of French works are often checked out by the French majors, of German works by the German majors, and so on.) If fluency in the language constitutes one of the aims of the course, then it should, of course, be tested. But if other objectives are also considered important, it is advisable at least once a semester to assign a paper or examination in the students' native language so that the content alone will be judged.

10.5.1b   LENGTH OF TEST

Within an hour, within even two or three, only a certain amount can be written by hand. Occasionally, teachers who feel that their examination insufficiently samples the material covered in class add an extra item or broaden existing questions at the last minute. The result is that many students are unable to finish the test within the allotted time, and the teacher —now feeling guilty about the length of the examination—debates whether to score the unfinished section zero or give it some credit.

The teacher can avoid this problem by choosing an essay topic whose scope can be covered within the allotted time. Not only does reliability in scoring increase—the speed factor is eliminated—but the students experience the satisfaction of handling the test question in a thoughtful, leisurely fashion. A set of multiple-choice questions or a series of short-answer questions could be added to examine those subjects not included in the essay.

10.5.1c VAGUENESS OF SUBJECT

Many times the essay subject is poorly defined. The students receive the impression—perhaps correct—that the teacher just thought up a topic on the way to class.

Here, for example, is a very broad subject:

Discuss seventeenth-century French tragedy.

Since each student may select different aspects to write about, there will be little common ground on which to base the scoring. Often this lack of focus can be corrected if the teacher spends sufficient time before the examination selecting the specific points he or she wishes to have covered in the essay. An improved question might read:

Explain the rules governing French classical tragedy and show their application in one of the plays you have read.

or:

Compare and contrast *Andromaque* and *Le Cid*, considering dramatic structure and each author's conception of tragedy.

In the latter questions, since specific information is asked for, the teacher can outline a more reliable scoring system.

10.5.1d NON-COMPARATIVE SCORING

Often the teacher will read one student's test in its entirety, assign a grade, read the next student's test, and so on. This type of scoring has the effect of reinforcing the teacher's prior judgments: the good student's paper is automatically considered very good, the average student's paper is consistently average. Let us consider a more equitable method.

When scoring a set of fairly long examinations, the teacher can read just the first question on each examination and then place that paper in one of three or four piles according to the merit of the specific essay. When all have been classified, the teacher peruses one group at a time, assigning the grades with + or − according to relative merit. Then the papers are scrambled and the second question is read. Again the papers are grouped according to merit. Since the teacher is concentrating on only one question at a time, he or she can more reliably and objectively compare the performance of the different students.

10.5.2   Essay-test validity

Essay-test validity depends on the test's relevance to the course objectives. All tests measure something; the teacher must determine whether the essay test given is actually measuring the type of performance that corresponds to the intended objectives of the course.

10.5.2a   KNOWLEDGE QUESTIONS: CLASS DISCUSSION

Frequently essay questions in literature courses are based on subject matter discussed in class. Let us look at the following question:

Describe the polemic struggle of the Jesuits and the Jansenists in the mid-seventeenth century and define Pascal's role.

While based on a literary work, it does not actually require the student to have read Pascal. Many students do well on such a question simply by studying their class notes. If the course objective is teaching *about* French literature, such a question is valid. But if the course objective is to have the students read and appreciate the texts, then such a question must be regarded as one of dubious validity.

Let us look at another question:

Describe the originality of Giraudoux's theatrical works.

This question, when given to a class of advanced students who have studied drama at length, would be a thought question. Too often, however, a question like this appears on a test in a survey of literature class or in a twentieth-century literature class. The students have probably read only one play by Giraudoux and very few plays from other periods. They will only be able to repeat what they have read about the playwight's originality or what they have heard the teacher mention in class.

10.5.2b   KNOWLEDGE QUESTIONS: READING

To encourage careful reading of the texts, many teachers ask identification questions. Here are some examples:

Identify the following characters and briefly describe their roles.

Identify the following quotations and situate them in the work as a whole.

As long as the passages cited are representative of the author's style and thought, such questions are valid tests of the students' familiarity with the texts.

10.5.2c   THOUGHT QUESTIONS

As we have seen, many questions, purporting to be thought questions, are really knowledge questions. The valid thought question presents the student with a problem, an interpretation, a comparison that has *not* been mentioned in class. At the same time, the problem is carefully defined so that, within the limits of his or her knowledge and his or her reading and within the time limitations of the test, the student can handle it satisfactorily.

Let us look at some possible thought questions.

Too broad:

> Discuss the problem of liberty as it presents itself to Roland, Tristan, Rodrigue, and Oreste.

> Discuss the theme of love in *Tristan et Iseut*, *Le Cid*, and *Andromaque*.

Within an hour the student cannot even begin to define "liberty" (in the first question), much less do an adequate job in relating the conception to four diverse protagonists. The definition of "theme" and "love" (in the second question) is also complex. The danger of such topics is that they encourage gross oversimplification on the part of the students.

Properly limited:

> Roland, Tristan, Rodrigue, and Oreste are not entirely free in their actions. Compare and contrast the factors that influence the decisions made by these protagonists.

> Describe the type of love presented in *Tristan et Iseut*, *Le Cid*, and *Andromaque*. What role does love play in each of these works?

It is also reasonable to offer the students some choice in their treatment of subject: they may choose two (or three) out of four protagonists or two out of three works.

In another version of the thought question, the students are presented with a quotation or a new idea that they must apply to what they have read:

> Baudelaire was impressed by Poe's classification of poetry as either descriptive or evocative. Apply Poe's distinction to the work of three poets we have studied this semester.

Recordings may also form the basis for thought questions. For example, the student might be asked to listen to three dramatized readings of

Baudelaire's "Invitation au voyage" and explain in an essay which one, in his or her opinion, best captures the spirit of the work. Or the student might listen to a taped discussion about a specific work and then make a detailed analysis of the points of view expressed.

The carefully prepared essay question provides a challenging finish to a well-taught advanced literature class.

part three
Current
Developments

outline

eleven
Directions
in Modern Language
Testing

Testing and evaluation play a multi-faceted role in the teaching of a second language. Even before second-language instruction begins, teachers are often concerned with measuring aptitude. If enrollments are limited, how can one select those students most likely to experience success? If enrollments are open, how can one best structure courses so as to place students into learning environments suited to their needs?

Once the second-language course is under way, teachers are anxious to determine how readily their students are progressing: What elements have been mastered and where is further instruction needed? To what extent can the students use what they have learned in communication situations? Do they understand the cultural parameters of the language under study? Are they able to interpret literature? If new students are entering the program, teachers would like to ascertain their level of language proficiency in order to place them in appropriate courses. In competency-based programs, teachers need to assess whether the goals of instruction have been met.

In addition to a concern for the subject matter itself, second-language teachers often want to evaluate the affective outcomes of their instruction. Do students have a positive attitude toward the new language and culture? Do they enjoy language classes so much that they wish to continue with other courses in the sequence? Are the students growing in self-confidence?

This chapter will touch lightly on some of the developments in language testing. The bibliography at the end of the book will point the way to further reading for those wishing to explore the area in greater depth.

11.1   MEASURING APTITUDE

The first language aptitude tests were developed after World War I, at the time when standardized objective tests made their entry into public education. Research into language aptitude rests on three basic assumptions: [1]

1. Certain talents or abilities (which are loosely termed "aptitude"), contribute to the "ease" with which a student learns a foreign language.
2. "Aptitude" is unevenly distributed in the population. Therefore, a student's degree of aptitude may be measured quantitatively.
3. The nature of "aptitude" may vary as instructional objectives change. The aptitude for learning to speak a language, for example, might not be the same as the aptitude needed for learning to read or translate.

11.1.1   Defining language aptitude

Research has not been able to uncover a single "language gift" possessed by some but not all members of society. On the contrary, the ability to learn languages seems to be a universal human trait. Of course, some people learn languages more quickly than others, and this observation led John Carroll to define language aptitude as the time needed for learning. [2] In other words, the student with high language aptitude will pick up a second language in shorter time than the student with low language aptitude.

Over the years, studies have attempted to isolate certain factors that contribute to successful second-language learning. The focus has almost always been on the formal classroom environment. The student with high aptitude, then, is the student who can learn a language quickly and well within academic constraints.

If languages are taught as school subjects, measures of IQ and measures of scholastic ability do correlate rather well with achievement in language classes. [3] That is to say, students with high IQ scores and good grade point averages tend to get good grades in foreign language courses. (The correlation is not always as high when language achievement is measured by

---

[1] Quoted from Rebecca M. Valette, *Directions in Foreign Language Testing* (New York: MLA and ERIC, 1969), p. 4. Further information on the topics mentioned in this section can be found in *Directions*, pp. 4–11. See also Leon A. Jakobovits, *Foreign Language Learning: a Psycholinguistic Analysis of the Issues* (Rowley, Mass.: Newbury House, 1970), especially Chapter 5: "Foreign Language Aptitude and Attitude" (hereafter cited as "Aptitude and Attitude," and *Psycholinguistic Analysis*).

[2] See John B. Carroll, "The Prediction of Success in Intensive Foreign Language Training," in Robert Glaser, ed., *Training Research and Education* (Pittsburgh: University of Pittsburgh Press, 1962), p. 122 (hereafter cited as "Prediction of Success" and *Training Research*).

[3] For a definition of the concept of correlation, see Section 4.1.3.

standardized achievement tests.) The correlation with prior grade point average is, however, highest with writing tests and is much lower with speaking tests. One might conclude that the qualities needed to obtain high scores in writing tests—good organization, attention to detail, ability to function well with written language—are the qualities that contribute to high grades in other courses.

The most recent language aptitude tests measure several interrelated factors. The Carroll-Sapon Modern Language Aptitude Test (MLAT), 1958, and the Carroll-Sapon Elementary Modern Language Aptitude Test (EMLAT), 1967, are built around the following factors:[4]

1. phonetic coding: the ability to "code" and "store" sounds so that they can later be retrieved
2. grammatical sensitivity: the ability to handle grammar
3. rote memory for foreign language materials
4. inductive language learning ability: the ability to infer linguistic patterns from new linguistic content.[5]

The Pimsleur Language Aptitude Battery (1966) is designed to evaluate the following factors:

1. verbal intelligence: familiarity with words and language analysis
2. auditory ability: ability to discriminate sounds and to make sound-symbol associations
3. motivation
4. verbal IQ (as measured by vocabulary size)[6]

Some teachers feel that musical ability is somehow related to language aptitude. There does not seem to be a definite measurable correlation, although research has indicated that perhaps the ability to discriminate pitch may be a factor in language aptitude.[7]

11.1.2 Prognosis: using aptitude tests for selection

The Carroll-Sapon and Pimsleur aptitude tests, which are the two batteries currently available commercially, predict student achievement rather reliably in courses where all students receive the same kind and the same amount of

[4] For complete descriptions of these tests and the Pimsleur Test, see the Appendix, p. 323.
[5] See Carroll, "Prediction of Success," *Training Research*, pp. 128–30.
[6] See Paul Pimsleur, "Testing Foreign Language Learning" in Albert Valdman, ed., *Trends in Language Teaching* (New York: McGraw-Hill, 1966).
[7] See Ralph R. Leutenegger and Theodore H. Mueller, "Auditory Factors and the Acquisition of French Language Mastery," *Modern Language Journal* 48 (1964), pp. 144–46; and M. Elizabeth Westphal, Ralph R. Leutenegger and Dorothea L. Wagner, "Some Psycho-Acoustic and Intellectual Correlates of Achievement in German Language Learning of Junior High School Students," *Modern Language Journal* 53 (1969), pp. 258–66.

instruction under similar conditions. As prognostic instruments, they are therefore most effective in selecting students for intensive language courses.

According to John Carroll's model for learning, five variables account for success in mastering a task:[8]

instructional factors: 1. adequacy of presentation (quality of instruction)
2. opportunity for learning (time allowed)
student factors: 3. general intelligence
4. motivation (perseverance)
5. aptitude (time needed to learn a task)

In an intensive language program, such as the language courses at the United States Defense Language Institutes, the quality of instruction is uniform, the time allowed is the same for all students, the candidates must demonstrate high general intelligence and strong motivation, and thus the only variable is measured aptitude. Because of the pace of the course, only students who learn languages quickly, that is, students with high aptitude, have a strong chance of being successful. It should be further pointed out that in the DLI program the military wants to produce a specific number of candidates able to handle a specific language: the concern is not the general education of all personnel. Hence prior selection is necessary, and the aptitude test helps to pick out those candidates who are most likely to do well.

In the typical secondary school or college language program, however, diversity rather than uniformity of course offerings and instruction is the general pattern; moreover, students are of different levels of general intelligence and show different degrees of motivation. Hence, measured aptitude is but one of five variables in predicting success. It should also be remembered that no test is perfect and that for any single administration of a test there is always a certain error measurement; the score that a student receives on an aptitude test usually is not an exact measure of his or her ability, but rather an approximation (see Section 4.2.2g, Standard Error). It is unfair, therefore, to keep a student out of a language course on the basis of an aptitude test score, especially if the student desires to take that course.

11.1.3   Diagnosis: using aptitude tests for placement

Commercial aptitude tests can make their most important contribution toward improving second-language learning in the area of diagnostic information. For instance, students with low scores in measured language aptitude might be placed into a slower track, while students with high

---

[8] Carroll, "Prediction of Success," *Training Research.*

aptitude scores might be scheduled into an accelerated class. (Of course, since aptitude is but one of the factors that contribute to success in a language course, the administration should consider these initial placements as tentative, and should move students up or down as their performance indicates.)

If the school has a general foreign language requirement, the aptitude test might provide useful information for determining whether a student could be allowed to omit the language course altogether. Some schools find it inhumane to require a student with serious learning difficulties to suffer through a required course in which lack of success is virtually guaranteed. It should be noted, however, that if this use of the aptitude test became known to the students, they might purposely strive for a poor score in order to avoid a course they do not like.

The scores on specific sections of the language aptitude test can also provide diagnostic information. Students with low scores in the aural portions of the aptitude test (phonetic coding or auditory ability) will probably do better in a course that presents reading and writing from the outset rather than one that places early emphasis only on listening and speaking. If such students were placed into an audio-lingual sequence, the teacher should be alerted to the fact that they might need special help in the initial phases of instruction. Similarly, students who scored poorly on the grammar sections of the aptitude test will require carefully sequenced presentations of structure, and might even do best initially in a more slowly paced audio-visual course.

Individual schools might wish to experiment by comparing language aptitude test scores (both global scores and part scores) with student performance in the various course options available. They may be able to discern certain patterns of correlation that would help in improving the placement of incoming students.

11.1.4 Identifying learning styles

Concern with the measurement of language aptitude is giving way to an investigation of learning styles. The first step is identifying learning styles and developing means of evaluation: does a student prefer working alone or in groups? does a student have a preferred sense modality: is the student "ear-minded" or "eye-minded"? does the student prefer a structured or an unstructured environment? Individual learning style is much more complex than the above "either-or" questions would indicate, and it is beyond the range of this handbook to explore the various approaches to the matching of learning styles to modes of instruction. However, schools with a sequence of varied language courses might wish to look into more effective ways of matching incoming students with learning situations most likely to produce a positive result.[9]

11.2 TESTING COMMAND OF THE SUBJECT MATTER

The central concern of language teachers when they think of "testing" is how best to evaluate the students' growing command of the second language. Ancillary concerns include the evaluation of the students' knowledge of culture and literature.

At the 1975 AILA (Association Internationale de Linguistique Appliquée) World Congress in a keynote speech entitled "Language Testing: Art or Science?" Bernard Spolsky identified three trends in the history of modern language testing: the prescientific trend, the psycho-structuralist trend, and the psycholinguistic-sociolinguistic trend.[10]

11.2.1 The prescientific trend

The prescientific trend characterized language teaching in the United States prior to the 1920s and is still the approach used by some teachers. There is a lack of concern for statistical analysis, for objectivity, and for test reliability. The tests themselves are mainly written exercises: translation, composition, or isolated sentences. In this "elitist" approach to testing, it is felt that the person who knows how to teach is obviously in the best position to judge the proficiency of the students.

The first edition of this handbook, *Modern Language Testing* (1967) was written primarily to help teachers without formal training in measurement to move from this "prescientific" method of evaluation to the more objective evaluation techniques of the "psychometric-structuralist" trend.

11.2.2 The psychometric-structuralist trend

The psychometric-structuralist trend saw the entry of the experts into the field of language testing. On the one hand, the measurement experts or psychometricians introduced their belief that measurement can and should

[9] For a more detailed introduction to the subject, see Carol Hosenfeld, "The New Student Role: Individual Differences and Implications for Instruction," in Gilbert A. Jarvis, ed., *Perspective: A New Freedom*, ACTFL Review of Foreign Language Education, vol. 7 (Skokie, Ill.: National Textbook, 1975), pp. 129–67.
[10] The following sections are a simplification of the views expressed by Bernard Spolsky, "Language Testing: Art or Science?", paper delivered August 27, 1975, at the Fourth AILA World Congress in Stuttgart, Germany.

be precise and scientific. Objective test techniques were developed, the most widely used being the multiple-choice item, and analytic scoring procedures were introduced. Statistical methods were improved to measure the reliability and validity of tests as well as their correlation with other types of measurement instruments. On the other hand, the language experts in the field of structural linguistics provided a scientific view of language and used contrastual analysis to identify the problems faced by the second-language learner: these problems, in Robert Lado's view,[11] are patterns and units that have either no counterpart in the native language or a different distributional pattern. The resulting language tests were "discrete point" tests, of which the best examples are the standardized language tests developed and administered by the Educational Testing Service: the College Entrance Examination Board Achievement Tests, the MLA Coop Tests, the Graduate Record Tests, and the Test of English as a Foreign Language (TOEFL).[12]

The proponents of the psychometric-structuralist trend have worked with the "traditionalists" of the prescientific trend to develop more objective and reliable means of scoring writing tests and oral interviews, such as the tests used by the Foreign Service Institute. The problem with these latter tests has been primarily one of economy: the scoring of essay tests and the administration of interview tests require trained scorers and significant amounts of time, whereas the multiple-choice objective tests are much easier to use.

11.2.3   The psycholinguistic-sociolinguistic trend

The psycholinguistic-sociolinguistic trend focuses on the integrative or "global" test, which takes into account the total communicative effect of the message. The psycholinguists insist that there is such a thing as overall language proficiency or language competence and that knowing a language is more than just knowing several thousand discrete elements. The sociolinguists place the emphasis on communicative competence and introduce the concept of a situational approach to testing.

In preparing language tests, the classroom teacher will want to take into account elements of both the psychometric-structuralist trend and the psycholinguistic-sociolinguistic trend. On the one hand, the teacher will want to test, in as objective a manner as possible, whether the students have mastered the vocabulary and the structures in a specific lesson. At the same time, the teacher is concerned with how well the students have assimilated

[11] See Robert Lado, *Language Testing: The Construction and Use of Foreign Language Tests* (New York: McGraw-Hill, 1964).
[12] For descriptions of these tests, as well as of the similar Pimsleur Modern Foreign Language Proficiency Tests, see the Appendix.

the elements of language and to what extent they can use the second language for communication. In each of the chapters of Part Two of this handbook, the first sections focus on "discrete-point" items. In the latter sections the emphasis shifts to the testing of communicative competence and suggestions about other global tests of language ability, such as dictations and cloze procedures, which measure the students' ability to function when there is reduced redundancy (that is, when elements are missing or difficult to understand).

11.3   MEASURING AFFECTIVE GOALS

Since the late 1960s, foreign language teachers have become increasingly concerned with the affective or humanistic outcomes of second language instruction.[13] Whereas only some teachers feel that the *main* goal of education should be the creation of better human beings, all teachers will agree that students are more likely to learn a second language if they are positively motivated, enjoy classroom activities, and feel that they are increasing their individual potential.

The most widely-used indirect measure of the extent to which affective goals are being met in the foreign-language classroom is the analysis of enrollment trends. With the abolition of language requirements in many, if not most, American schools and colleges, students no longer feel obligated to study a foreign language, or if they do begin a second language, they drop the course after two years. In a school where language enrollment figures are increasing more rapidly than the size of the student body, the teachers may conclude that they are indeed meeting the affective, or humanistic, goals of their students.

In 1970, under the sponsorship of the Northeast Conference, Leon Jakobovits prepared the Foreign Language Attitude Questionnaire (FLAQ).[14]
The items on the questionnaire ask the students about their linguistic background, their reasons for studying a foreign language, the skills they wish to develop, and their views about the benefits of knowing a second language.

[13] For a review of these trends, see Renée S. Disick and Laura Barbanel, "Affective education and foreign language learning" in Gilbert A. Jarvis, ed., *The Challenge of Communication*, ACTFL Review of Foreign Language Education, vol. 6 (Skokie, Ill.: National Textbook, 1974). See also R. C. Gardner and W. E. Lambert, *Attitudes and Motivation in Second-Language Learning* (Rowley, Mass.: Newbury House 1972).

[14] A study of motivation in foreign-language learning and a presentation of the FLAQ are to be found in Joseph Tursi, ed., *Foreign Languages and the "New" Student*, Reports of the Working Committees of the Northeast Conference on the Teaching of Foreign Languages (New York: MLA Materials Center, 1970). See also Jakobovits, "Aptitude and Attitude," *Psycholinguistic Analysis*. For a description of the test, see the Appendix.

Teachers do not have to use the entire questionnaire, of course; they may select only those sections which are most relevant to their own school situation.

In addition to evaluating the attitudes of students enrolled or about to enroll in second language classes, the teacher may wish to draw up a brief dropout survey to identify the reasons for which students decide not to continue with foreign language instruction.[15]

[15] See, for example, the short questionnaire "Reasons for Discontinuing Foreign Language Study" described by John Dusel in his article "Diagnosing the Decrease in Foreign Language Enrollment," *Tennessee Foreign Language Bulletin* 16, no. 2 (1969), pp. 20–22.

outline

twelve
Testing
in Bilingual
and ESL Programs

ilingual programs and courses in English as a Second Language (ESL) present certain testing needs that go beyond the suggestions made in the previous sections of this handbook. Teachers and supervisors in bilingual programs want to determine to what extent and in which contexts a bilingual child can operate in each of the two languages concerned; questions are also raised with respect to the appropriateness of standard examinations. Teachers of ESL programs work with much more heterogeneous groups than their colleagues who teach a foreign language at the secondary or university level; the broader the ESL program, the more critical the matter of student placement.

12.1 MEASURING LANGUAGE DOMINANCE IN BILINGUALISM

Very few bilinguals are equally proficient in two languages. In admitting students into a bilingual program, teachers need to ascertain the degree of bilingualism of each candidate in order to ensure optimum placement in the courses offered.

12.1.1 Factors in describing bilingualism

Bilingualism is a complex phenomenon. The following factors must be taken into consideration in measuring linguistic dominance.

12.1.1a LANGUAGE DOMAINS

Bilinguals frequently prefer one language over the other in specific contexts or language domains. These domains include home, neighborhood,

313

and school for younger children, and may extend for older speakers into other areas such as music, politics, religion, sports, and hobbies.

12.1.1b SKILL AREAS

Bilinguals are not always equally competent in the skill areas of listening, speaking, reading, and writing. A child may be able to write in one language and not in the other. An adult may be able to read technical reports in a second language, but not to write them. An amateur radio fan in Mexico may be able to comprehend English messages without having a highly developed speaking ability. A literature professor may be able to lecture in the second language and yet have difficulty understanding casual conversations.

12.1.1c LEVELS OF FORMALITY

The bilingual may have limited levels of formality on one or both languages. For instance, a worker who has learned the second language by talking to other workers on the road crew will have a very informal style and may be uncomfortable or incompetent in a formal situation. Of course, not even all monolinguals develop the entire range of levels of formality ranging from slang and vulgarity at one end of the scale to eloquent lecturing ability at the other.

12.1.2 Individual oral tests

Individual oral tests assess bilingual communicative competence. These interviews typically include matching native language and target language segments to permit a comparison between the two languages.

The most difficult aspect of the interview test is putting the candidate at ease, for unless the candidate is relaxed, his or her speech will not indicate true language competence. When children are being tested, it is advisable to have the interviewer be of the same ethnic and linguistic background as the child. Sometimes better results are obtained if the interviewer is of the same sex. It has also been found that mothers of the children in bilingual schools can be trained to administer individual interviews.[1]

The following item types have been used in interview tests for language

---

[1] See Bernard Spolsky, Penny Murphy, Wayne Holm and Allen Ferrel, "Three Functional Tests of Oral Proficiency," in Leslie Palmer and Bernard Spolsky, eds., *Papers on Language Testing: 1967–74* (Washington: Teachers of English to Speakers of Other Languages, 1975). Reprinted from the *TESOL Quarterly* 6, no. 3 (September 1972); hereafter cited as "Three Functional Tests" and *Papers on Language Testing*.

dominance. (Most such items, by their very nature, sample only child-to-adult language. A broader measure of language ability would also include child-to-child language.)

SAMPLE ITEM TYPE *1*   SELF-EVALUATION

The student is asked to describe his or her ability in the two languages according to domain, skill area, and level of formality. If the student is not consciously or subconsciously trying to veil his or her bilingualism, such self-evaluations are usually rather accurate. Questions are generally asked in both languages in order to allow the interviewer to assess relative fluency.

SAMPLE ITEM TYPE *2*   WORD-NAMING

The student demonstrates his or her vocabulary fluency by naming all the words that come to mind in a certain domain.

Spoken Cue: Think of your house and tell me all of the things you can see in the kitchen. (pause) Now tell me all the things you and your family do in the kitchen. (pause)

Visual cue: Look at this picture of a house. Tell me all the things you see in the picture. (pause) Now look at the people and tell me all the things they are doing. (pause)

Tests of this sort usually cover several domains (such as home, school, and neighborhood), and are administered in two languages. A comparison of the results allows the examiner to determine overall language dominance and to note whether this dominance varies from domain to domain.

SAMPLE ITEM TYPE *3*   SENTENCE REPETITION

The student is asked to repeat a series of everyday sentences, first in one language and then in the other. An occasional incorrect sentence may be included to see how the student reacts to inappropriate usage.

SAMPLE ITEM TYPE *4*   ORAL QUESTIONS—PICTURE CUES

The student is asked questions about cartoons or pictures, first in one language and then in the other. The questions may be arranged so as to elicit specific structures. An analysis of the results reveals the degree of the student's proficiency in both languages and indicates whether the student is structurally dominant in one of them.[2]

[2] Items of this type form the basis of the *Bilingual Syntax Measure* (*BSM*) developed by Marina K. Burt, Heidi C. Dulay and Eduardo Hernández Ch. For a description of this test, see the Appendix.

SAMPLE ITEM TYPE 5 BILINGUAL INTERVIEW

Two interviewers, each using only one of the two languages, ask the student personal questions and background information. The student's performance is rated on a five-point scale, for instance:

S: Student speaks only Spanish
S-e: Student speaks mainly Spanish, but knows a little English
S-E: Student is equally proficient in Spanish and English
s-E: Student knows a little Spanish, but speaks mainly English
E: Student speaks only English.

(With children, the questions may be asked less formally by integrating them into a general conversation.) [3]

SAMPLE ITEM TYPE 6 PICTURE DESCRIPTION

The student is shown a picture or series of pictures showing activities in familiar settings and is asked to describe, in his or her own words, what is happening in the pictures, first in one language and then in the other. If desired, these free speech samples can be recorded and scored at a later time. A comparison of the two samples will show whether one language is dominant.

SAMPLE ITEM TYPE 7 FREE SPEECH—CAMERA STIMULUS

John Hollomon used a camera to elicit speech samples in a bilingual test. [4] His free speech test is divided into three parts. For the first part of the test, the child is given a Polaroid snapshot of himself or herself and is asked to talk about it. The child is asked questions eliciting different tenses: where he or she was when the picture was taken, what he or she plans to do with the picture after the test, and so on. For the second part of the test, the child is shown how to take a picture with the camera and is then asked to talk about it. For the third part the child is asked to explain to one or two peers how the camera works and how to use it. In each part of the test the child uses first one language and then the other.

The combined use of the three parts assesses the child's ability to use the two languages in a variety of situational contexts. It measures linguistic dominance as well as the ability of the child to switch from one language to the other.

---

[3] This approach was refined for the *Navajo-English Dominance Interview* developed by Wayne Holm and Bernard Spolsky. For more complete information, see Spolsky, Murphy, Holm and Ferrel, "Three Functional Tests" in *Papers on Language Testing*, pp. 80–83, 87–88.

[4] For further information, see John W. Hollomon, "A practical approach to assessing bilingualism in young Mexican-American children," *TESOL Quarterly* 10, no. 4 (December 1976), p. 394.

12.1.3   Group tests

Although individual oral interviews, when well conceived and administered, are the most valid type of language dominance test, conditions sometimes require a school to use group tests. This is particularly true in situations where relatively large numbers of students must be tested in a relatively short period of time.

When group tests are administered to young children, it is important to make sure that each child is at ease and knows how to respond. A flustered child will receive a test score that does not accurately reflect his or her language ability. The following guidelines may be of help:

1. Keep the test short. Twenty minutes should be an absolute maximum.
2. Try to use familiar surroundings. Children are more relaxed in their own classroom, with their own teacher present.
3. On one or more days preceding the test, let the children work with sample items. In this way the format is familiar and they know how to respond correctly.
4. Have enough monitors present so that you can be sure each child is working on the correct item. With very young children, you may want to print an answer booklet with only one item per page, alternating the color of the paper. (For instance: items 1, 5, 9 etc. on red paper; items 2, 6 and 10 on yellow paper; 3, 7, 11 on pink paper; 4, 8 and 12 on blue paper.) At a glance the monitors can be sure that all children are answering the right question.

When working with older students, it is equally important to present the test in a non-threatening context and to develop clear instructions.

The group tests often focus on listening comprehension, using items such as those suggested in Chapter 5. With young children, picture items are used: the children hear a statement or question and mark the corresponding picture on an answer sheet. The test consists of two parts, half in one language and half in the other. The items are of equal difficulty and lexical range. A comparison of the scores reveals whether one language is stronger than the other.

12.1.4   Home interviews

In bilingual programs for young children, the teaching or administrative staff may wish to explore the home setting of each student. Not only does the home interview establish communication between the parents and the school, but it enables the staff to answer questions such as:

Which languages does the child hear at home?

Which language or languages do the parents understand? Which do they use at home? Which do they use with the child?

(If appropriate) Which language or languages does the child hear on radio and/or television?

The interviewer may also ask the parents to evaluate the language ability of their child. A more complete interview would also touch on the family history and socio-economic background, including parental education.[5]

12.2   USING STANDARD PSYCHOLOGICAL TESTS

Care must be exercised in using standard psychological tests, such as IQ batteries or reading readiness tests, with children in a bilingual program. It is obvious that if the tests are administered in the child's weaker language, the results will give an unreliable picture of IQ or reading readiness. The low score reflects a language barrier rather than low ability.

Even if the standard psychological test is administered in the child's dominant language, two other factors must be taken into account: conditions of administration and culture bias.

When a standardized test is given very early in the school year, some children may be intimidated by the entire testing situation. Under such circumstances, their low test scores again will not reflect their true ability. It may be advisable to postpone standard tests until several weeks into the term, when the children are more at ease in the classroom and have come to know the teachers.

The content of the psychological test must also be studied to determine whether any items would be culturally inappropriate for the children. Navaho children, for instance, might not have developed the same concepts as a middle-class suburban child and might be puzzled by test items that refer to things outside their life on the reservation. It is further possible that children of two linguistic groups may possess similar concepts, but that these are expressed quite differently in the two languages. In such cases, it is almost impossible to translate a test from one language to the other without changing the focus of many of the items.[6]

---

[5] For more information on home interviews and a sample interview form, see Muriel R. Saville and Rudolph C. Troike, *A Handbook of Bilingual Education*, Revised Edition (Washington: Teachers of English to Speakers of Other Languages, 1971), pp. 68–69.

[6] For a further discussion of this problem, see Anabelle R. Rosenbluth, "The Feasibility of Test Translation Between Unrelated Languages: English to Navaho," *TESOL Quarterly* 10, no. 1 (March 1976), pp. 33–43.

12.3   PLACING STUDENTS IN AN ESL SEQUENCE

The placement of students is a matter of concern for administrators of most English courses for secondary students and adults. When students are well placed at an appropriate spot in the sequence, the courses function more smoothly and there is a lower dropout rate.

The form of the placement test varies from situation to situation. When small groups of incoming students are involved, face-to-face interview tests are feasible. With large groups of students who must be placed within a day or two, however, some form of group testing is required.

The content of the placement test directly reflects the parameters of the English program concerned. If the program is a small one with clear-cut beginning, intermediate, and advanced courses, it is not necessary to develop a highly refined placement battery: one needs simply a measure that will divide the students into three groups. In a large program with a broad range of possible courses, the placement procedure becomes more complex.

12.3.1   Analyzing placement needs

The first step in preparing a placement test is the analysis of the needs of the program. The following set of questions may be used as guidelines:

1. *Size of program:* How many students are involved? How many teachers?
2. *Scheduling of classes:* How are classes scheduled? If several different levels meet at the same time on the same day, it is easy to transfer students from one class to another. If the different levels meet at different times or different days, switching students from one class to another becomes more difficult. In the latter case, proper placement is essential.
3. *Time of entry:* Do all students enter the program on the same date? Or can they begin the program at any time? Placement in the latter case is easier, for the new students can visit ongoing classes as part of the registration process.
4. *Nature of the courses:* Is there a linear progression from one course to the next? If so, it is important to place each student properly. Or does each course have its own character and is the amount of material covered simply determined by the teacher as a function of how the students are doing? In such cases, accurate placement is less important.

The second step is to define the parameters of the placement procedure. Here the questions are:

1. How much time is available for placing an incoming student? Is there time for an interview? time for a written test? for a recorded test?

2. What personnel is available for placement procedures?

Each school or program will have to determine the best placement procedure to meet the needs of the incoming students.

12.3.2   Using commercial tests

In some programs, commercial ESL tests are used for placement. In courses for foreign students that are given as part of the university program, the scores on the TOEFL test [7] may furnish useful placement information. Many incoming students have already taken this test, so that these scores may already form part of the student's dossier.

The new *Structure Tests—English Language* (STEL) by Jeanette Best and Donna Ilyin have been developed as placement and/or achievement tests. Students read sets of three sentences and mark the one in correct English. For example:

A. Paul is coming.
B. Paul am coming.
C. Paul are coming.

The tests are grouped into three levels of structural difficulty: beginning, intermediate, and advanced.

Each program must determine whether the commercial tests available do indeed work as effective placement instruments for incoming students. Many schools have found that the best solution is either to use commercial tests in conjunction with local measures or to develop a completely local placement instrument.

12.3.3   Using local placement tests

Hundreds, if not thousands, of schools have developed their own ESL placement tests. Some of these are discrete-point tests that evaluate vocabulary and structure as well as one or more skills, such as reading. Others are global tests, such as interview tests (Section 6.5), dictations (Section 8.5), noise tests (Section 5.7), cloze tests (Section 7.8). Occasionally the end-of-course examination is recycled the following semester as a placement test: for instance, students who do well on the final examination for Course 3 may be placed into Course 4.

The following item type has also been used with ESL students.

---

[7] For descriptions of the TOEFL and STEL tests, see the Appendix.

SAMPLE ITEM TYPE *8*   OPEN COMPLETION

The student reads a series of incomplete sentences and writes in any word or group of words that forms a logical completion.[8]

1. Where did they _____ ?
2. You are the _____est.
3. Which is the one with the _____ ?

The students will produce a variety of answers, and any acceptable completion is counted as correct.

If an open completion test were developed as a placement test to accompany a specific course, the type of structures required in each blank could be sequenced to parallel the course content. The easy structures would be placed at the beginning of the test, and the sentences would get progressively more difficult. The point at which the student is unable to continue further would indicate the place of entry into the ESL program.

[8] This type of test in experimental form is briefly described by Virginia French Allen in "Toward a Thumb-Nail Test of English Competence," in Palmer and Spolsky, *Papers on Language Testing*, pp. 3–5.

appendix
Commercial
Language Tests

Commercial language tests may be classified under six headings: prognostic tests, progress tests (to accompany a specific set of instruction materials), achievement tests, proficiency tests, bilingual tests, and attitude questionnaires. While the following list in no way pretends to be complete, it does include descriptions of the most widely used tests published in the United States.[1]

A.1 PROGNOSTIC TESTS

A.1.1 *Modern Language Aptitude Test* (MLAT), J. B. Carroll and S. M. Sapon (The Psychological Corporation, 757 Third Avenue, New York, NY 10017), 1959.

Age group: English-speaking persons, Grade 9 to adults
Forms: two
Administration: by school
Tape: yes (not needed for the Short Form)
Length: 60–70 minutes (Short Form without Parts I and II—30
    minutes)
Description: The test has five parts:
    Part I: Number learning. Students learn numbers in a new language.
        This part measures auditory memory and auditory alertness (tape).
    Part II: Phonetic script. Students learn phonetic script and select the

---

[1] Consult Oscar K. Buros, *Foreign Language Tests and Reviews* (Highland Park, N.J.: Gryphon Press, 1975).

correct transcription for words spoken on the tape. This part measures sound-symbol association ability (tape).

Part III: Spelling clues. Students select the correct meaning of coded English words (a high-speed section). This part measures English vocabulary and, to some extent, sound-symbol association.

Part IV: Words in sentences. Students handle diverse aspects of grammar in English, without using specific terminology. This part measures sensitivity to grammatical structure.

Part V: Paired associates. Students memorize pairs of words. This part measures ability to learn rapidly by rote.

A.1.2 *Elementary Modern Language Aptitude Test*, J. B. Carroll and S. M. Sapon (The Psychological Corporation, 757 Third Avenue, New York, NY 10017), 1967.

Age group: English-speaking students in grades 3–6
Tape: yes
Length: 61 minutes (may be given in two or more sessions)
Administration: by school
Description: The test has four parts:
  Part I: Hidden words. Students find synonyms or definitions for groups of letters that, when spoken, approximate an English word. Example: "silns," correct answer "quiet." This part measures vocabulary and sound-symbol association.
  Part II: Matching words. Students see two sentences and find the word in the second sentence that has the same grammatical function as the underlined word of the first sentence. This part measures sensitivity to grammatical structure.
  Part III: Finding rhymes. Students select the word from a list that rhymes with the cue word. This part indirectly measures sound discrimination.
  Part IV: Number learning. Students learn numbers in a new language. This part measures auditory memory and auditory alertness (tape).

A.1.3 *Pimsleur Language Aptitude Battery*, P. Pimsleur (The Psychological Corporation, 757 Third Avenue, New York, NY 10017), 1966.

Age group: English-speaking students in grades 6–12
Tape: yes
Length: 50–60 minutes
Administration: by school
Description: The test has six parts:

Part I: Grade-point average. Using a four-point scale, students indicate the grades they last received in English, social studies, mathematics, and science.

Part II: Interest. Using a five-point scale, students evaluate their interest in studying foreign languages.

Part III: Vocabulary. Students select synonyms for twenty-four English words.

Part IV: Language analysis. Presented with a limited number of words and phrases in an unfamiliar language, students are asked to select the foreign-language equivalents of various English sentences. This part measures ability to draw appropriate analogies and to reason logically using foreign-language materials.

Part V: Sound discrimination. Students learn to discriminate orally between similar sounds in a new language. This part measures the ability to learn new phonemic distinctions and to recognize them in different contexts.

Part VI: Sound-symbol association. From groups of four similarly spelled nonsense words, students select the ones that agree with the sounds heard on tape. This part measures ability to associate English-language sounds with their written symbols.

A.2 PROGRESS TESTS

Progress tests are designed to accompany a specific set of instructional materials. Most of the major publishers are now producing tests to accompany their language textbooks. Teachers are advised to request a copy of the commercial test and study it in the light of their own course objectives. Only then can they decide whether or not to order such tests for their classes.

A.3 ACHIEVEMENT TESTS

A.3.1 *Common Concepts Foreign Language Test* (California Test Bureau, Del Monte Research Park, Monterey, CA 93940), 1962.

Languages: French, German, Spanish (and English)
Levels: One (all grades)
Forms: two
Administration: by school
Skills tested: listening
Tape: yes
Length: 40 minutes

Description: Students hear sentences in the foreign language. They indicate their understanding of what they have heard by selecting from sets of four colored pictures the ones that have been correctly described.

A.3.2 *MLA Cooperative Foreign Language Tests* (Educational Testing Service, Princeton, NJ 08540), 1963.

Languages: French, German, Italian, Russian, Spanish
Levels: L (One–Two) and M (Three–Four)
Forms: two
Administration: by school
Skills tested: listening, speaking, reading, writing
Tape: yes
Length: listening—25 minutes; speaking—10 minutes; reading—35 minutes; writing—35 minutes
Description:

Listening. The first few items of the Level L test use pictures. Thereafter students select from the printed selections in their answer booklet the correct rejoinders or correct answers to taped questions. The following types of items are used: discrete statements or questions, questions about a recorded conversation, appropriate rejoinders for a telephone conversation, and, in Level M, questions about a longer recorded passage. The tests do not measure listening comprehension independently of reading.

Speaking. Item types involve repetition of recorded sentences, reading aloud, answering questions about pictures, and free oral description of a picture.

Reading. The types of items include fill-in-the-blanks, substitution of words or phrases, and questions on short reading passages. The entire test is multiple-choice.

Writing. The items differ somewhat from language to language. In general the following types are used: fill-in-the-blanks, transformation of sentences (to the past, to the plural, etc.), dehydrated sentences, and directed composition.

A.3.3 *Pimsleur Modern Foreign Language Proficiency Tests*, P. Pimsleur (The Psychological Corporation, 757 Third Avenue, New York, NY 10017), 1967.

Languages: French, German, Spanish
Levels: One and Two
Forms: one
Administration: by school

Skills tested: listening, speaking, reading, writing

Tape: yes

Length: listening—20 minutes; speaking—20 minutes; reading—35 minutes; writing—35 minutes

Description:

Listening. Part I contains 20 phonemic-accuracy items in the form of complete sentences. In Part II students select the most appropriate response to a spoken stimulus from among four printed responses. This test may be used only for classes with reading skill.

Speaking. In Part I students identify objects pictured in the test booklet. In Part II students hear a number of sentences on tape and then read them aloud. In Part III students repond orally to questions presented on tape.

Reading. All the reading-comprehension items are based on short passages. The entire test is multiple-choice.

Writing. The types of items vary somewhat from language to language. At both test levels, however, there is a progression from fill-in-the-blank items to controlled sentences (transformation and substitution) to free composition based on pictures.

A.3.4 *Regents High School Examinations* (The State University of New York, The New York State Education Department, Albany, NY 12224), revised annually.[2]

Languages: French, German, Hebrew, Italian, Spanish

Level: Three

Forms: one

Administration: on specified dates in the state of New York

Skills tested: listening, reading, writing

Tape: no (teacher reads script)

Length: three hours

Description: A typical examination has five parts:

Part I: Listening comprehension. Students hear short paragraphs and select the correct answers to questions printed in their test booklets; reading skill is necessary.

Part II: Listening and writing. Students write answers to oral questions.

Part III: Reading comprehension. Students answer multiple-choice questions based on printed paragraphs.

Part IV: Completion. Students answer multiple-choice testing of grammar and vocabulary.

Part V: Directed compositions. Students write an essay based on a brief outline given in English.

[2] Retired forms of Regents examinations are reprinted and sold by Amsco School Publications Inc., Box 351, Cooper Station, New York, NY 10003.

A.3.5 *College Board Achievement Tests* (Educational Testing Service, Princeton, NJ 08540), revised annually.

Languages: French, German, Hebrew, Russian, Spanish
Levels: Two through Five (one test)
Forms: varied
Administration: in specified centers on dates announced in advance
Skills tested: reading
Tape: no
Length: 60 minutes
Description: Since the College Board Achievement Tests are written by rotating committees of professors, the format and item types may vary somewhat from year to year. All items are multiple-choice reading items. Typically such tests include the following item types:
Situation questions. This printed test measures familiarity with the spoken language. Students select the appropriate statement from four or five options.
Usage questions. This part includes substitution and fill-in-the-blank items, occasionally with English cues, and completion sentences.
Vocabulary questions. This part includes discrete items that usually test vocabulary in context in the target language.
Reading-comprehension items. Passages are given, followed by questions on content and items on particular words and phrases, sometimes requesting the most appropriate English equivalents.

A.3.6 *College Board Supplementary Achievement Tests* (Educational Testing Service, Princeton, NJ 08540), revised annually.

Languages: French, German, Italian, Russian, Spanish
Levels: Two through Five (one test)
Forms: varied
Administration: annually, on a specified date
Skills tested: reading (Italian), writing (Italian), listening (French, German, Italian, Russian, Spanish)
Tape: yes
Length: Italian Achievement Test (reading and writing)—90 minutes; Listening-comprehension tests—30 minutes
Description:
Italian Achievement Test. This test is similar to the College Board Achievement Tests in other languages (see A.3.5) but includes a final section that measures student proficiency in writing.
Listening-comprehension tests. The types of items include short conversations followed by oral questions and printed responses, short

questions with printed responses, long passages with oral questions and printed responses.

A.3.7 *Comprehensive English Language Test for Speakers of English as a Second Language* (CELT), D. P. Harris and L. A. Palmer (McGraw-Hill Book Company, 1221 Avenue of the Americas, New York, NY 10020), 1970.

Language: English
Levels: Two through Five
Forms: one (although the three parts are entitled Form L-A, Form S-A, and Form V-A)
Administration: by school
Skills tested: listening, reading
Tape: yes
Length: listening—35–45 minutes; structure—45–55 minutes; vocabulary —35–45 minutes
Description:
   Listening (Form L-A) Students hear brief recorded passages and select the appropriate response from among the four printed in the test booklet.
   Structure (Form S-A) Students select the appropriate sentence from among the options printed in the booklet.
   Vocabulary (Form V-A) Students select the appropriate synonym from among options presented.

A.3.8 *Test of English as a Foreign Language* (TOEFL) (Educational Testing Service, Princeton, NJ 08540), prepared annually.

Language: English
Level: candidates for admission to American colleges
Forms: one
Administration: in specified centers on specified dates
Skills tested: listening, reading
Tape: yes
Length: two and a half hours
Description: Since the TOEFL is written by a committee, the format and item types may vary somewhat from year to year. All the items are multiple-choice items. Typically such tests include the following subtests:
   Listening comprehension. This subtest has three parts: direct questions, statements followed by questions, and a "lecture" followed by comprehension questions.
   Structure. Students read a segment of a dialog and select the appropriate completion.

Vocabulary. This subtest has two parts: sentence completion and selection of synonyms or definitions.

Reading comprehension. Students answer multiple-choice content questions on a reading selection.

Writing ability. The first part of the subtest consists of sentences in which four phrases are underlined: students select the one that is incorrect. The second part contains sentence completion items, in which students select the appropriate expression from the four options.

A.3.9 *Structure Tests—English Language* (STEL), J. Best and D. Ilyin (Newbury House Publishers, 68 Middle Road, Rowley, Mass. 01969), 1976.

Language: English
Levels: beginning, intermediate, and advanced
Forms: two for each level
Administration: by school
Skills tested: reading
Tape: no
Length: 30 minutes
Description: Each test contains 50 items that measure the students' ability to identify correct structures. Students read three sentences, which are similar except for one underlined element, and mark the sentence that is grammatically accurate.

A.4 PROFICIENCY TESTS

A.4.1 *College Board Advanced Placement Tests* (Educational Testing Service, Princeton, NJ 08540), prepared annually.

Languages: French, German, Spanish
Level: Five
Forms: one
Administration: annually, on a specified date
Skills tested: listening, reading, writing
Tape: yes
Length: three hours
Description: These tests are administered to high-school seniors who have followed a specialized course of language study. For the literature version, the specific works to be covered are announced at the beginning of each school year. Recent tests have included a section that measures listening comprehension (oral questions with printed responses) and sections that test note-taking (a recorded lecture),

reading comprehension (passage items), and textual compositions on literary topics.

A.4.2 *Graduate Record Examinations* (Educational Testing Service, Princeton, NJ 08540), prepared annually.

Languages: French, Spanish
Level: candidates for graduate study
Forms: one
Administration: in specified centers on specified dates
Skills tested: reading
Tape: no
Length: three hours
Description: The Advanced French Test and the Advanced Spanish Test use reading-comprehension items to examine knowledge of literature and general familiarity with culture and civilization. These items also test vocabulary and grammar as well as sensitivity to style and the ability to follow the development of an author's thoughts.

A.4.3 *MLA Proficiency Tests for Teachers and Advanced Students* (Modern Language Association, 62 Fifth Avenue, New York, NY 10011), 1961.

Languages: French, German, Italian, Russian, Spanish
Level: present and prospective teachers
Forms: two (HA, HB)
Administration: by school
Skills tested: listening, speaking, reading, writing
Tape: yes (listening and speaking)
Length: listening—20 minutes; speaking—15 minutes; reading—40 minutes; writing—45 minutes; applied linguistics—40 minutes; civilization and culture—30 minutes; professional preparation—45 minutes.
Description: These tests are administered in three different combinations: (1) all seven tests, (2) the four skills tests, or (3) the three tests on linguistics, culture, and professional preparation. The professional-preparation test is in English and is the same for all five languages.

A.4.4 *Graduate School Foreign Language Tests* (Educational Testing Service, Princeton, NJ 08540), 1963–64.

Languages: French, German, Russian
Forms: one
Administration: four times a year at participating graduate schools

Skills tested: reading

Tape: no

Length: two versions—80 and 100 minutes

Description: These tests are designed to evaluate the foreign-language reading proficiency of graduate-level degree candidates. Part I tests control of structure through both discrete items and passage items, all in the target language. Part II presents reading passages in the target language with questions in English; students select passages with subjects from the biological sciences, the humanities, the physical sciences, or the social sciences.

A.4.5 *Ilyin Oral Interview*, D. Ilyin (Newbury House Publishers, 68 Middle Road, Rowley, Mass. 01969), 1976.

Language: English

Levels: upper elementary school to adult, beginning and intermediate

Forms: two

Administration: by school; individual administration

Skills tested: listening and speaking

Tape: no

Length: variable—the full form consists of 50 questions, but the interview may be terminated earlier when a frustration level is reached.

Description: The interviewer asks the student prepared questions relating to a series of drawings depicting activities and clock faces with specific times. The interviewer rates each response on a 2-1-0 scale using a prepared answer sheet.

A.5 BILINGUAL TESTS[3]

A.5.1 *Bilingual Syntax Measure/Medida de Sintaxis Bilingüe* (BSM), M. K. Burt, H. C. Dulay, and E. Hernández Ch. (The Psychological Corporation, 757 Third Avenue, New York, NY 10017), 1975.

Language: English (BSM-E) and Spanish (BSM-S)

Levels: Kindergarten to Grade 2

Forms: one

Administration: by school; individual administration

Skills tested: listening and speaking

Tape: no

---

[3] This appendix does not list the Spanish-language editions of intelligence tests, personality tests, attitude tests, etc. For a complete catalog of available tests of this sort, write to the major test publishers.

Length: 7–10 minutes

Description: The interviewer asks the student prepared questions about seven cartoon-type pictures. The test is administered first in one language and then in the other. The test may be used to measure language dominance with respect to basic syntactic structures, as well as structural proficiency in either English or Spanish.

A.6   ATTITUDE QUESTIONNAIRES

A.6.1   *Foreign Language Attitude Questionnaire* (FLAQ), L. Jakobovits (Northeast Conference, Box 623, Middlebury, Vt. 05753), 1970.

Age group: elementary school to adult

Forms: two (S1 for students with foreign language study, S2 for students who have not studied foreign languages)

Administration: by school

Tape: no

Length: 15–20 minutes

Description: The questionnaires ask about the students' language background and their attitudes toward the foreign language and their reasons for study. Most responses are formulated in a multiple-choice format, with the opportunity for further comments in writing.[4]

---

[4] For further information on the FLAQ, see Joseph A. Tursi, ed., *Foreign Languages and the "New" Student* (Reports of the Working Committees of the Northeast Conference on the Teaching of Foreign Languages), 1970.

Selected
Bibliography

This bibliography is limited to selected books and research monographs on the general topic of second language testing. It does not contain magazine articles: for extended bibliographies consult the works indicated with an asterisk (*).

*Allen, J. P. B., and Davies, Alan, eds. *Testing and Experimental Methods*. Edinburgh Course in Applied Linguistics, vol. 4. London: Oxford University Press, 1977.

Bloom, Benjamin S., Hastings, Thomas J., and Madaus, George F., eds. *Handbook on Formative and Summative Evaluation of Student Learning*. New York: McGraw-Hill, 1971. Of specific interest to language teachers is Chapter 22: "Evaluation of Learning in a Second Language" by Rebecca M. Valette.

Buros, Oscar K., ed. *Foreign Language Tests and Reviews*. Highland Park, N.J.: Gryphon Press, 1975. A reprint of the foreign language sections of the *Seven Mental Measurements Yearbooks* (1938–1972) and *Tests in Print II* (1974).

*Clark, John L. D. *Foreign Language Testing: Theory & Practice*. Philadelphia: Center for Curriculum Development, 1972.

*———. "Measurement Implications of Recent Trends in Foreign Language Teaching," in *Foreign Language Education: A Reappraisal*. Edited by Dale L. Lange and Charles J. James. The ACTFL Review of Foreign Language Education, vol. 4. Skokie, Ill.: National Textbook, 1972.

Davies, Alan, ed. *Language Testing Symposium: A Psycholinguistic Approach*. London: Oxford University Press, 1968.

*Fehse, Klaus D., and Praeger, W. *Bibliographie zum Testen in der Schule (Schwerpunkt: Fremdsprachenunterricht)*. Arbeitsmittel für den Unterricht, vol. 3. Freiburg: Becksmann, 1973.

Harris, David P. *Testing English as a Second Language*. New York: McGraw-Hill, 1969.

*Heaton, J. B. *Writing English Language Tests: A Practical Guide for Teachers of English as a Second or Foreign Language*. London: Longman, 1975.

Jones, Randall L., and Spolsky, Bernard, eds. *Testing Language Proficiency*. Arlington, Va.: Center of Applied Linguistics, 1975.

*Jorstad, Helen L. "Testing as Communication," in *The Challenge of Communication*. Edited by Gilbert A. Jarvis. The ACTFL Review of Foreign Language Education, vol. 6. Skokie, Ill.: National Textbook, 1974.

Lado, Robert. *Language Testing: The Construction and Use of Foreign Language Tests.* London: Longman, 1961; New York: McGraw-Hill, 1964.

Motte, Jean-Claude. *L'évaluation par les tests dans la classe de français.* Paris: Hachette/Larousse, 1975.

O'Brien, M. C., ed. *Testing in Second Language Teaching: New Dimensions.* Dublin: Association of Teachers of English as a Second or Other Language and Dublin University Press, 1973.

Palmer, Leslie, and Spolsky, Bernard, eds. *Papers on Language Testing: 1967–1974.* Washington: Teachers of English to Speakers of Other Languages, 1975.

Savard, Jean-Guy. *Bibliographie Analytique de Tests de Langue.* Québec: Presses de l'Université Laval, 1969.

Schrand, Heinrich, ed. *Testen: Probleme der objektiven Leistungsmessung im neusprachlichen Unterricht.* Berlin: Cornelsen-Velhagen & Klasing, 1973.

Upshur, John A., and Fata, Julia. *Problems in Foreign Language Testing, Language Learning.* Special issue no. 3, August 1968.

*Valette, Rebecca M. *Directions in Foreign Language Testing.* New York: MLA/ERIC, 1969.

*————. "Testing," in *The Britannica Review of Foreign Language Education*, vol. 1. Edited by Emma Marie Birkmaier. Chicago: Encyclopaedia Britannica, 1968.

————, and Disick, Renée S. *Modern Language Performance Objectives and Individualization: A Handbook.* New York: Harcourt Brace Jovanovich, 1972.

Index

Index

A 7
B 8
C 9
D 0
E 1
F 2
G 3
H 4
I 5
J 6